Edited by **ZAHRA HANKIR**

ESSAYS BY

ARAB WOMEN

REPORTING

FROM THE

ARAB

WORLD

OUR
WOMEN
ON THE
GROUND

Foreword by **CHRISTIANE AMANPOUR**

D0050400

SACRAMENTO PUBLIC LIBRARY
828 "I" Street
Sacramento, CA 95814
08/19

WITHDRAWN

"A compelling and gripping read."   —*Middle East Monitor*

"Out of the gloom of the Middle East, this book brims with new voices—Arab women reporting on their world as no one else has seen it, with courage, inspiration, and resilience. A terrific read, full of insight and surprise."

   —David E. Hoffman, former foreign editor of
     The Washington Post and Pulitzer Prize–winning
     author of *The Billion Dollar Spy*

"A remarkable book that fills a tremendous gap, as mainstream media coverage of the Middle East and Arab world has long been dominated by men or outsiders. The voices of these trailblazing women are even more vital today, when the region's upheaval cannot be explained without local, and especially female, perspectives."

  —Hassan Hassan, *New York Times* bestselling co-author of *ISIS*

"This astounding, affecting collection offers a sweeping panorama of the contemporary Arab experience—heartland and exile; repression and liberation; violence and love. I struggle to think of any work of reportage that has so fully depicted the many-layered recent history of this vibrant and traumatized region. Rich with understanding and sincere emotional connection to the people and places that drive the news, this book contains voices that are both fresh and necessary."

   —Megan K. Stack, author of *Women's Work*

"A dazzling book that elegantly demonstrates how to tell stories with humility, affection, and truthfulness."

   —Azadeh Moaveni, author of *Lipstick Jihad* and
    Honeymoon in Tehran

"The stories of how these women crossed boundaries and pushed the limits professionally, culturally, and personally are stark and haunting. I loved this book, for its courage but also for the fact that the future of news will be told by local correspondents whose passion for justice and truth shines through. A must-read for anyone who wants to see a side of news from the Middle East they would never see by watching the nightly news."

—Janine di Giovanni, author of *The Morning They Came for Us*

"With steely courage and pens of fire, these *sahafiyat*—Arab female journalists—tell the stories of their country's conflicts, providing rigor, depth, and insight few outside commenters could match."

—Molly Crabapple, author of *Drawing Blood* and illustrator of *Brothers of the Gun*

PENGUIN BOOKS

OUR WOMEN ON THE GROUND

ZAHRA HANKIR is a Lebanese British journalist who writes about the intersection of politics, culture, and society in the Middle East. Her writing and journalism have appeared on BBC News, *Bloomberg News*, *Vice*, and Al Jazeera English, and in *Roads & Kingdoms* and *Literary Hub*, among other media outlets. She was awarded a Jack R. Howard Fellowship in International Journalism to attend the Columbia Journalism School and holds degrees in politics and Middle Eastern studies from the American University of Beirut and the University of Manchester.

CHRISTIANE AMANPOUR is CNN's chief international anchor and host of the network's award-winning, flagship global affairs program *Amanpour*, which also airs on PBS in the United States. She is based in the network's London bureau. Christiane's illustrious career in journalism spans more than three decades. After joining CNN in 1983, Amanpour rose through the organization, becoming the network's leading international correspondent reporting on crises in the Gulf, Iraq, Afghanistan, North Korea, Palestinian territories, Iran, Sudan, Israel, Pakistan, Somalia, Rwanda, the Balkans, Egypt, and Libya. Amanpour has interviewed most of the top world leaders over the past two decades and has received every major broadcast award, including an inaugural Television Academy Award, eleven News and Documentary Emmys, four Peabody Awards, and nine honorary degrees. In 2014, she was inducted into the Cable Hall of Fame and in 2018 into the Broadcasting & Cable Hall of Fame. She is a member of the American Academy of Arts and Sciences, a Commander of the Most Excellent Order of the British Empire, an honorary citizen of Sarajevo, and a UNESCO Goodwill Ambassador. Amanpour is a graduate of the University of Rhode Island.

OUR
WOMEN
ON THE
GROUND

Essays by Arab Women
Reporting from the
Arab World

EDITED BY **ZAHRA HANKIR**

FOREWORD BY **CHRISTIANE AMANPOUR**

PENGUIN BOOKS

PENGUIN BOOKS

An imprint of Penguin Random House LLC
penguinrandomhouse.com

Introduction and selection copyright © 2019 by Zahra Hankir
Penguin supports copyright. Copyright fuels creativity, encourages diverse voices,
promotes free speech, and creates a vibrant culture. Thank you for buying an
authorized edition of this book and for complying with copyright laws by not
reproducing, scanning, or distributing any part of it in any form without
permission. You are supporting writers and allowing Penguin to continue to
publish books for every reader.

The essays in this book are the copyrighted property of the respective writers.

"What Normal?" by Hwaida Saad, "Words, Not Weapons" by Shamael Elnoor,
and "Between the Explosions" by Asmaa al-Ghoul are translated by Mariam
Antar. Translation copyright © 2019 by Mariam Antar.

Excerpt on page 69 from "Dedication" from *Bilingual Blues* by Gustavo Pérez
Firmat (Bilingual Press, 1995). © Gustavo Pérez Firmat. Used with permission.
Photograph on page 94 by Ellen Emmerentze Thommessen Jervell. Used with
permission.

LIBRARY OF CONGRESS CATALOGING-IN-PUBLICATION DATA
Names: Hankir, Zahra, editor. | Amanpour, Christiane, writer of foreword.
Title: Our women on the ground : essays by Arab women reporting from the
    Arab world / edited by Zahra Hankir ; foreword by Christiane Amanpour.
Description: New York, New York : Penguin Books, 2019. |
    Includes bibliographical references.
Identifiers: LCCN 2018052511 (print) | LCCN 2019012777 (ebook) |
    ISBN 9780143133414 (paperback) | ISBN 9780525505204 (ebook)
Subjects: LCSH: Women journalists—Arab countries—Biography. |
    Reporters and reporting—Arab countries. | Women in journalism—
    Arab countries. | Women in the mass media industry—Arab countries. |
    Women—Arab countries—Social conditions.
Classification: LCC P94.5.W652 (ebook) | LCC P94.5.W652 A737 2019 (print) |
    DDC 070.4082—dc23
LC record available at https://lccn.loc.gov/2018052511

Printed in the United States of America
10 9 8 7 6 5 4 3 2 1

Set in Wile Roman Pro
Book design by Sabrina Bowers

Penguin is committed to publishing works of quality and integrity.
In that spirit, we are proud to offer this book to our readers; however,
the stories, the experiences, and the words are those of the authors alone.

To Atwar Bahjat, Mayada Ashraf, Layal Nagib, Malika Sabour,

and the Arab and Middle Eastern women journalists and

photojournalists who lost their lives while reporting from their

homelands.

Contents

EXILE

TRANSITION

Foreword

I began my career as a foreign correspondent in the first Gulf War, and somehow, serendipitously, CNN paired me up with an all-female camera crew. That was the summer of 1990, in Saudi Arabia. Suffice to say we were an unusual-looking team! But somehow it worked; our gender and our professionalism actually opened doors instead of slamming them in our faces.

Since then I have worked alongside many great female journalists from all over the world, from my fellow anchors and correspondents to producers and photojournalists. I have discovered them to be some of the bravest, most inspiring, provocative, energetic, and resourceful of my colleagues.

The Balkan wars of the 1990s represented a game-changing shift in the rules of our road. It was during those conflicts that our reporters' immunity ended; no longer were we considered neutral objective witnesses. We became deliberate targets. Ever since, journalists have been swallowed up into the tribal politics of the global environment, pulled—usually against our will—into one ideological corner or another.

My late colleague Margaret Moth, a camerawoman, was shot by a sniper and almost killed in Sarajevo. The van in which she was traveling was clearly labeled as a press vehicle, but it didn't matter. The bullet shattered her jaw, blew out her teeth and part of her tongue. All of us were immensely angry at what had happened to her, but Margaret was philosophical. "I don't blame anyone for firing at me," she said. "They're in a war and I stepped into it." She returned to Bosnia as soon as she was physically able. She was utterly fearless and a source of inspiration for journalists across the world. I see Margaret's attitude and spirit in many other women who live and work amid the unrest and oppression that the world endures today.

The journalists in this book have demonstrated the highest professional achievements and courage. Of course, many of these journalists are local, covering their own homelands. Many of their stories are in the Middle East and the Arab world, where societal norms and traditions continue to place complex obstacles in the paths of women. To become a journalist in some of these places takes a special kind of courage for a woman. It can mean defying family and community, and it brings unique challenges and entails sacrifices specific to women.

But women's voices are crucial to gaining a full understanding of a story. Without the female perspective the full picture simply cannot be painted, and often—particularly in the Middle East and the Arab world—female protagonists can be given a voice only by other women. Women can enter places and speak to people their male colleagues simply cannot. Sometimes they can ask questions that would not be tolerated from their male counterparts.

Conflict zones today are even more dangerous than those that I experienced decades ago in Bosnia. Lines are more blurred, actions less predictable, the consequences of mistakes more dire. Those who choose to enter these theaters, both male and female, deserve our respect and admiration. As professional journalists we must continue to nurture, encourage, support, protect, and fight for those who make this choice. We must also make sure more women are among their ranks, because without them the stories of today and tomorrow will remain only partly told.

CHRISTIANE AMANPOUR

Introduction: Sahafiya

I come from there
and I have memories.
—MAHMOUD DARWISH

When I first visited Ruqia Hasan's Facebook page, in 2014, I was struck by her profile photo. The Syrian woman had paired a black hijab with a figure-hugging top that was embroidered with gold sequins. Her eyebrows were impeccably groomed, and bronzer contoured her cheekbones. It was a daring look, considering she lived in Raqqa—the northern Syrian city that was, at that time, controlled by the most brutal Islamist group in the world. Most striking, though, was the defiant expression on Ruqia's face, a defiance reflected in each one of her Facebook posts. Everything about the petite woman screamed: "I am here and I will not be silenced."

Ruqia was a *sahafiya*—a woman journalist—who secretly reported on the crimes of ISIS from inside Raqqa. But she was no ordinary reporter, at least by mainstream media standards. The thirty-year-old of Kurdish descent* wasn't employed by a major

---

* It's important to note that Ruqia was of Kurdish, not Arab, descent, though she was Syrian by nationality. While this book centers on women of Arab ancestry, many women of the broader Middle East share the exact same social, political, and cultural challenges. That said, by using the catchall term "Arab," we by no means aim to present the twenty-two countries that comprise the Arab world as monolithic, nor do we want to depict the experiences of its more than 400 million people as one and the same. On the contrary: we wish to illustrate just how rich and wide-ranging this area of the world is. Our decision to categorize the authors in this book as Arab is in part due to their shared linguistic heritage, although it's worth acknowledging that even then, across the Arab world, dozens of dialects are spoken.

news outlet. She never had a byline or a dateline and was never trained to cover warfare. She hadn't conducted any interviews, and she certainly wasn't impartial: she'd participated in antigovernment protests and openly criticized Syrian president Bashar al-Assad.

Online, Ruqia was fearless, even though vocal opponents of ISIS were often swiftly executed. The citizen *sahafiya* wrote in chilling detail under a pen name, Nissan Ibrahim, about the atrocities the group was waging on the people of Raqqa. She shared her reports on Facebook, sometimes posting several times a day. As Ruqia amassed a large social media following, her friends advised her to take down the photos of herself that were viewable to the public to protect her identity, but she refused.

A philosophy graduate of the University of Aleppo, Ruqia was known for the personal, poetic, and somber tone of her social media posts, which were always written in Arabic. She wavered between reporting what she'd witnessed and writing about how she felt. In December 2014, less than a year after ISIS declared Raqqa the capital of its caliphate, she posted the following: "In Syria, life and dignity have become two parallel lines that never meet."

Ruqia mostly referred to ISIS as Daesh, an acronym for *al-Dawla al-Islamiya fi al-Iraq wa al-Sham* (the Islamic State of Iraq and Greater Syria), which has reportedly drawn the ire of some ISIS commanders as it strips the terror group's label of its reference to Islam.

"Daesh has closed all internet cafés in the countryside, and most likely in the city, too," the citizen *sahafiya* wrote in June 2015. "Without the internet, we will lose our only way of communicating. Dear God: Emigration is a loss of dignity and a form of humiliation, while staying here is hell. Dear God: Where should we go?"

What Ruqia presented in her harrowing posts was an authentic account of the events unraveling on the ground in Raqqa. Those accounts came at a time when few Westerners could report from within Syria, but they nonetheless commanded the international journalistic narrative on the country from afar.

One of Ruqia's final posts on Facebook was also her most unsettling. "I'm in Raqqa, and I've received death threats," she wrote on July 20, 2015. "When ISIS soldiers arrest me and kill me, it will be okay, because while they will cut off my head, I'll still have dignity, which is better than living in humiliation."

Shortly after that post, Ruqia was abducted by ISIS and never heard from again. In January 2016, her brother received confirmation from the terror group that she had been murdered along with five other women. At the time of this writing, Ruqia's body had not been returned to her family.

Well before Ruqia was killed, I wondered what her story was. Why did she turn to writing and citizen journalism, despite knowing that death would be a very likely outcome of her outspokenness? Why did she choose the pen name "Nissan," which means "April" in Arabic? How did she reconcile the identity she presented online with what was expected of her at home or by the society she lived in?

Much like Ruqia, scores of women in or from the Arab world and broader Middle East have quietly and courageously risked their lives to write about the coming apart of their region. These women are fierce reporters who have helped shape the narratives of perhaps the most important moments in their homelands' modern history, a time of failed revolutions and violent warfare, widespread political and social upheaval, and the worst refugee crisis since the end of the Second World War. And yet, despite their access, expertise, and the obstacles they must overcome in order to do their jobs, they haven't received as much attention as their Western and often white male peers.

Our Women on the Ground presents intimate and rarely heard accounts of what it's like for a woman to report on a region she hails from. The stories of the nineteen *sahafiyat* whose essays make up this collection are crucial—not only because they have contributed to our understanding of what is transpiring in some of the most dangerous countries and protracted conflicts in the world, but also because they intrepidly crush stereotypes of what it means to be an Arab or Middle Eastern woman today, especially in the era of U.S. president Donald Trump, the rise of populism and the far right in Europe and elsewhere, and ISIS.

Arab women are indeed misunderstood on multiple levels and by multiple groups. On one hand, an Arab woman may be victimized or pitied by outsiders who think her to be "submissive," "oppressed," or "subjugated." She is occasionally boxed into one identity, whereby, for example, her Arab identity is (incorrectly) conflated with a Muslim one. And she is frequently exoticized or superficially celebrated. On the other hand, an outspoken Arab woman is sometimes deemed improper, or an anomaly, by both outsiders and the society around her. Professionally, she might be considered less of a "threat" than her male peers, or not taken seriously. And she is sometimes actively silenced or passively unheard.

This anthology is, in part, an effort to disrupt such flimsy stereotypes. The *sahafiyat* come from different generations, faiths, and nationalities, reflecting the diversity of an entire region. They are writers, reporters, broadcast journalists, and photojournalists who work for newspapers, websites, magazines, and television networks. The women are reporters employed by international and local media outlets, as well as independent, freelance, and citizen journalists. They started their reporting careers in the 1980s, 1990s, 2000s, and 2010s—some are veterans, while others are emerging. Four have stepped away from the field. Their countries of origin include Lebanon, Syria, Egypt, Morocco, Yemen, Libya, Palestine, Sudan, and Iraq.

Some of these women have been sexually assaulted, threatened, propositioned, detained, or even shot at while on the job, but have persisted nonetheless. They've contributed to dispelling the many myths saturating an often basic depiction of the region they have cultural, linguistic, and personal ties to, while fighting patriarchy and sexism. At the same time, they've also been able to use gender to their advantage, managing to conduct harrowing interviews with other women precisely because being female has given them access a male reporter would not have been able to secure as easily, if at all. Some have even lost loved ones while on the field.

What binds them all is the fact that they are unwavering in their pursuit of truth and their desire to disseminate it. That relentlessness is the thread that runs through this book's pages. The *sahafiyat* have helped write history. Together, their stories offer a stunningly complex patchwork narrative.

When I learned of Ruqia, I added her name to a long list of journalists covering the Middle East that I'd started compiling in a Google doc titled "Mideast Reporters" in December 2010. I created the document shortly after Tunisian street vendor Mohamed Bouazizi self-immolated, sparking the beginning of what would later be dubbed the Arab Spring. News on the Middle East, already a hotbed for foreign reporters, subsequently imploded. I wanted to keep track of who was reporting what and from where, often following the journalists on Twitter and Facebook and adding their names to my Google Alerts. This "journo-list" endeavor was, in part, because at the time I was a *sahafiya* writing about the ramifications of the Arab Spring and monitoring regional media for *Bloomberg News*.

For as long as I can remember, I had wanted to be a journalist. My fascination with news and the Arab world was born in a small living room in the United Kingdom in the early nineties. My father used to record the BBC's dispatches from Iraq and Kuwait on VHS during the first Gulf War, in addition to political developments in our home country, Lebanon, which was still reeling from a deadly sectarian conflict and an Israeli invasion. Over the years, his tapes piled up. When I was growing up, my mother and father would nostalgically tell my siblings and me that they missed home, even as images of armed men, injured civilians, and bombed-out buildings covered the TV screen. As phone lines were frequently down in south Lebanon, my parents were rarely able to communicate with their families, whose safety they continually feared for, and they relied on journalists for updates on the calamitous situation.

Fourteen years later, during my tenure as the editor in chief of my university's student newspaper in Beirut, I was thrown into reporting on Lebanese politics at a time of unending turmoil. Rafiq al-Hariri, Lebanon's former prime minister, was assassinated in a massive car bombing by unknown assailants, an event that marked the start of what many called the Cedar Revolution. Its upshots, which included the departure of Syrian troops from the fragile country, altered the course of modern history in Lebanon and perhaps the region. As the newspaper's editor, it was my duty to commission, write, and edit stories on the student body's reaction to the assassination and the instability that ensued. Though the newsroom was full of men, some of the most tenacious and determined reporters on my team were women, one of whom—Nour Malas—wrote a piece for this book.

In January 2010, soon after graduating from Columbia Journalism School, I joined *Bloomberg News* as a reporter. The move was an unusual one for me: given my background in literature and politics, I wasn't especially interested in finance. Within twelve months, however, the Arab Spring would erupt, and the position would come to involve reporting on how the financial markets and economies across the Middle East and North Africa were reacting to the upheaval.

The underpinnings of the Arab Spring were indeed largely economic. But because I was reporting from the air-conditioned skyscrapers of Dubai instead of on the ground in countries including Egypt, Syria, Libya, and Tunisia, I felt like a fraud.

At one point in June 2011, along with a Syrian stringer, I interviewed the head of Syria's stock market about his outlook for the year. His country was already on the path toward implosion, but he was choosing to turn a blind eye to the situation—he said he expected several businesses to take an interest in the market, and that the violence would quickly dissipate. That was the moment I reached peak cognitive dissonance.

My reporting was so far removed from what was unfolding from a humanitarian and political perspective that when Nour Malas casually referred to a "fundic" in a conversation we were having about the uprisings, I'd assumed she meant a fund manager. She was, of course, referring to an Islamic fundamentalist.

I was certain I belonged on the streets of Cairo and Benghazi, yet there I was, desktop daydreaming in the luxurious halls of the Dubai International Financial Centre. I sat in front of four *Bloomberg* terminal screens with a skinny latte, a Rolodex of investment banking and trading contacts, and two BlackBerrys close by. (My family was, of course, comfortable with this arrangement. I was in the Middle East, but nowhere near the violence. I was reporting on the Arab Spring without having to speak to rebels or strongmen. And my prospects of marriage to a banker were reasonably high.) In hindsight, I wish I had dropped everything on the spot and rushed to the front lines, but that would have required courage I admittedly did not yet have— courage the women in this anthology exemplify.

That's not to say the story of how the Arab Spring eventually touched the oil-drenched gulf wasn't fascinating to observe from an economic perspective. Countries that had been mostly insulated from protests and considered "safe havens" began to witness dissent, prompting generous handouts, salary increases for state employees, and affordable housing programs from the government to placate activists and dissidents. Though that dissent was almost immediately crushed—in the case of Bahrain, the quashing was of a particularly deadly and violent nature—fear of it potentially breaking out again or of any spillover from neighboring countries continues to influence policy making and economic strategy in some of the world's most prosperous nations, and to weigh heavily on human rights.

While at *Bloomberg*, I was occasionally placed on "Arab Spring monitoring" duty, which quite literally entailed monitoring state-run websites, the pan-Arab news channel Al Arabiya, and other Arabic-language media outlets for breaking news. Initially, we spotlighted the brewing conflict in Syria with a barrage of death-toll headlines. But we soon stopped flashing news on the fatalities: there were simply too many to keep up with.

To overcompensate for that cushy financial reporting job, I voraciously consumed news on the Arab Spring whenever I had a spare moment, closely following the work of reporters I had quickly come to admire. Many of those journalists are featured in this book. When I added their names to my ever-growing journo-list, it didn't take long for me to notice the considerable gender and background discrepancy. As the list grew, so, too, did the imbalance. Soon I observed that not only were there more men than women reporting on the region for international media, but most of the reporters were Western. (It's worth noting that many excellent women reporters of Western origin have been leading Middle East coverage in the past decade or so, particularly that of Syria—including, of course, the indomitable Marie Colvin, who died while covering the siege of Homs.) The gap came as no surprise to me, but to see it in such plain form was a shock nonetheless.

As this book demonstrates, Arab *sahafiyat* all over the world are doing incredible and vital reporting during this era of unrest, and they understand the region deeply. In fact, one of the most significant challenges I faced in creating this book was having to cap the number of contributors and conflicts; there are far too many brilliant women reporters whom I reluctantly had to exclude, and, sadly, there are far too many conflicts in the region to include them all. And yet, these women's voices aren't heard enough in the global discourse on the Middle East. This absence can be attributed, at least in part, to gender bias. Add to that an *Arab* woman writing about the *Arab* world, and the problem is compounded.

The problem is hardly recent. In the past century, some of the journalists and media activists who have left an indelible mark on the region were women who challenged societal norms and risked their lives as they sought to document and challenge disturbing truths and political developments. But, perhaps unsurprisingly, they are little known, even in the Middle East.

Nabawiya Musa, a writer, editor, and founding feminist of modern Egypt, devoted her entire career to furthering women's education and eliminating their exploitation. Born in 1886 in Zagazig, Egypt, she became the first Egyptian woman to complete secondary school exams. Musa passionately believed that most perceived differences between men and women were nothing but social constructs that could be eroded with time, and embarked on a career in writing and education to convey that message. In addition to editing a woman's magazine and writing for *al-Balagh al-Usbu'i*, or the *Weekly News*, she penned a number of seminal articles, including "Women and Work" in 1920.

Across the Mediterranean some twenty-five years after Musa's death in 1951, Ghada Salhab, a young Lebanese *sahafiya*, traveled to the front lines of a ferocious civil war to report on it for a national news magazine. Lebanese women are markedly active in the journalism space, partly because the country has the freest press in the Arab world and is, as a result, a regional media powerhouse relative to its small size. But during that devastating and drawn-out war, which raged from 1975 to 1990, and the Israeli invasion of 1982, few Lebanese women reporters were on the front lines.

Salhab, originally from Tripoli, the second-largest city in Lebanon, bravely covered violent battles between Christian and Muslim militiamen in Beirut. She also covered culture extensively, wanting to highlight the layers of Lebanese life beyond the front lines. The *sahafiya* later wrote four volumes in Arabic on the civil war, *The Black Box of the Lebanese Disaster*, in which she exposed details on the conflict that hadn't been documented elsewhere. She wrote the books, she once said, so the youth could learn from mistakes of the past.

(Another one of the trailblazing women who covered the war was the esteemed Nora Boustany, who wrote for the *Washington Post* and other publications and who currently teaches journalism at the American University of Beirut. Sadly, Boustany was unable to contribute a chapter to this book, but we would be remiss not to note her illustrious career.)

Musa and Salhab are little known, even in their regions of origin, and yet they helped shape and document twentieth-century Egyptian, Lebanese—and Middle Eastern—history.

My intention in creating this anthology was to help ensure that the voices of the women who are striving to shape and document Arab history now are amplified, and to give them the space to speak for themselves, without projecting themes of women's issues and patriarchy onto them. The result is a unique combination of memoir, history, politics, cultural criticism, and war reportage.

In these essays, the *sahafiyat* confront issues surrounding gender, nationality, tradition, and authenticity. They explore their struggles with conflicting identities, reflect on the unexpected friendships they've formed with their sources, or describe the ways in which their job has changed throughout the years of covering a rapidly transforming country. A few of them write about the consequences of being a woman on the field—from experiencing misogyny to the uncomfortable truth of how being a female reporter sometimes helped them secure access to male sources in conservative settings. These journalists, some of whom are Middle Eastern by ancestry but have strong ties to the West due to displacement or other factors,* have played a

---

* The notion of a dual, or split, identity isn't uncommon among those of Arab or Middle Eastern origin, given waves of emigration spurred in part by warfare and forced exile—demonstrated heartbreakingly by the mass exodus of Syrians to surrounding Levantine countries, Europe, and

crucial role in helping to narrow a geographical and cultural gap with the rest of the world by way of their linguistic skills and network of contacts in the Arab world.

Some of the women are independent journalists or "media activists," like Ruqia. For them, their work has directly opposed the regimes or movements they report on, and often involves expressing opinions or taking stances, a brand of journalism that would be deemed unacceptable to traditional Western media outlets, most of which mandate high standards of impartiality. Many of the other women work, or have worked, with international media outlets, and have therefore had to contend with that expectation of neutrality despite harboring strong personal views on the conflicts they have reported on.

To be a *sahafiya* in the region can entail engaging in some form of defiance against state or nonstate actors—not by choice, but simply by doing one's job. To be a woman war reporter in this part of the world can sometimes mean you are defying not only the state but also your society, family, and the role you are expected to play within your home.

A *sahafiya* is twice burdened. As a Middle Eastern or North African woman in her homeland, she is among some of the most mistreated women in the world when it comes to her basic rights: while there have been improvements, the region continues to rank last globally among eight on the World Economic Forum Gender Gap Index.

And as a native *sahafiya*, she is among some of the most repressed reporters in the world. The Middle East and North Africa is the most difficult and dangerous area for journalists to operate in, according to Reporters Without Borders, which has also listed Syria as the second-deadliest country for journalists after Afghanistan.

A journalistic and historical narrative on the Arab world and

---

beyond following the onset of the Syrian civil war. I intentionally wanted to reflect this reality in my selection of contributors in the "Crossfire" section.

the broader Middle East dominated by male or Western talking heads is, simply put, incomplete. Failing to expand that narrative to sufficiently incorporate the voices of Arab and Middle Eastern women in the global media landscape obstructs an inclusive dissemination of ideas about the region. And yet the public needs precisely that diversity of voices to formulate insightful views on the area and its people.

I created this long overdue anthology because it's a book I desperately wanted to see on bookshelves everywhere, one that brings attention to underreported tales and the women who tell them. Arab and Middle Eastern women aren't heard enough in this space. But they're living and breathing the region, reporting on it from the front lines in Sana'a and Mosul and from Riyadh and Cairo—even from their living rooms in Raqqa.

These are *our* women on the ground.

I invite you all to listen to what they have to say. They may surprise you.

ZAHRA HANKIR

REMEMBRANCES

The Woman Question

Hannah Allam

When I speak before Western audiences about my years covering the war in Iraq as a journalist for McClatchy Newspapers, someone inevitably asks, "What was it like to be a woman over there?"

"Well, I've never been there as a man, so I'm not sure I can compare," is the clever way some of my friends reply to the same question.

I remind myself to borrow the line, but I can never quite remember to use it because when I hear the question, I see faces. Ban. Shatha. Sahar. Faten. Huda. Alaa. Jinan. Raghad. I think of the slivers of Iraq that they and many other women showed me, spaces that were off-limits to my male colleagues. Kitchens where meals were prepared without electricity. A bedroom with a mortar crater in the ceiling. A beauty salon that banned political talk so customers could get their hair done in peace. "Ladies' hours" at the Babylon Hotel swimming pool, where sunshine hit bare skin and the war lurked just over a tall concrete barrier.

Reporting on Iraq through the eyes of its women was illuminating, but, perhaps more important, it was more representative of the population as a whole. Years of bloodshed had left Iraq with a population that was more than half women, many of them heads of households because their men were dead or missing or exiled. When the "woman question" comes up at public talks, I explain the importance of covering women's stories by evoking the grisly math of car bombings.

At the height of the sectarian war, in 2006, car bombings were so commonplace that we stopped reporting on them unless twenty or more people were killed. For a year I didn't bother to set my alarm before going to sleep because I knew I'd be awakened every morning by a thunderous boom. It wasn't unusual to record daily car bomb death tolls of eighty or more. Because the most frequent targets were government and police buildings, the vast majority of the casualties were men.

Consider those numbers for a moment: eighty dead men meant eighty new widows and dozens of newly fatherless children. Every day. That meant that each week, more than five hundred Iraqi women suddenly became the sole providers for their families, setting their own devastation aside to keep their children fed and housed. They sold their wedding gold to buy bread. They felt like burdens on the extended families who took them in.

At their most desperate, some women entered into so-called temporary marriages that weren't intended to last long. Essentially, these marriages were prostitution with a thin religious veneer: men with money to spare would pay the women in exchange for sex, but because the couple was technically "married," however briefly, the arrangement was deemed legitimate according to some Shi'a Islamic rulings.

A widow named Nisreen told me her hands shook and her face reddened with shame when she signed a temporary marriage contract in exchange for fifteen dollars a month plus groceries and clothes for her five children.

"My son calls me a bad woman, a prostitute. My children have no idea I did this for their sake," Nisreen said.

Before I first traveled to Iraq in the summer of 2003, I read an article in *Rolling Stone* in which a U.S. military officer marveled at the toughness of Iraqi women and mused that the advance might not have been so easy had U.S. forces faced the country's women.

It was a comment meant to emasculate the men as much as it praised the women, and I would hear many versions of it when I was around U.S. troops.

Even in the Middle East, where there is no shortage of heartache, Iraqi women are known to be particularly tough. The guttural Iraqi accent only underlines that reputation. Nelly, a chain-smoking, melodramatic Egyptian hairdresser in Baghdad, once whispered to me that Iraqi women were the region's most beautiful—until they opened their mouths.

I observed that tough exterior in hundreds of Iraqi women I met over the years. The elderly women trudging through the southern marshes with heavy sacks of reeds strapped to bowed backs. The stoic mothers looking for their sons among the corpses strewn at the scene of a suicide bombing. The pregnant militant who put a gun to my head in a Sadr City alleyway, and my Iraqi female friend who calmly swatted it away and lectured the attacker about her terrible manners.

Those sorts of stories accumulated until they formed an archetype: the tragic yet resilient Iraqi woman, a metaphor for the country itself. In hindsight, it seems so facile to see Iraqi women only through the prism of their war-ravaged lives, but how else do you report a story where pain is etched on the face of every woman you interview?

Even though several women correspondents covered Iraq, there was an unspoken understanding that if you delved too deeply into women's lives, you risked being labeled as soft, or missing the point. And the point, at least for many of our male colleagues, was the combat, the "bang-bang," in the parlance of war photographers. I'll never forget the sting when one of my male colleagues let out a deep sigh as I told him about a piece I was writing on civilians: "Oh, Hannah and her PIPS." The acronym, he said, stood for "Poor Iraqi People Stories."

The PIPS captured the gloomy reality of war, but not the women themselves, at least not in a three-dimensional way. Amid the nonstop carnage, I seldom got to write about how witty or sweet or vulnerable Iraqi women could be. Those were the private memories, written in my heart if not in my notebook, and the ones that I recall more easily than any I published under a Baghdad dateline.

Of course, Iraqi women were more than capable of telling their own stories, and did so whenever they had the chance. Our bureau for McClatchy Newspapers was unusual: it employed three consecutive Arab American women bureau chiefs and more Iraqi women reporters than any other Western news agency. When the local staff saw how rarely civilian life made it into news stories that focused on the bloodshed and political turmoil, they started a blog, *Inside Iraq*, for which they wrote pieces using their own experiences to illustrate the human impact of war and occupation. The blog gained a following of loyal readers from around the globe.

In 2007, the International Women's Media Foundation awarded six Iraqi women from our bureau the prestigious Courage in Journalism Award. They were the first winners from Iraq in the history of the prize. The honorees included a woman who had to retrieve her nephew's dismembered body from a morgue because militants would've killed any man who showed up; one who had nearly died in a bombing but returned to work a couple of days later, her hearing still impaired from the blast; and one who commandeered an ambulance to sneak into a hospital that was on lockdown because the Iraqi government was trying to hide the civilian deaths from a disastrous operation.

The women received their awards from Angelina Jolie and Meg Ryan at glitzy ceremonies in New York and Los Angeles. They basked in the moment, but knew their fairy tale would soon be over. There was still so much to do back home. Sahar, one of the honorees and a gifted writer with an unfailing moral compass, delivered the acceptance speech, explaining why she chose such dangerous work.

"It's because I'm tired of being branded a terrorist; tired that a human life lost in my country is no loss at all," she told the audience. "It is our responsibility to do our utmost to acquire the answers, to dig them up with our bare hands if we must."

I wish I could convey how devilishly funny my Iraqi girlfriends were, but the problem with sharing such memories is context. Things people find hilarious in wartime come off as odd or in poor taste in normal life. And nobody does gallows humor like Iraqis. As the years stretched on without the restoration of power, a popular joke was that a distraught boy runs up to his mom and sobs that his father had touched a wire and been electrocuted. The mother replies: "Thank God! There's electricity!"

To pass the time in traffic snarls, my friend and translator Ban, a literature buff who used to tell me Iraq was waiting for Godot, invented a game called Is That the One? We'd sit in the backseat and peer out the windows, looking for cars that sat a little too low. "There it is!" I'd yell, spotting a Mercedes that seemed suspiciously heavy, as if it were crammed with explosives. "Is that the one?" I'd ask Ban, meaning, "Is that the car bomb that's about to blow us to smithereens?" "No! *That's* the one!" she'd reply, pointing out a flatbed truck stacked with unmarked boxes. At the time, we found this endlessly entertaining and not the least bit macabre.

When your days hover so closely to death, the pursuit of fun becomes thrilling and a little reckless. It's as if you know you're on your way out, so why not really live it up? After the U.S. military imposed a curfew in 2003, Iraqi women friends would often crash in my room. We'd play music and dance our hearts out, twirling until we forgot that we were in a dingy hotel room with shatterproof tape on the windows and flak vests by the door. A few Iraqi women I knew swallowed black-market pain pills or smoked hashish mixed with tobacco. They got manicures even when insurgents began tossing Molotov cocktails through the salon windows. Some undergrads at Baghdad University wore tight skirts and left their hair uncovered in defiance of flyers promising death for girls who didn't veil.

I knew one young woman, the daughter of a cherished friend and a recent dental school graduate, who refused to let "the situation"—Iraqis' preferred euphemism for sectarian slaughter—deter her from pursuing her dream. She went door-to-door in Baghdad neighborhoods, offering free checkups and minor dental procedures. Her mother, who'd already lost a son to crossfire, was fearful but proud.

"This is madness!" I would tell her. "Who knocks on strangers' doors in a civil war?"

"I do," the young dentist replied.

It was the tiny, ordinary pleasures that were most missed: a shopping excursion without fear of kidnapping, sipping chai on a balcony without the crackle of sniper fire, going for a leisurely drive uninterrupted by checkpoints.

Ban's husband, Selwan, the love of her life who later was gunned down by insurgents, bristled under the traditional customs of his homeland. He was proud that his wife earned the same salary he did, and he found it amusing that Ban and I would steal his car keys and go for joyrides at a time when many families thought it too risky for women to drive.

Our favorite route was along the Tigris River, looping back to the highway and then across Jadriyah Bridge. At a certain stretch, there was a big bump in the road, and if you hit it fast enough, the whole car would lift a little, like in action movies. We lived for that bump, for that fleeting feeling of being airborne and free, Thelma and Louise in Baghdad.

One beautiful spring day in 2004, Ban and I coasted along the bridge, belting at the top of our lungs a song we both loved by the Tunisian pop star Latifa. We whizzed past funeral banners, past the remnants of palm groves the Americans had chopped down to deter snipers, past a sand-colored mosque. The bump was coming up and we were excited for it, cranking the music up as high as it would go.

We barreled toward our favorite spot, ready for that familiar rush, when I saw a black flash out of the corner of my eye. I looked in the rearview mirror and saw that we were being forced off the road by a massive, Blackwater-style American security convoy. The lead SUV was inches from ramming the back of our car. A man with an assault rifle angrily motioned for us to move, and it was clear the convoy had been trying to pass us for a while. We hadn't heard the honking over our music.

My legs went to jelly and I swerved out of their way as fast as I could. I'd seen a convoy like this shoot an unarmed man right in front of me, and had heard dozens of similar stories from Iraqis. I have no idea why they didn't shoot us; maybe they were close enough to see we were women.

Badly shaken, Ban and I drove home in silence, going so slowly that hitting the bump was anticlimactic. We made a pact not to tell Selwan for fear he wouldn't let us take the car out again.

Later that evening, after our nerves had calmed, we started giggling about what a dumb move it was, nearly sacrificing our lives for a pop song and a bump in the road. But given all the gruesome deaths we had seen in Iraq, we agreed that rocking out with your best friend in a moment of sheer bliss wouldn't have been such a bad way to go.

What was it like to be a woman in Iraq? The women I met worked tirelessly to keep day-to-day life functioning smoothly, even when they were living in the midst of a weeks-long battle, as was the case in the summer of 2004 inside the Imam Ali shrine.

The shrine is a shimmering monument of gold and peacock-blue mosaic topped with an onion-shaped dome that looks like the turban of a pasha from long ago. On calm days, pigeons mill about, looking for scraps of food from the Shi'a Muslim pilgrims who come to the Iraqi holy city of Najaf in droves.

But in the awful summer of 2004, the U.S. military surrounded the compound in an attempt to drive out Mahdi Army insurgents who were camping out inside. The pigeons had flown

away—nature's early warning system—and most Western reporters had left the shrine. Only a handful remained inside with
the Mahdi Army guerrillas, including me, along with dozens of
Iraqi civilians seeking refuge; they were hoping that even if the
Americans flattened the city, they wouldn't dare violate the
sanctity of one of Islam's most revered sites. One night, when
U.S. bombing raids shook the compound so violently that it felt
as if our skeletons would push through our skin, I feared they
had bet wrong.

In my memories of that August, heat and fear are intertwined,
each making the other worse. Even in wartime, women in Najaf
wear abayas, long billowy robes that leave only their faces,
hands, and feet exposed. I remember sweat trickling down my
back as I crouched in the courtyard listening to gunfire. Running
in an abaya was a special skill that we honed each time we had
to take cover: you use your left hand to hold the silky fabric
under your chin to keep it in place and your right hand to hike
up the bottom to free your feet. Then you run in a zigzag pattern
to avoid giving a clear shot to the snipers.

There wasn't much food, but everyone was too hot and terrified to eat anyway. At night, I locked arms with my dear friend
and translator Huda, and we debated which was more horrifying: the actual ground-shaking impact of an air strike or the
dread of waiting for the next one. Once, a tiny mouse scurried
across the floor where Huda and I lay. We shrieked, then burst
out laughing at the absurdity of being startled by a mouse while
bracing for a thousand-pound bomb.

Most of the men were outside fighting the U.S. troops, so it
was the women who kept the compound in order, cooking,
cleaning, and helping care for the wounded men brought in by
comrades who then rushed back to battle. Women's voices were
the ones I heard praying aloud each time the name of a new
"martyr," a Mahdi Army casualty, was announced over the compound's loudspeaker.

The only respite from the war was the washroom, where cool

water—a precious commodity at the time—still flowed from taps that were built for worshippers to make ablutions before prayer. Following the example set by the Iraqi women, I learned to take off my headscarf and hold it under the faucet before putting it back on my head still soaking wet—a miracle antidote to the heat.

One day I grew so hot I began hallucinating. I sat in the washroom, dizzy, as the mosaic tiles faded away, and found myself in my mother's kitchen in Oklahoma, the smell of her pancakes so vivid that I expected a plate to appear before me.

The spell ended when I heard someone whispering prayers from another corner. A middle-aged cook named Saleema was cleaning out her ringing ears with a matchstick. She was crying. "Don't worry, Auntie," I told her in Arabic. It wasn't her own safety she was thinking about. She said she couldn't take seeing any more mangled bodies of young Najafi men coming through the doors of the shrine.

She was also troubled by the U.S. casualties, refusing to think of them as faceless enemies. "And what about the poor American boys out there?" she asked. "Don't they also have mothers who want them home?" I was moved by her empathy and jotted down notes from our encounter so that I could include the scene in my report from the shrine, if we ever made it out.

After dawn the next morning, Huda and I fled the compound during a lull in the fighting. We stumbled through the old city's labyrinthine streets, finding a corpse lying in one alley, an American armored vehicle in another. We flagged down the only car that was out, a red sedan carrying two Iraqi women who were on a dangerous ride to check on their relatives after the overnight air strikes.

The driver, Leila, was surveying the smoldering, zombie-movie ruins of her city and wondering aloud how long Iraqis would suffer.

"It's a calamity beyond all calamities," she said. "Every day I tell myself it'll end and we can be happy. But it won't end and we won't be happy."

Leila dropped us off at a hotel, and their red sedan continued on its grim mission. I thought a lot then, and have since, about how Leila was simultaneously heartbroken and resolute, a combination I saw again and again in the women I met in the decade I covered Iraq. The women at the shrine that bloody summer. The women on staff in our Baghdad bureau. The mothers and sisters and aunties who quietly fought to retain a measure of humanity on the margins of a grinding war.

Their experiences were woven into the stories I filed, but I never wrote the truth as plainly as this: Every time Iraq began to unravel, it was women who worked the hardest to stitch it back together.

Love and Loss in a Time of Revolution

Nada Bakri ◆

It was a cold and damp evening in February 2012 when my son, Malik, and I landed in Adana in southern Turkey. Our journey from Beirut had been long and we still had a two-hour drive to reach Antakya, a picturesque city near the border with Syria, where we would meet my husband and Malik's father, Anthony Shadid.

By the time we got in a taxi, darkness had fallen over everything. Night lights shimmered, but it was still difficult to make out the contours of the landscape.

"Go see Daddy," Malik said, clapping his hands in excitement. I felt a pang in my heart; I suspected Anthony might not get to Antakya until the next morning, and I did not want Malik, who was only twenty months old, to be disappointed when we arrived at our hotel and his father wasn't there.

Anthony had told me he would call me only when he thought it was absolutely safe for him to do so. He had entered Syria illegally from the southern Turkish border in order to interview armed rebels and opposition activists for the *New York Times*. Cell phone calls could be detected, and he wanted to err on the side of caution and avoid them if possible.

But as fate would have it—mine and Malik's—we never saw Anthony again. Not alive, at least.

What happened that night changed my life in ways I could never have imagined. Until that day, I had been working in

Beirut as a reporter covering Lebanon and the Middle East for almost a decade. They were some of the happiest and most rewarding years of my life: I loved being a reporter and was proud of my work. I was married to the man I loved. I became a mother.

That night in Antakya, I became a widow.

I don't remember precisely when I first realized I wanted to become a journalist, but it was sometime during high school. To be completely honest, there might have been an element of vanity involved as I imagined the excitement of covering major events and the satisfaction in knowing that people would read or listen to what I had to say.

But my real motivation was linked to my upbringing. I grew up in Lebanon, a country always at war with itself, in a politically savvy family. I didn't witness any of the heavy fighting on the streets of Beirut in the 1980s, nor do I remember the Israeli invasion of 1982 or the infamous massacre in two adjacent camps for Palestinian refugees on the outskirts of the city a few months later. But I have heard enough about these events to write a book.

I do remember the sounds and smells of war, and the fear. I remember crouching with my siblings and my mother in a makeshift shelter—a corridor in our apartment—during an evening of fighting in 1990 that was very close to our home. I also remember the frightening sound of Israeli warplanes before they dropped their bombs.

The street in Beirut on which our apartment building was located was blocked at one end by a small mountain of sandbags, which my mother and I once climbed over on our way to my grandmother's house a couple of blocks away from us. We walked on streets that were narrowed from the debris of shelled buildings and avoided others that were hot spots for snipers who often targeted pedestrians randomly.

The Lebanese civil war officially ended in 1991, when Parliament issued an amnesty law pardoning all but two warlords and all militias were disarmed. An Arab-brokered deal between opposing Lebanese political factions underlined the importance of "mutual coexistence" among the eighteen recognized sects of Lebanon's Muslim and Christian communities. It also restructured their political representation.

But though in some ways the deal brought peace and stability back to Lebanon, it didn't heal the wounds of war. The nation remained deeply divided and extremely precarious.

By the time I graduated from the Lebanese American University in Beirut in the spring of 2002, I had lived through a decade of intermittent fighting between Lebanese Christian and Muslim militias and their foreign allies. Major regional and international events also unfolded during that period, including the second Gulf War in Iraq, the September 11 attacks on the World Trade Center, and the war in Afghanistan. The Arab-Israeli conflict was always there, sometimes a leading story and sometimes a distant murmur.

A few years later, in 2007, I found myself in Beirut again, this time as a reporter. The streets were full of fighting and debris, much as they had been in my childhood.

The new turmoil had been set off by the assassination of former prime minister Rafiq al-Hariri in February of 2005 by a massive car bomb in Beirut. His death, widely blamed on Syria and its allies in Lebanon, split the country into two camps: a Shi'a one backed by Syria and Iran and led by Hezbollah, and a Sunni one backed by the West and led by Hariri's supporters. Christians were divided between the two camps. The results were a seventeen-month-long political stalemate and a string of political assassinations.

The first round of fighting broke out on January 23, 2007. A protest that day turned violent when Hezbollah supporters blocked roads leading to Beirut with burning tires and cars and clashed with loyalists of the Sunni government.

At the time, I was a reporter for a Lebanon-based English-language newspaper called the *Daily Star* and a stringer for the *New York Times*.

I had heard reports that morning of men in black balaclavas brandishing batons and blocking access to and from Rafic Hariri International Airport, Lebanon's only civilian airport. I hitched a ride there on a scooter driven by an old acquaintance and Hezbollah supporter, a man in his midfifties named Abu Ali who had fought in the civil war.

When I arrived, the scene was tense as passengers begged and pleaded with protesters to be let in and out of the airport. Black smoke filled the air and young men were feeding pits of fire with rubber tires and trash. I approached a group of protesters, introduced myself, and asked why they were rioting. As I listened and took notes, a man suddenly came charging at me, trying to grab my notebook. But I was quick, holding it close to my chest and running toward Abu Ali, who was a few meters away with his back turned to me. The other man and a couple of other protesters were chasing me, but as soon as I started calling Abu Ali's name and they realized I had come with him, they let me leave with my notebook. If not for him, I don't know what might have happened to me that day.

A few months later, during a funeral procession for victims killed in another round of clashes, a friend of mine who was a foreign freelance photojournalist got in a fight with a mourner over the photos he was taking. Since neither of them spoke the other's language, I went over to them to help mediate. The argument quickly escalated as more mourners got involved, and I was pushed and shoved violently. I don't remember how the fight was broken up, but I do remember sobbing hard as soon as I was alone. I did not cry because I feared for my life. I cried because I felt very vulnerable and completely unable to defend myself physically as a woman.

As much as I loved my job, there were many times between

2005 and 2008 when I wished to be someone else or somewhere else. I was once looking for the phone number of a contact in my phone book when I noticed that I had written the word *dead* in parentheses next to his name. The person was Samir Kassir, a prominent columnist critical of Syria who had been killed in June 2005 in a car bomb outside his home. I counted eight other men, politicians and activists, whom I had interviewed many times and who were killed in the span of two years. The conflict was starting to take its toll on me.

Then, in May 2008, I had a very close call with death.

The government of Lebanese prime minister Fouad Siniora, who was backed by the West, had recently discovered a private telecommunication network used by Hezbollah. Hezbollah had fought against Israel in July 2006 in an asymmetrical war that devastated Lebanon, known in Lebanon as the July War; the party considered the network a crucial part of its resistance against Israel. (Hezbollah is credited for liberating south Lebanon, home to the majority of its Shi'a population, from an Israeli occupation that lasted from 1982 until 2000.) Siniora announced that steps were being taken to dismantle the network, as it violated the sovereignty of his government. Hezbollah was enraged.

On May 8, the group's leader, Hassan Nasrallah, said the government's announcement was "a declaration of war." No one believed Hezbollah would use its weapons domestically. But the unimaginable happened.

In scenes reminiscent of the civil war, men with machine guns battled on the streets of Beirut, snipers took positions, and neighborhoods were littered with burned cars and debris. Government supporters, however, were no match for Hezbollah's military power, and they quickly retreated. The three days of fighting left at least eleven people dead and nineteen injured.

On Saturday, May 10, I went with my colleague Raed Rafei, who was working for the *Los Angeles Times* then, to cover the funeral of a young Sunni man who had been killed by a sniper two days prior.

It was another emotionally charged scene in which sectarian allegiances served to stoke violence. The Sunni mourners vowed to take revenge on the Shi'a and called Hezbollah, which means the "Party of God," "an enemy of God." As the pallbearers approached a store owned by a Shi'a man, mourners urged him to close his shop. He refused, and they smashed his windows with chairs and rocks.

He responded by opening fire on the procession. I immediately got down and crawled to take cover behind a garbage container. Raed was walking next to me, and when the gunfire erupted, he also hid. When everything had gone quiet, I emerged from my hiding place and saw the two men who had been standing right next to me moments earlier lying on the ground in a pool of blood. Raed was standing over a body with a point-and-shoot camera. We had both survived and they had not. Their names were Ali Masri and Moussa Zouki.

I later sneaked into the hospital where the bodies of Masri, twenty-three, and Zouki, twenty-four, had been taken. I found Mr. Masri's father, Mohammad, lying on a bed in an emergency room. When he heard that his son had been shot, he had passed out and was brought to the same hospital.

"Tell me what happened to Ali," he begged between sobs. "My heart is telling me he is dead. A father's heart knows. He's dead. Don't tell me he is not dead. I know he is. Ali, my son, can you hear me?"

He pulled a picture of Ali from his wallet and kissed it. "Answer me, Ali," he said, looking at the photo. "Are you dead? Don't die."

I walked out of the room when I could no longer hold back my tears. I went outside and tried to collect myself. When I walked back into the hospital, I saw Ali's mother. "Ali is here," she said, pointing in the direction of the morgue. "I want to stay here. He told me this morning he wanted to sleep more. He is going to sleep forever now."

Ali and I were strangers. But I still can't shake off the memory of that day or how senseless his death was.

I first met Anthony in September 2006, shortly after the July War, at a popular rally held by Hezbollah in the southern suburbs of Beirut to mark its "divine victory" against Israel. Because they had held their own for thirty-three days, the conflict was considered a victory by many Hezbollah supporters, despite the fact that at least twelve hundred Lebanese civilians had been killed, entire villages in south Lebanon had been destroyed by aerial strikes, and every major bridge and highway in Lebanon had been bombed.

I had read Anthony's coverage of the Middle East, beginning with the U.S.-led invasion of Iraq in 2003, with great admiration. So when he called to ask me out on a date a few days after the rally, I was very happily surprised. On our second date, we went to the movies. By the third time I saw him, being together felt more like being with an old friend than with a romantic interest, and so we became friends instead.

But six months later, he asked me on a date again. "What do you mean?" I remember asking him, a little confused. He said, "You told me on our first date that you are more comfortable dating someone you are friends with, so I wanted us to become friends first."

By the end of May, I had had enough of Beirut and its protests, bombs, street fights, and never-ending political bickering. Like the toxic fumes of burning tires that constricted my lungs, the conflict had become psychologically suffocating. I decided to take a break and enrolled at the Graduate School of Journalism at Columbia University in New York City. I had been flirting with the idea of graduate school since finishing college, but I hadn't felt ready to go back to school until that spring.

There was very little that we didn't do together. I was happy and in love. When it was time for me to leave for graduate school, Anthony asked me to marry him and I said yes.

In June 2009, after graduating from Columbia University, I moved to Baghdad to work as a reporter for the *Washington Post*. Anthony, now my husband, was the bureau chief. We had been married for a year but hadn't lived in the same city yet.

I had been to Iraq once before, in December 2002—three months before the U.S.-led invasion, in a time of peace. But the country had changed a lot since then.

As Anthony had put it in the *Washington Post* in 2009, "The war in Iraq is indeed over, at least the conflict as it was understood during its first five years: insurgency, communal cleansing, gangland turf battles and an anarchic, often futile quest to survive, in other words, civil war—though civil war was always too tidy a term for it."

But the situation on the ground was still very complex. I was anxious about my new job, and about working with Anthony, who was widely considered the most successful foreign correspondent covering the Middle East. I fretted about the stories I would write and those I would miss and whether anyone would read anything I wrote at all. Our living arrangements were not ideal since we had to live and work in a house that served as bureau and home for the newspaper's local and foreign staff.

Anthony was a great partner, in marriage and at work. We made a good team and I leaned on him to understand the complexities of Iraq. Together, we brainstormed ideas, planned reporting trips, and sounded out the best translations of quotes from Arabic to English. If I was working late on a story, he stayed up until I finished it. Neither of us ever filed a story before the other read it.

Our bedroom was on the second floor overlooking a wild garden with palm trees. We decorated with paintings and framed photographs and an antique Persian carpet. It felt like home.

On quiet evenings, we watched American television shows

while eating pints of vanilla ice cream. *Desperate Housewives* was still on the air at that point, and downloading an episode over the very slow internet connection sometimes took a whole day. But it was worth the effort because the simple pleasure of watching a TV show each week gave our life there a sense of normalcy and routine.

Sometimes, we went out on date nights. Once we came across a tiny restaurant in an upscale neighborhood of Baghdad called al-Reef, where a man played a medley of Eastern and Western tunes every night on the piano. It remains one of my fondest memories from my life in Baghdad, where both pianists and music venues were scarce.

I woke up one day in August feeling sick. Anthony and I walked to a small pharmacy and asked for an at-home pregnancy test. The salesperson looked at us disapprovingly, and I knew he assumed we were not married. "Made in Syria" was written in big Arabic letters on the box, which looked like a cheaper version of Clearblue. It cost the equivalent of two dollars.

My Iraqi colleague once took me to visit his wife's doctor for a routine obstetric checkup in my first trimester. The doctor was puzzled as to why I chose to stay in Baghdad when I could carry my pregnancy in a safer and healthier environment abroad. I pointed out that Iraqi women delivered healthy full-term babies every day. "But they don't have a choice," she said. She ordered an ultrasound, and although everything was normal she told me I would have to spend the rest of my pregnancy in bed to avoid a miscarriage. I suspected it was her attempt to convince me to leave. I ignored her advice and never saw her again.

I did think of her when, five months into my pregnancy, I got in a car accident. My car skidded when I tried to slow down before a blind curve. The road was wet and the vehicle spun out of control, flipped, and landed on its roof. I was unscathed.

In January 2010, three massive car bombs exploded within minutes of one another in three separate neighborhoods in the city. The targets were hotels frequented by foreign correspondents and businessmen. The third blast exploded at 3:37 p.m. on January 25 and was close enough to our house to shatter many of our windows.

The blast struck the Al Hamra Hotel, which was across the street from the *Washington Post* building and home to many of our friends and colleagues. Anthony and I had left the *Post* in December and joined the *New York Times* bureau in Baghdad; we were living about a mile away. I was seven months pregnant that day, and for the first time since the 2005 explosion in Beirut that killed Hariri, I did not want to go to the bombing site. At that moment I felt a bigger commitment to motherhood than to any news story, no matter how important it was.

By the end of 2010, Anthony and I, along with our newborn son, Malik, were living in Beirut, where Anthony had been appointed the bureau chief for the *New York Times* and I was a reporter. The situation there and in the Arab world in general—save for Iraq—was stable.

But on December 17, 2010, a young fruit vendor set himself on fire in a Tunisian village following a dispute with the local police. The incident sparked protests that were captured on video and seen by millions across the world. A popular rebellion soon broke out, and twenty-eight days later President Zine el-Abidine Ben Ali stepped down after twenty-three years in office.

Protests then spread to Egypt, Libya, Bahrain, Yemen, and Syria. Before the popular revolutions, most Arab countries had lived under repressive regimes that restricted freedoms and violated basic human rights.

In January 2011, Anthony called me from Cairo's Tahrir Square, where he was on assignment for the *New York Times*, so that I could listen with him to the jubilation that had erupted among protesters when President Hosni Mubarak's regime was felled. I was in Beirut and he wanted to share with me this epic moment in the history of the Arab world. Many, including Anthony and me, could not believe it was happening.

Encouraged by the successful revolutions in Tunisia and Egypt, activists on social media soon called for Syrians to take to the streets of Damascus in what they called a Day of Rage against the government of Bashar al-Assad. Assad had inherited power in 2000 from his father, Hafez, who had ruled the country for nearly three decades with an iron fist.

I drove to Damascus on February 4, 2011, to cover the potential protest for the *New York Times* and headed to the parliament building, where it was scheduled to be held. But no one showed up. "Syria is the last country where regime change will occur," a political activist and dissident told me later that day.

I visited Syria again in September with a Syrian friend and colleague who was working and living in Beirut. By then, more than twenty-six hundred people had died since the uprising, which had eventually erupted in mid-March in the poor southern town of Dara'a. The capital was yet to witness any unrest, but the general mood was somber, and many feared that the struggle to dislodge Mr. Assad could turn into a civil war, unleashing sectarian bloodshed in a country where ethnic and religious minorities had long coexisted.

The Syrian rebellion marked its seventh year in March 2018. Hundreds of thousands have been killed, and the regime still seems as strong as ever.

Syria is not the only country where the popular uprising failed to achieve its goals. Despite the bloodshed, many regimes managed to survive rebellions against them. Some rulers implemented modest reforms, while others violently silenced dissidents. Yemeni and Libyan leaders were overthrown, but the countries degenerated into chaos. A stricter military government rules Egypt now and fighting continues daily in Syria.

I sometimes think of Anthony's death as an unintended consequence of the Arab revolts. So was the week he spent in captivity in Libya in March 2011. His car was stopped at a military checkpoint manned by soldiers loyal to then Libyan leader Colonel

Muammar Gaddafi. He and three other *New York Times* colleagues who were traveling with him along the eastern coast of Libya were arrested and held captive for almost a week. I was in Beirut with Malik at the time, and for four days no one knew anything about their fate.

Anthony later said that one soldier had wanted to execute them on the spot. He told me he really thought he was not going to make it out alive. But instead, he and his colleagues were sent to a detention center in Tripoli that was under the control of the foreign ministry. The ministry released them six days after they were arrested to Turkish diplomats serving as intermediaries between Libyans and American officials.

Six months later, in August 2011, Anthony went to Syria to cover the uprising. Unable to enter legally (he had been blacklisted after a reporting trip he made in 2005 that angered the regime), he crossed the eastern Lebanese border into Syria sitting on a scooter behind a young smuggler. He made it home safely a week later.

A second trip was arranged for February 2012. This time he would sneak into the country from its northern border with Turkey. My friend and *New York Times* colleague in the Beirut bureau, Hwaida Saad, worked her contacts and organized the trip. The smugglers who agreed to take him arranged to hike and travel by horseback across the mountainous border between the two countries.

Anthony had asthma and was allergic to horses. When he called me from Antakya in southern Turkey the night before he left, he was worried about being near horses, but told me he had his inhalers and had never needed more than that. He was also angry about a comment a colleague in New York had made. "This is going to be a great workout for you," the editor had told him over the phone. "I could die on that trip and he is saying it is a great workout," Anthony said to me.

The last time I spoke with my husband was on February 14,

2012. He was in northern Syria and called me from his satellite phone to wish me a happy Valentine's Day. He said he was to leave Syria in a day or two, again traveling by hiking and horseback, and that the trip had been the best one of his entire career.

When Malik and I finally reached Antakya on the night of February 16, I checked into a boutique hotel called Al-Liwan. The place reminded Anthony, ever so nostalgic, of the family house he had rebuilt in south Lebanon. His grandmother had lived there as a little girl during the Ottoman occupation of the Levant, and he often joked that he wished he had been born a Turkish gentleman in the days of a tolerant and cosmopolitan Levant.

I was awakened shortly before midnight when my cell phone rang. It was Jill Abramson, the executive editor of the *Times*.

"Anthony had a fatal asthma attack," she said. I repeated the sentence in my head, but I could not understand what she was trying to tell me.

"What do you mean, a fatal asthma attack?" I asked.

Nothing I had ever been through prepared me for that moment.

"Anthony is dead," she said.

I curled up on the bathroom floor and cried. I wanted to scream but Malik was asleep, and I didn't want to startle him.

The Spanish author Javier Marias writes in his novel *The Infatuations* that death is hard to overcome because the finality of it is hard to accept:

> It's incomprehensible really, because it assumes a certainty, and being certain of anything goes against our nature: the certainty that someone will never come back, never speak again, never take another step—whether to come closer or to move further off—will never look at us or look away.

I remember shaking Anthony very hard when I was finally allowed to see him uncovered the next day—I had to wait for the autopsy to be done and for him to look like himself again. As ridiculous as it sounds to me now, I shook him to wake him up, to get him to stand up and walk out of that cold morgue, which smelled of everything malignant.

Many colleagues and friends traveled from all over the world to pay their respects and attend a memorial service in Anthony's honor. I was very appreciative of and grateful for their presence.

I suppress, as much as I can, my memories from the night he died and the following two days I spent in Turkey in hospitals, morgues, courtrooms, and police interrogations. On the flight from Adana to Istanbul, I screamed like a madwoman. Malik was sitting on my lap, agitated, and Anthony was in the cargo hold lying in the only coffin we could find in Adana. It had belonged to a German man; Muslims don't bury their dead in coffins.

In *The Year of Magical Thinking*, Joan Didion writes that "people who have lost someone look naked because they think themselves invisible." Invisibility is a comforting feeling when your heart is so heavy. After he died, I preferred places where I knew no one and where no one knew me. Places where I felt most invisible and completely anonymous.

It has been more than six years since Anthony passed away. And yet on some days, it still feels as raw as it did that night in Turkey. I quit journalism, left my home in Beirut, and moved thousands of miles away from everyone I knew and everything familiar. Along the way, I became someone I don't recognize. I lost my balance and the discipline I once had. Anything that requires the smallest mental effort is now daunting, including writing these lines.

I am thankful for being a mother. In so many ways, I think it saved me from making the wrong choices and forced me to get out of bed when I had no energy, will, or desire to do so. Raising a happy and healthy child will always be my biggest and most rewarding achievement.

I turned thirty-seven in January. But the last birthday I remember was my thirty-first. I cannot account for the last six years of my life. I have forced myself into an exile and an isolation that is now so strong I cannot seem to break free.

What Normal?

Hwaida Saad

There's a scene from a Syrian TV show in which one woman detainee at a Syrian prison asks another what had happened to a person they both knew named Taym. The first prisoner had been detained during the early stages of the Syrian crisis in 2012, while the other had been taken in more recently.

The second detainee answers, "Taym works at a field hospital in the liberated areas."

"What? The liberated areas?" the first woman asks. "We have liberated areas in Damascus now?! Why are you upset?"

"In theory, yes, we have liberated areas," the newcomer responds with a faint smile, traces of blood on her lips.

The first detainee is surprised by the second woman's rather subdued answer and her lack of enthusiasm. It's obvious she hasn't an inkling as to what had been going on beyond the prison walls during her detention. She claps excitedly, demanding more information about the so-called liberated areas.

"You must tell me everything, especially about the liberated areas! Is the war coming to an end, then?" she asks.

The newcomer maintains the cold, expressionless look on her face.

It's a short scene, but to my mind, it sums up the events in Syria from 2011 to 2018. By now, I feel as though the story of the country has become a long and unending saga. The second detainee's sarcastic smile says it all.

When I first sat down to write this essay, I hesitated. I was forced to think about the past seven years and the numerous exchanges I have had with individuals on social media. I have so much in my head: events, names, and places I've been. There is so much to remember.

Yes. It has been seven years of the Syrian conflict already, and we've now entered its eighth. Yes. The years that have passed us by are a string of moments, and I've lived through them all, every detail. The events I've followed have grown bigger and bigger.

There are the countless stories that I've reported for the *New York Times*. There are the accounts of people I met and corresponded with through Skype, WhatsApp, or Facebook. Where do I start? How do I start? And the bigger question: What happened between 2011 and 2018?

Anthony Shadid was part of the story in the beginning, although he wouldn't make it to the end.

It was 2010. The *New York Times* had hired Anthony to take over as Beirut bureau chief from Robert Worth. For years, I'd been covering Syria from afar, occasionally taking trips into the country with Robert. Entering Syria as a journalist wasn't easy, even back then. Arranging a trip would involve days or even weeks of waiting, since international and particularly American media weren't welcome in Syria. And there were complications involved at every stage, from applying for a visa to crossing the border. But it was nonetheless still possible to enter the country legally as a journalist at that point.

Anthony had an attractive personality. He was always smiling, very sharp, and, most important, he spoke Arabic fluently and had a deep understanding of Middle Eastern culture. At the time, the newspaper's local office doubled as a work space and a home for Anthony and his wife, Nada Bakri, who was also a reporter at the *Times*. The couple converted one of the house's five rooms into an office for us, with four chairs and joined tables. Anthony insisted that we work together, in the same room, rather than in separate ones. We had a very good relationship; I often helped organize his trips to Syria.

Beirut was quiet back then, and early 2011 was uneventful. The demonstrations in Tunisia were broadcast on almost all the TV channels, and I watched them with Malik, Nada and Anthony's son. I didn't think much of them at the time. I thought they were just protests, nothing more than a passing event.

By the time the war erupted, entering Syria to report from the ground had become an increasingly dangerous endeavor. And in any case, it would have been too risky for me to get information from my sources in person.

In the early days of the uprising, I communicated with Syrians I had already met during previous assignments in Damascus by phone. Later, some of my colleagues at the *New York Times* who were also covering the uprising shared with me a list of phone numbers belonging to prominent Syrian opposition members as well as protesters, suggesting I reach out to them. Some of those individuals were active on Skype, so I also connected with them there. One Skype contact led to another, and the list grew longer and longer. Later, the Syrian government blocked Anthony's and my mobile and landline numbers, so we could no longer make any phone calls to Syria. I resorted to the virtual world for the crux of my reporting, communicating with Syrian citizens through Skype, WhatsApp, and other social media.

I don't know where they all were before the war started: Mohammad, Bilal, Maysara, Abu Al-Baraa, Abu Al-Majd, and the others.

Perhaps they were at school or university. Perhaps they were street vendors or owned stores in Syria's old souks. Perhaps I walked past them, or bought from them. Perhaps they were laborers in Lebanon, toiling the land or working menial jobs. They were Syrian citizens, their full names known to all. They were ordinary people going about their daily lives.

But the beginning of 2011 changed all that. Names morphed into pseudotitles whose origins could be traced back to long-gone eras.

Mohammad became Abu Moaz Al-Shami (Abu Moaz of Damascus); Bilal became Abu Bilal Al-Homsi (Abu Bilal of Homs); Nour became Thaer Al-Dimashki (Damascus rebel). Their faces changed, and their jobs did, too.

Yahya used to be a car mechanic in Beirut. He joined the revolution early on, growing a beard and joining an extremist group. He says he remembers Beirut, but doesn't like it.

Abu Taym, also from Homs, used to work in agriculture. He later became a commander. He's torn between his love of Lebanon and his duty as a commander of a battalion in the Free Syrian Army.

Rami Al-Sayyid of Yarmouk, the Palestinian refugee camp in the Damascus district, lived in Achrafieh, Beirut—just steps away from me—in 2000. He chose to stay in Yarmouk at the beginning of the revolution, and lived through it all. Now he's trapped in the conflict, and reminisces about his beautiful days in Beirut. He wishes we had met in those days, before the war, a wish I share with many others I've spoken with. I became obsessed with that idea, too.

Even the chef became a battalion leader. He changed his name from Hadi to Abu Al-Laith (Father of the Lion). He describes himself as *moujahid fi sabeel illah*, "a fighter for the sake of Allah." He used to spend his holidays between Beirut and Damascus, dancing late into the night with his friends. But now he deems a woman's voice *'awra* (a blemish or weakness). Sometimes, Abu Al-Laith slipped and forgot that he was a *moujahid*—he would send me flirtatious messages accompanied by heart and rose emojis on Skype. He was once a professional at making Arabic sweets and kebabs; he's now a professional at making hand grenades.

In the beginning, my exchanges with these men were filled with humor. Our Skype chats were a much needed break from the long days of protesting, and later, when the peaceful demonstrations turned violent, from the battlefields. Reading the words or hearing the voice of a woman made the men nostalgic for their loved ones after having been disconnected from them for various reasons. For the most part, they weren't bothered by the fact that I was Lebanese; they loved the personal questions, such as my age and social status.

But after President Bashar al-Assad issued a general amnesty in May 2011 that applied to all detainees belonging to political movements, including the outlawed Muslim Brotherhood, violence rose dramatically. Armed factions started surfacing, and non-Syrian parties, mainly Hezbollah of Lebanon, began to enter the fray, too.

As the conflict spread its tentacles, the questions from my online sources took an ugly turn. The men wanted to know what my political affiliations, religion, and sect were. That infuriated me. Most explained that their questions were necessary for them to establish trust and ensure their safety, especially after sieges on "liberated areas" had begun, metaphorically.

"Don't misunderstand my question," one of my contacts said. "You know that the situation is critical and that we must be wary of the regime."

Some were diplomatic. Others, not so much.

"Honestly, I do not love or trust the Shi'a, nor the Iranians, and we fear you might be one of them," one contact told me.

Their questions bothered me a great deal, and I insisted on not mentioning religion or sect whatsoever. I didn't want to play their game, especially as the "sect game" in Lebanon had already exhausted me. (Syria was once a haven for my family; we'd often visit in order to forget my country's sectarian, doctrinal complexities. But today, Syria has become a place that reminds me of all those complexities.) My defiance was a great obstacle in both my emotional state and my career: it sometimes meant I'd lose the contact altogether, or that they'd cross me off their Skype list.

And yet some were still prepared to play the "love game" with me, even taking risks and crossing the siege to come to Beirut to meet me in person.

One of those men was a Syrian from the Homs countryside who was educated in Lebanon, at the Beirut Arab University, and opposed the regime. He adored the Lebanese accent and remembered Beirut fondly, but hated the Dahieh—a mostly Shi'a Muslim southern suburb of Beirut.

He had tried hard to rise above the sectarianism; his city, which is situated along the border with Lebanon, was under siege by regime forces and Hezbollah. He didn't ask about my sect. Perhaps he didn't insist on finding out because he thought we were of the same denomination. Or maybe he had come to his own conclusions based on the fact that I lived in Achrafieh, a predominantly Christian area in Beirut.

We didn't talk about religion. He was enthusiastic about the revolution. But his enthusiasm wore off as the number of armed factions operating in his area increased and corruption spread. Our chats were a mix of his rendering of Lebanese pop star Elissa's songs—even though he didn't like music—and the sounds of regime shelling and propelled grenades pouring down around him. He was highly educated and witty.

As the war took a different direction in Homs, and Hezbollah came onto the Syrian scene, our banter began to change. The ongoing shelling and siege in his hometown had a negative impact on him. His mind was swinging between his loyalty to the revolution and his hatred toward the Lebanese militia. He started reflecting on the differences between the doctrines of Sunni Islam and Shi'a Islam as the political schism between them deepened.

After a year, he grew tired of virtual chitchat and decided to take a risk and come to Beirut to meet me, the Lebanese *houri-yyat al-bahr,* or "Beautiful Mermaid." (The term *houriyyah* in Arabic wasn't widely used before the days of Daesh; the group popularized it as it had promised its soldiers that if they martyred themselves, they would be granted "pretty women" in heaven.) I found the nickname beautiful. It reminded me of a film I love, *A Fish Called Wanda.* The man sold his laptop—one of the only valuables still in his possession after he'd lost nearly everything—to pay for the trip's expenses.

When we met in person, he didn't hide his resentment toward Hezbollah and Shi'a Muslims: he criticized them strongly and freely. I had brought a Syrian friend along to the meeting, and we listened to the man silently. His comments were blunt to the point of being offensive. My friend and I tried to take the edge off with faint smiles, after which we exchanged knowing glances. The man seemed confused by our behavior, and doubt filled his soft face as he realized that one of us "could belong to the enemy's sect," or be a supporter or member of "the other party." In his eyes I saw struggle and confusion between his loyalty to the revolution and his infatuation with a reporter who had drawn him to Beirut and whose political and religious affiliations he knew nothing of. After all, I might have belonged to a sect he considered his biggest enemy.

His first cause was the revolution. Later, matters became increasingly mixed up. His brother was killed by a Shi'a neighbor. He lost his city, which had fallen into the hands of the regime and Hezbollah in the spring of 2013. The price of his revolution was high. His anger and bigotry fluctuated, but his passion strengthened. A counterrevolution was brewing inside him.

He decided to emigrate and live elsewhere with his depression. We stayed in contact for a while after he arrived in Sweden, where he was seeking refuge. There, he began to suffer in different ways, as he had to contend with a new language, a new community, and new traditions.

After the crisis in Syria turned bloody, some regions were "liberated." In other words, they came under siege. During the siege, ideas changed, and so did faces—many of which grew beards. On the radio, jihadi songs replaced those of Elissa. Innocence gradually disappeared. Tired of demonstrating, some decided to join armed factions.

Death edged closer and closer, touching everything and taking everything. For me, it started with the passing of Anthony on February 16, 2012, during his reporting trip to Idlib, which had just been announced as liberated by the Free Syrian Army.

My Skype list started shrinking one name at a time: the little green dots began disappearing, until finally very few were left after seven years of conflict. It was like the tale of the ten little monkeys—*and then there were none*. A picture of a cake on Skype, however, reminds me of them once every year on their birthdays.

Abu Bilal Al-Homsi was around twenty-eight when the protests started in his hometown, which came under siege from 2012 to 2014. He took part in the demonstrations, recording what he was witnessing and sharing it with Arab and international media.

We communicated through Skype. He was quiet and had a fair complexion, sleepy eyes, and full cheeks. His reserved personality didn't stop him from joking around. He often added smiley emojis and kisses to his Skype messages. He once didn't even hesitate to propose to me. He thought of himself as a Syrian citizen who was fighting for change in his country and defending his neighborhood. He was religiously conservative, but seemed open to the outside world.

He adapted to the siege, sharing pictures of his home in Bab al-Dreib with me. One was of his rooftop plants: tomatoes, lettuce, and eggplants. Even as he became more conservative, he retained his sense of humor. He liked to call me Um el-'Ayoun (literally, "the mother of the eyes," meaning "the one with the eyes"), sometimes sending me the eyeglasses emoji.

But something happened during the siege. Goals shifted. Religion turned to bigotry. Over time, Abu Bilal committed to his faith wholeheartedly.

In April 2014, Assad forces and rebel groups reached an agreement to evacuate old Homs under UN supervision, allowing the government to take full control of the city. Abu Bilal couldn't hide his anger at the leaders of the factions who had signed the evacuation agreement, describing the deal as "criminal," according to Sharia (Islamic law). He decided to stay in the suburbs of northern Homs, pledging allegiance to Daesh. I never thought that he would become a Daesh fighter.

He kept in touch with me through Skype. He wasn't a foreign fighter, but a national who had decided to join the most extreme and bloody faction in the Syrian war, cheering Daesh's victory when the group barged into Palmyra in 2015. He was put in charge of "the prisoner file," and started negotiations for the release of the state's detainees with the regime.

When Abu Bilal joined Daesh, he asked me for the first time about my sect.

"I'll give you some lessons about Islam to save you on the day of judgment," he said soon after he pledged allegiance to the group. He talked with his usual shyness about a Lebanese girl who used to send him pictures dressed in not-so-modest "modern" clothing. He was trying to introduce her to Islam and heaven. "I convinced her to pray and read the Qur'an," he once said jokingly, in his sharp Homsi sense of humor.

I shocked myself when I agreed to visit his empty home in Bab al-Dreib during a reporting trip a few months after the regime had gained control of old Homs and after he had fled.

When I arrived at the house, I took photos of it to send over to him. Water had flooded the home. Abu Bilal searched for his plants in the images, but couldn't find them; they were gone. The old Bab al-Dreib mosque, which was a few yards from his home, brought memories back to him.

"You took me back to past memories, Hwaidita!" (as he used to call me). "I thought you'd never find your way to my house!"

Abu Bilal went from sending news about besieged old Homs to international news organizations to reporting on Daesh's victorious battles against the "infidel nation."

"I am now very happy living the jihad," he told me. "The Middle East is changing, Islam is stronger. It is the road to heaven. I want the Americans to hit their heads against the wall."

"Are you scared of us?" he asked me the day after Daesh took Palmyra. "One day, you will come visit us in Palmyra for a reporting trip."

Over time, the frequency of Abu Bilal's Skype messages decreased, until finally they stopped altogether, a few months before his suicide mission.

The last things he wrote were exultations of Daesh's foreign operations, such as the attack on the offices of the French satirical magazine *Charlie Hebdo* in January 2015. He called the attack "a blessed operation in retaliation to those who participated in bombing Muslims and in response to the crusade alliance."

In January 2016, an explosion shook the Al-Zahraa area in the heart of Homs, which had an Alawite majority. It was a suicide attack carried out by none other than Abu Bilal Al-Homsi. He killed more than thirty citizens and wounded about a hundred others.

Abu Bilal, the man whom I had been chatting with for months, had become the "Knight of Martyrs," according to Daesh. Ever since, his green icon on Skype has been permanently shut off.

While I met some of my sources online, I knew others in real life, too. Abu Al-Majd, who was a twenty-year-old officer in the state's military police when we first met, was one of these contacts.

When Anne Barnard was named the Beirut bureau chief of the *New York Times* in 2013, our Syria reporting entered a new, challenging era—one that entailed meeting with and interviewing people living in government-controlled areas. Anne took the lead and I followed in her footsteps.

I went on a reporting trip to Palmyra with Anne the following year, just before Daesh's attack on the area. This particular expedition was one of the most bizarre trips we'd ever taken. Security forces accompanied us to monitor our movements, as well as the interviews we were conducting. A local sheikh, Ahmad Dagher (known as Abu Ali), was with us every minute of the visit. He complained when we stayed in the city of ruins longer than expected. People at the souk looked at us from afar. Clearly, they found it odd that a group of foreigners was visiting the city considering the security situation, despite the fact that prior to 2011, Palmyra had been a major tourist attraction. Some seemed anxious about the security vehicles that had been trailing us. They tried to avoid talking to us, or answering our questions. Only the children were excited to see us. Dozens of them walked with us in groups, and they didn't leave until late at night.

We conducted a lengthy interview with one of the clan's sheikhs, known as Sheikh Faisal Al-Katran, at his house. When we left, we were met by an army of people, military as well as civilians; it appeared that they had been waiting for us. It was a dark night and there were no streetlights. Suddenly, a voice from the middle of the crowd asked for my phone number. I shouted it out, even though I didn't know whose voice it was.

Months later, I received a message from an unfamiliar Syrian number.

"Hello, this is Abu Al-Majd. Do you remember me?"

The name didn't ring any bells.

"I'm the voice who asked you for your number that night."

Abu Al-Majd had been part of our security escort. He was

one of the first members of the Syrian military who dared to speak to me and, in turn, to an American newspaper. It wasn't easy to establish a line of communication with members of the military. I was excited.

The man was twenty, but when I spoke to him via Skype, his soft features made him appear even younger, and he behaved like a teenager.

"I loved the jeans you were wearing," he said when we started our correspondence, which lasted through May 2015, nearly a year in total. "When you gave me your number that night, dozens of people in the crowd wrote it down."

Abu Al-Majd messaged me almost daily, either by WhatsApp or on Facebook. He talked about everything: his service in Palmyra, his holidays in Old Damascus, his love of music, his love for his cousin, his romantic escapades, and even his salary and experiences as a soldier. His favorite movie was *Behind Enemy Lines*, he once told me, because it reminded him of his own story. He spoke nostalgically about his life before the conflict and about his house, which had been destroyed in Yarmouk.

Palmyra was a form of exile to him. He spent hours at checkpoints, at the front line with the enemy—Daesh. There was no electricity, and no television; he was completely cut off from the outside world. He considered himself "dead, a dead human being."

"The city has a negative effect on me," he often said. "It's arid; there's nothing but tents, palm trees, and clan chiefs."

His mood fluctuated as events changed.

Sometimes he'd seem happy, and would send me love songs by the Lebanese singer Wael Kfoury. Other times, when he was feeling morose, he'd send me depressing messages about how low his salary was—the equivalent of one hundred dollars a month. He'd talk about his long shifts, and share with me the nightmares he had about Daesh capturing him or ambushing his group. He was only truly happy when he was reunited with his mother during the holiday season in Damascus, he said.

One of Abu Al-Majd's nightmares came true when Daesh attacked the Shaer mountains along the outskirts of Homs in 2014. He lost a number of his companions in that ambush.

By May 2015, Abu Al-Majd increasingly felt the enemy advancing toward Palmyra, and his distress grew by the day. He hated Palmyra, he hated Damascus, and he even hated himself. "I don't know who is against whom in Syria," he told me repeatedly, referring to the state of complete and utter loss that the country was enduring.

He was proud to be a soldier serving his country. To his mind, the concepts of the "opposition" and regime "supporters" were illusions. There were two sides—with the state, or with terrorism—but he didn't hide his sarcasm regarding how the state treated its foot soldiers.

"We get everything here," he said once, with sarcasm and ridicule. "We even pay for bread! What a shame." He resented those who lived happily while he was deprived. He even wished his life were like mine. "Try to enjoy your life as much as you can," he told me. "You'll regret every moment you lived which you did not enjoy."

Abu Al-Majd was coming of age. He continued messaging me via WhatsApp and Facebook, either by sending me photos—in which he was evidently trying to make himself look cool—or by sending me his favorite songs. He sometimes sent me voice messages containing the sounds of his battalion exchanging fire with Daesh.

He felt certain that we'd never properly meet. "We're in two different countries," he once said. "Only these messages bring us together."

Between March and May 2015, there were signs that the end was nearing.

On May 13, 2015, Daesh started executing people in Sukhna, located some forty-five miles from Palmyra. At the time, Abu Al-Majd was on leave in Damascus. More than seventy military men, most of whom were his friends, were either killed or slaughtered when Daesh suddenly attacked their police center in the area.

Daesh was edging closer and closer to Palmyra. Abu Al-Majd's morale was at its worst. He could've been one of those whose throats were cut.

He used to send me pictures of the dead bodies of his friends. He once sent me a picture of his friend, the daughter of an officer, whose throat had been slit. She was beautiful, he had told me.

He decided to never go back to Palmyra.

"No one can force me to [go back]," he told me on May 14. "I'm not a coward, but I am a human being and I have the right to be scared. Right?"

A day later, Abu Al-Majd was instructed to move from Damascus to Homs city, where the situation was less dangerous. He seemed somewhat relieved, but his relief didn't last long. The feeling that he'd imminently be sent to Palmyra occupied his thoughts.

"I feel lonely, but if I was ordered to go to Palmyra, I'd go," he said in one of his last messages to me. "I have no choice. I'm not happy at all. Quite honestly, I'm headed toward suicide," he told me.

The following day, what he had predicted did indeed happen: the order from the army headquarters to head to Palmyra arrived. The evening of May 17 was the first and last time Abu Al-Majd ever called me.

"I'm in Homs; tomorrow I'm heading to Palmyra," he said. His voice was weary, and he asked me to refrain from asking any more questions. He told me they would leave Homs for Palmyra in the morning by bus.

That day, Abu Al-Majd had seen a fortune-teller; she had read his cup of Turkish coffee. As she was reading the cup, he recounted, her voice changed suddenly, and she started mumbling.

She told him he had many enemies. She spoke about his suffering, and said that although he was now in a desert, he would soon move with four others to a "safe green place."

The fortune-teller scared Abu Al-Majd, but he wanted to know more, so he decided to see her the following day before setting off to Palmyra.

The instructions he received from his senior commanders were clear: if he didn't go, he'd be "punished." He knew he was marching toward death.

"I wish I won't wake up tomorrow," he said. He repeated what a friend of his had posted on Facebook:

> Alas, a country whose heroes die in graves and [whose] thieves live in mansions.

On May 18, Abu Al-Majd left Homs in a military vehicle, but the road was riddled with land mines, so they headed back to the city. But fate had other plans.

The following day, he sent me two pictures via WhatsApp. One of them was of him smoking *sheesha* in his green fatigues. The other was of him posing. With the pictures came a short message:

> I took these pictures on purpose. They might be my last.
> We are moving to Palmyra shortly.

After that, Abu Al-Majd's messages stopped for good. I tried to reach him via WhatsApp before his final journey, but he didn't reply.

Days passed. I followed the stages of Daesh entering Palmyra closely, and its impromptu executions of both civilians and the military, often documented in their press releases. But there was no news of Abu Al-Majd.

Before we were disconnected, Abu Al-Majd had introduced me to his cousin, whom he had intended to marry. I tried to get in touch with her. It was she who finally gave me the news, via a message on WhatsApp:

> Abu Al-Majd's throat was slit by Daesh, days after he arrived in Palmyra.

The news was shocking. Death is death, but the manner in which Abu Al-Majd had been killed came as a shock nonetheless.

After a long search on Facebook, during which I contacted many people in Abu Al-Majd's network, one of his friends agreed to reveal exactly what had happened to him.

According to the friend, on May 19, sixty soldiers and policemen, along with one officer, headed by bus to Palmyra's military airport. Abu Al-Majd begged the driver to head back, but it was too late. The men were dropped off at the airbase, while the driver and the officer drove back to Homs. Within hours, Daesh fighters raided the airport, killing anyone they could find.

Abu Al-Majd managed to flee along with some of his friends, finding refuge in the home of a local family who had agreed to host him and allowed him to communicate with his family intermittently.

He was petrified, and his father told him to read the Qur'an. Prayers failed him.

Four days into his stay, Abu Al-Majd decided to leave the home, telling his parents that he didn't want to further endanger the family that had taken him in. He disguised himself in a woman's abaya and wandered into Palmyra's souk, which at the time was teeming with Daesh fighters. It was time for midday prayer, and since Daesh required men to drop everything they were doing to go to the mosque, his only choice was to make his way there to avoid arousing suspicion.

When he entered the mosque, he uncovered his face for the first time. A civilian recognized him and asked if he was Abu Al-Majd, to which he replied, "Yes, but I haven't done anything." The man was an informant. He wasn't convinced of Abu Al-Majd's innocence, so he called a Daesh fighter.

As if he'd already assumed his own fate, Abu Al-Majd handed over a letter to a civilian, asking him to deliver it to his mother, so she would know that he had died in martyrdom.

Later that same day, Abu Al-Majd's throat was slit by Daesh fighters in front of the mosque. According to eyewitnesses, his body was left in the streets for several days. It was the same street through which he had escorted me and my colleagues during our visit to the city a year earlier.

When I learned of Abu Al-Majd's death, I wondered if Abu Bilal had documented it, as he reported on Daesh's victories. The answer isn't certain. What is certain, however, is that both men overlapped in Homs in 2015. While one chose death voluntarily, the other was forced into it.

These stories won't be the last.

Following Lebanon's fifteen-year civil war, which erupted in 1975, and theoretically ended in 1990 after various Lebanese political parties signed a peace accord, people claimed to have resumed their normal lives. But there was always a big question mark following the word "normal."

I could never figure out what they meant by "normal."

Today, seven years after the beginning of the Syrian war, despite all that has happened, some people speak enthusiastically about how the situation in the country has started to improve.

An acquaintance of mine who lives in Beirut, for example, always tells me with conviction whenever I return from my reporting trips to Syria that things are "back to normal" in Damascus.

His comment takes me back to that scene in the Syrian TV show between the two female detainees.

With a skeptical smile on my face, I reply, "What normal?"

TRANSLATED FROM ARABIC BY
MARIAM ANTAR

On a Belated Encounter with Gender

Lina Attalah

Amid the gloom of your imminent departure, you brought a big smile to my face when you remembered who I was and the media I had helped create. In the throes of your delirium, your pain, and your struggle to catch every breath as your organs failed you, you pointed at me while talking to your nurse and said to him, "You know who this little girl is? She's a journalist. She founded a newspaper."

It's not quite a newspaper, *baba*, I said, smiling, habitually uncomfortable when I receive praise. It's just a website. Something intangible, inside the internet. I didn't want to disregard the little things that made you feel good in the moment. But, *baba*, you didn't tell the nurse I was your daughter. Perhaps you assumed he already knew. Or perhaps at that point, at the curious stage when you were on death's doorstep, you were finally disowning me? I am struck by how you chose to identify me as a journalist—a media founder—and not your daughter.

I tried to write this essay during your lifetime, or rather, in your final moments—when you were dancing between the world we know now and an afterworld that seemed near, judging from the occasional smile in your sleep. But I failed. When you left us, I could write this only as a letter to you, an absent you.

Unlike most people writing to their departing loved ones, I do not wish to reduce you to an angelic figure, the first man in my life who helped make me what I have become today. Instead, I remember two specific incidents that demonstrate how our relationship—its presences and absences, its tensions and silences—embodies the word that my coeditor Naira Antoun says best describes the world: *paradoxical*.

Remember when you used to carry me when I was a little girl screaming in pain from an infected eardrum, whirling me around the dining table and humming a song slowly, your lips at times meeting my right ear? I don't remember which song you were singing. But I remember feeling safe, even from that horrid introduction of physical pain in my early life. That moment marked my first encounter with your masculinity and a very specific tenet of our relationship. For years in my childhood, you'd return from your work travels, clothed in your policeman's uniform, with a toy I had desperately wanted in hand. I'd be faced with the conflation of your engulfing virility as a robust young man and your tender softness as a loving, gift-carrying father. I understood that you had been out in the deep south, fighting a ferocious fight against armed militants in the ranks of a security apparatus that had enforced a broader fatherhood—a patriarchy—over Egypt. I thought, no one can be braver than you, and no one can give me more security than you. Even in your absence back then, you were so present. At the time, I had no relationship to speak of with the nation.

Fifteen years later, you set fire to a book I had been reading by a Syrian writer. As you randomly sifted through the pages, you caught sight of a passage that contained a graphic sex scene. You were so vehement about not wanting me to read the book that you forcefully disappeared its words into ashes. At that point, you had retired and mostly spent your time at home, completely disengaged from and disapproving of the life of activism and journalism that I had chosen for myself.

My bitterness that day made me wonder how the sea of love and comfort that I had once felt around you had disappeared. I pondered how the intense feelings I'd identified as love as a young girl had started morphing into feelings of estrangement as I grew older. Somehow, your enchanting presence had become an absence. Had you changed, *baba*, or had you reserved your tender softness for the younger version of me, treating me with the strictness of a man, a patriarch, and a policeman once I became a young woman, journalist, and activist—just as you were slowly walking out of your career? Was this transformation your choice, or had you been socialized into it? Had a layer of you retreated into the background?

Or was it I who ultimately grew up not wanting the dolls you'd always gifted me, and losing faith in that engulfing sense of security, simply because I didn't need them anymore? My growth might have been a natural evolution, a coming-of-age. It also could have been tainted by the ways in which I sometimes associated fatherhood with notions of societal patriarchy and the violence of parenting.

Have I conflated your subject into that of the state in my growing up? With our patriarchal families being an inspiration for political authoritarianism and a site for the embodiment of its control, did you come to represent for me the very type of control I intended to fight against?

The first time I saw policemen brutally beat protesters during the 2003 demonstrations against the Iraq War in Cairo, I found that I didn't want to go back to my parents' house. I wanted to remain outdoors, as the street and the protesters felt like a home and family I had chosen. I felt that fights at home about my curfew or safety or not focusing enough on my studies were trivial compared to the bigger struggles that were taking place outside the household.

At that time, both contentious politics at home and the antiwar movement—occupying public spaces, grappling with the state's crackdown, tying regional and international causes to local ones—were interfering with my personal life and the different sentiments that governed it. They were a constellation of guilt, obligation, and fear, among other things, which were first and foremost nurtured at home and somewhat made more prominent by the fact that I was a daughter.

But I couldn't live one life. I had to carry on living these two lives, bouncing between constant negotiation, compromise, and resistance. One was a life of choice, with an open-ended shimmering horizon, while the other was a life drawn solely in the imagination of one's parents, an imagination that at times can seem like a prison of some sort. Living two lives meant constantly guarding them from each other, safely insulated, for one risked defacing and assaulting the other. It was exhausting.

All the same, I was perhaps engaging in some form of escapism or coping mechanism in choosing to ignore the realities behind these two lives. I found the consciousness of gender troubles psychologically daunting and somewhat unconstructive. I thought sidelining this consciousness and thinking of myself as genderless was, in a way, an act of resistance—a passive resistance, manifested by walking down the street, into the workplace, inside public institutions, and then back into my family's home without the baggage of associated gendered expectations and assumptions. This was potentially fueled by a rather Marxist political environment of activism, which largely considered gender troubles to be subordinate to class struggle. I wasn't paying much attention to the superficiality of this form of resistance. I simply closed my eyes to the fact that while moving forward as women, we continue carrying a piece of that oppression to which we are turning our backs.

Later, as I began working as a journalist in Egypt, I ascribed a more articulate political meaning to my attitude. Women in Egypt, as well as in other Arab and Middle Eastern countries, are often depicted by the Western world as nothing but victims of patriarchy. Through the privilege of social status, and, more specifically, my family's middle-class insistence to invest in a good-quality education (in other words, a French school and an American university), I had direct access to that Western world.

I worked in English, the lingua franca of the globe. I became an extension of the object of the typical Western gaze in that context, albeit an exciting extension because of the irregularities I presented: I was an Arab woman whose activism was visible to the public, against the odds of the prevalent conservatism and patriarchy associated with the region. Speaking and writing invitations on the back of my gender started rolling in one after another. You may even consider this essay to be one of them.

These invitations often made me feel trapped in place, identity, and body. I felt as though a form of bourgeois or liberal feminism was being imposed upon me and I had to constantly free myself from it. I almost never had something smart to say as an answer to that nagging question: What is it like to be a woman journalist in Egypt nowadays? I didn't want to recount stories of sexism, patriarchy, and oppression that would feed into commonplace Orientalist essentialism and render me a heroic survivor. Nor did I want to engage in a short-sighted defense of the Arab. But I had no third story to tell, no nuanced explanation of how we live a life of public engagement through the lens of gender. Rather than trying to challenge the question with my answer, I gently sidestepped it, acting a bit like the compliant yet skeptical copyist in Herman Melville's "Bartleby, the Scrivener," who was famous for responding "I would prefer not to."

My tongue spoke a lingua franca, but my mind was refusing to speak its dominant mind-set, which tends to represent the society I come from as static. Hence, there were moments of silence. At that time, I had not yet read the Egyptian poet Iman Mersal's illuminating text "The Displaced Voice." Mersal posits that speaking a second language with an accent is a way for the mother tongue to be present—to be immortal—to the point of "sabotaging" that second language in some way. But instead of allowing for this duality, I worked on perfecting the sound of my second language, while muting its troubling implications. Remember the duality of the family home and the street home? In language, too, I silently lived this discomforting duality.

With time, I came to understand how that duality might have been my own manifestation of second-wave feminism, one of whose suggestions is that the personal is political. Like Carol Hanisch, a radical feminist and one of the first to have expressed this thought, once said, "I have been pressured to be strong, selfless, other-oriented, sacrificing and in general pretty much in control of my own life. To admit to the problems in my life is to be deemed weak." Had I been conscious of feminist approaches to activism in my early life, perhaps I would have acknowledged and navigated my two lives more graciously, rather than fanatically rendering one invisible in the presence of the other.

At the transformative moment of Egypt's 2011 revolution, when masses took to the streets demanding the fall of the regime and chanting for freedom, justice, bread, and human dignity, I became the chief editor of a Cairo-based English-language newspaper called *Egypt Independent*. I had been working there since 2009, when the newspaper was led by a woman named Fatemah Farag, whose leadership was truly inspiring. Farag had created a space that allowed for experimentation and self-growth in the workplace, all the while managing her team's complex personalities. I had learned a lot from her, but never associated the nuance of her leadership style with her womanhood.

The political developments at home and my engagement with them through the lens of journalism distanced me even further from the entire body of identity politics. Shortly after the magic of the uprising, which engulfed much of our thinking and work, not to mention our emotional states, the country's struggles were split along the fault lines of Islamic and secular rule. Supporters of secular rule often flirted with a strain of conservatism, while remaining in fierce opposition to the political Islamic project. It was difficult to be a woman or to cover women's issues without getting caught up in the Islamist-secularist polarization. Paying attention to gender was seen as a power play against the Islamist political elites, even though that wasn't something that many of those invested in a serious conversation about gender were interested in, especially given the conservatism of the secular side.

As Arab Spring activism began to shift closer to identity politics, I chose instead to align myself with those calling for basic human rights and, especially, the right to resources. I constantly reminded myself that when Mohamed Bouazizi had set himself on fire in December 2010 in Sidi Bouzid, a Tunisian village, sparking entire revolutions with his ashes, he wasn't fighting for the right to drink beer. He was drowning in debt because he wasn't allowed to sell his produce on the streets of the town and had no other avenue for employment. My early years of activism had been marked by the antiwar movement in the wake of the U.S. invasion of Iraq, which would leave behind it the shadow of a country mired in sectarian strife. A similar fate would later unfold in Syria. In early 2011, when the uprising escalated into an armed conflict, I covered what unraveled on the ground by shadowing a multisect revolutionary brigade in Aleppo. There, the people were fighting for dignity and freedom, not the triumph of one sect over another.

But there was another reality to reckon with, a stifling reality that couldn't be negated by the simple denial of identity politics. The newsroom I was leading had already been established as a space run by women editors, Farag being its founding editor. However, it was part of a bigger media organization, where the power structure was more traditionally constructed and where men held most of the power. To many of them, our newsroom was irrelevant, perhaps because we were less experienced—we had been attracting mostly young journalists. A leak or a scoop coming out of our newsroom wouldn't be treated seriously by the higher-ups, and our different way of producing content—one that encouraged less traditional, more innovative, experimental, surprising, and at times artistic forms of storytelling—was frowned upon. I'd spent so long attempting to look away from my womanhood that I failed at first to connect the dots.

At the time, I often attributed our marginalization to age, rather than gender, as though such abuses of power can be deciphered. It helped that in a wider context, the state had categorized the youth as a threat: revolutions are usually associated with the young and their able bodies. The older men of my organization, I thought, were probably stuck wondering how they could manage the troublesome youth of our newsroom.

For financial reasons, in early 2013, *Egypt Independent*'s print edition folded. In an editorial, the management's representative, a seventy-year-old man, wrote that the newspaper hardly ever published useful content anyway.

The struggle to keep the newspaper alive and its eventual failure unsettled my tendency to turn away from identity politics. I didn't suddenly choose to espouse them wholeheartedly, but through negotiation and resistance with the older men of the administration, I came to better understand those identity politics and the ways in which they sat systemically in the collective consciousness. They had to be dealt with, not denied altogether.

In mid-2013, during another heightened period of political polarization, I cofounded the website *Mada Masr*—the news website my father would refer to while in the hospital five years later.

The forces of Islamism, spearheaded by the Muslim Brotherhood, had been reigning over the country for just over a year. Confronting the Brotherhood was a powerful military institution. Most Egyptians, anxious about an Islamist regime that had promised to interfere with their everyday social lives, threw their support behind the military, who ultimately won, ousting the Muslim Brotherhood from power. But first, there had to be violence.

Supporters of the Muslim Brotherhood set up protest encampments, and in August 2013, one of those camps was the site of a massacre. Security forces killed at least one thousand men, women, and children in broad daylight. This massacre and the violence written on the bodies of the victims in a battlefield marked by the annihilation of the other pushed me to reinvestigate the question of identity and identity politics.

I saw how massacres can be a spectacular demonstration of the Foucauldian idea that power is manifested ubiquitously in daily life and over the human body. Witnessing violence and connecting it to the idea of power over bodies challenges the limiting, essentialist, and undeveloped binary of female subordination to male power. In other words, bodies are constructed and reconstructed to serve different functions, chief among which is the exertion of power. Instead of simply focusing on male-female gender dynamics, we have to look at the forces behind the constructions of these identities. Only by addressing those forces can we deal with subjugation, including gender-based subjugation.

But the notion of modern power is commonly critiqued by those who argue that humans can be reduced to "docile bodies," changeable objects that are acted upon by force or subject to different forms of systemic violence. The possibility of violence, spectacular or structural, confirms the docility of our bodies. At the same time, our bodies have possibilities to be reckoned with. Away from the newsroom, from politics, broader and personal, from state and family, I turned to the arts, where I always found room for these other possibilities. Together with Kinda Hassan, an audiovisual artist whose work centers on the body and its collisions with self-image, instincts, and impulses, I lived, conversed, and cowrote texts on the body's journey to new realities. Hassan's immersive practice as an artist opened up introspection into how the body can mobilize subversive roles that can unsettle common understandings of gender. From her work, an aura of possibility was constantly unfolding in association with gender, and the body was central to such possibility.

Later, I sat on my balcony reading through philosopher Judith

Butler's writings on how gender is a bodily discourse—repetitively performed, so as to become real and accepted—as opposed to a sheer identity that requires a fixed representation. A fixed-gender identification, I learned, is not a natural disposition, but rather a process of cultivation. In this notion of subjective gender construction, I came to see how gender could be different from identity politics.

I returned to the newsroom at *Mada Masr*—a space essentially designed to cater to possibilities—with a certain sense of awakening, gleaned from textbooks, exhibition halls, and living room chats. From my coeditor, Naira Antoun, and other colleagues, I learned about intersectionality, a framework that analyzes the ways in which different institutions of power can overlap. We could use this framework as a tool with which to investigate stories through a lens of gender instead of focusing only on gender itself. We engaged, for example, with state institutions, looking into how class differences changed the amount of control those institutions wielded over the people. We asked questions such as: How and why have homosexuals of different social classes been targeted differently by the state? How does class interfere with women's experiences when undergoing abortions?

I learned to venture into questions of gender in coverage across the board, questions that were at times direct and at others subtle. What does thinking through a gender lens mean in terms of people's modes of coping and resistance in the wake of unprecedented austerity measures and economic hardship, for example? What kind of possibilities emerge from gendered roles and constructions within these attempts to survive?

These might be natural questions to ask for many progressive editors in chief. But it took me time to start asking them. In all my years running newsrooms, I had never been known as an editor who encouraged the coverage of gender issues, women's issues in particular. But through my educational process, which was mostly mediated in shared spaces of love filled with progressive feminist women, I slowly embraced the challenging task of activating a gender lens in the way I view and engage with my surrounding world.

Before getting there, I might have been the subject of Arundhati Roy's disdainful gaze, when the writer, in conversation with Aishwarya Subramanyam, said she felt annoyed when "cool young women" say they aren't feminists. Roy spoke of a battle between those who sidle up to power and those who have an adversarial relationship with it, and how it is through these battles with power that many freedoms are won.

While I believe myself to be naturally averse to power, I also subscribe to its complexity, best described in the academic Avery Gordon's text *Ghostly Matters*. "Power," she writes, "can be invisible, it can be fantastic, it can be dull and routine. It can be obvious, it can reach you by the baton of the police, it can speak the language of your thoughts and desires." In subscribing to the complexity, at times invisibility, of power, I made peace with a trajectory that started off with a constant distancing from the troubles of gender and ended with a confrontation with them and all the nuances they come with.

One night shortly before my father passed away, I climbed over his hospital bed like a child would to sing a song into his left ear. I wanted to distract him from his delirium so that he would give up trying to leave his bed—he was bedridden at that point due to tubes in his body that the doctors had hoped would keep him alive for a little while longer. It worked: he left his delirium temporarily to sing along to a Sayed Darwish song that he loved. Neither of us had experienced such victory together during the time we'd shared when he was in good health.

I don't know yet if it was that particular encounter with the body—a frail, departing corporeality—that opened up the uncharted territory of revisiting my personal history and unearthing its murky origins. At the end of the day, my encounter with death was a reminder that we often can't quite trace the beginnings, but we do see the end. It was also perhaps a reminder of what philosopher Walter Benjamin was talking about when he wrote "Death is the sanction of everything the storyteller can tell."

From the window of that end, however, I can trace a continuum of a set of biological realities: of birth, reproduction, and death, of a toddler being carried around a dining table and an immobile corpse on a deathbed. One day, that corpse had helped create a body that it thought it owned, similar to how power is imagined before it can be practiced. In the face of that power, that body was unarmed and unwanting to fight for its freedom. Yet, paradoxically, it kept running away to other, bigger battlefields, standing fragile under the open sky, until it found freedom within itself.

CROSSFIRE

Maps of Iraq

Jane Arraf

It was a lovely spring morning in 2004; the air that would soon heat up to the temperature of a hair dryer was still a caress rather than an assault. I was heading out of the office with an Iraqi colleague to cover the annual Shi'a pilgrimage to the Kathimiya shrine in Baghdad. I remember saying out loud that nothing bad could possibly happen on such a beautiful day. As we approached the streets thronged with pilgrims, we heard the sirens. Ambulances and pickup trucks were racing away from the shrine with bodies of the dead and wounded piled in the back. Three bombers had detonated suicide belts at one of the most sacred sites in Shi'a Islam.

We walked toward the shrine, even as people ran from it. Waved in by distraught guards, we found an imam standing in the courtyard. He was surrounded by severed limbs in pools of blood on the white marble tiles. I offered condolences in both Arabic and English, telling him, "I'm so sorry." "You're sorry!?" he roared back in English. And then he burst into tears. In either language, the words of comfort couldn't begin to encompass the enormity of the unfolding tragedy.

With one foot in the Arab world and one foot in the West, my Iraqi producer and I were the ones trying to explain to viewers Iraq's shocking slide into violence.

———————

Hoping to improve relations with the U.S. government, Saddam Hussein had invited American television networks to open bureaus in his tightly controlled country in the midnineties. CNN's idealistic founder, Ted Turner, took him up on the proposition, and I opened the network's first Baghdad bureau in 1998. For almost three years I was the only Western journalist based in the country.

As a Palestinian Canadian, I was expected by Iraqi citizens to be more Palestinian than Canadian. The Iraqi government saw me as a U.S. agent, while the U.S. government saw me as an Iraqi apologist. I was kicked out of Iraq a few months before the start of the war for coverage that was less sympathetic than the Iraqi government demanded, but made my way back through Kurdish-controlled territory to northern Iraq through Iran to cover the conflict for CNN.

A few months after Baghdad fell in 2003, invasion turned to occupation, and the soldiers on the ground—generally well-meaning guys from small towns in America—realized how far they were in over their heads.

Embedded with the army and the marines, I covered the battles for Samarra, Tel Afar, and Fallujah and smaller battles in almost every Iraqi province live from the front lines.

"I didn't imagine you'd look so ethnic," a marine said to me in 2004. We were lying in a schoolyard in western Anbar Province watching the sun come up. Before dawn, we had run across a bridge that the marines had warned us could be wired with explosives. He had never seen me on CNN, but had heard my middle-American accent on the radio. He was Italian American—an ethnic group that, unlike Arabs, had become part of the American mainstream generations ago.

My Arabic was far less than perfect, the product of listening to parents who spoke the language to each other but never required their children to speak it. In 2003, though, it was often considered the best Arabic in the army squads I was covering.

Would it have been equally painful to watch the train wreck

unfold had I not been Arab? I think the tragic miscalculations of the war would have been. But I might not have been as conscious of the depth of misunderstanding as worlds collided.

In Diyala Province, an al-Qaeda stronghold and one of the centers of the growing insurgency, I covered American soldiers as they raided houses and arrested military-age men en masse in their search for al-Qaeda fighters.

The U.S. had invaded Iraq with a severe shortage of interpreters, which made their mission much more difficult. Along with their rifles, most soldiers and marines were sent off to war with a laminated cheat sheet called the Iraq Culture Smart Card. "*Ihna* Amerkan" (we are American) was one of its helpful phrases, along with transliterations of "turn around" and "drop your weapons." But other terms on the card, such as *mullah* (religious leader) and *madrasa* (religious school), were rarely even used in Iraq.

In one house, a soldier urgently questioned the bewildered Iraqis with a single word from his smart card—mujahideen, or "jihadist fighters"—to try to determine whether any of them had seen al-Qaeda fighters. In another, the soldiers asked Iraqis whether there were any Palestinians with them. (There are tens of thousands of Palestinians in Iraq.)

At the beginning of each raid, there was an adrenaline rush: we didn't know what would be behind the gates once the soldiers had kicked them down and shot the locks off the doors. But after that, the raids took on a numbing regularity.

Men and women were separated, and the men and older boys were forced to lie on the floor with their hands behind their backs. They were often blindfolded so they wouldn't recognize the Iraqi informant, who would point out people they were looking for.

The more indiscriminate raids were sweeps of entire villages where blindfolded men, their hands cuffed behind them with plastic ties, would be woken up in the middle of the night, loaded onto trucks, and driven away for questioning. Most were taken away while wearing long robes and no shoes—they weren't given a chance to get dressed first.

I was there as a journalist to bear witness and report on the war. Embedded with American forces for an American news organization, I was required by regulations and common sense to wear body armor. The garment looked as different as possible from the military vests.

But the squad didn't have an interpreter or an Arabic-speaking soldier, and the terrified Iraqi women who were herded into a room while their men were forced to lie motionless with their hands behind their heads couldn't tell the difference. They assumed I was a soldier or one of the Arab American contract interpreters who would arrive in droves later on in the conflict.

With their children screaming in terror, weeping women would ask me where the men were being taken, or beg me to tell the soldiers that their sons, husbands, and brothers had done nothing wrong, and that there were no insurgents hiding among them.

I could offer only vague reassurance that the men would likely be released soon. I could see how humiliated the men and older boys felt about being treated as if they were criminals in their own homes; they seethed silently while they complied with the demands being shouted at them.

The language might have been a puzzle to American soldiers, but in some ways the culture was even more so. The essential Arab concept of maintaining dignity seemed alien to all but the savviest of soldiers.

But, then again, it wasn't just soldiers who didn't understand the culture. The Americans moved into Saddam's palaces. L. Paul Bremer, a diplomat, was appointed head of the Coalition Provisional Authority, a transitional government that took charge of Iraq. Less than two weeks after he arrived in his suit jacket, he signed an order disbanding the Iraqi army, believing—mistakenly—that he was dismantling the system that had kept Saddam in power. His decision proved to be the most misguided of the war. It created a security vacuum, stripped hundreds of thousands of men of their livelihoods and dignity, and fueled the insurgency that tore Iraq apart.

At the entrance to Saddam's former palace complex, which had become the headquarters of the U.S. military, I watched as former Iraqi army generals—who hadn't resisted the U.S. invasion but who were now out of work—gathered in front of the barbed wire to try to talk to someone in a position of authority. As spring turned into summer, they stood there, dressed in their best suits in the blazing heat, only to be told by young American soldiers in unwashed uniforms that they couldn't come in. Inside, U.S. State Department contractors, who were paid for by Iraqi government assets and earning danger pay, threw parties by the palace swimming pool. Sometimes, I realized, stereotypes are true.

The most effective American officers and soldiers were those who realized the extraordinary importance of reaching across the cultural divide. While there were some enlightened generals who tried to make sure their troops realized that the Iraqi people were not the enemy, the officers and soldiers who made the biggest difference were the less senior ones on the ground.

In a conflict where hasty arrests were common and apologies rare, one brigade commander took our camera crew with him when he went to deliver a public apology to a local sheikh who had been wrongfully arrested. The colonel left his body armor—and his boots, as is Arab custom—at the door. The sheikh welcomed him, and us, into his home. We were seated in upholstered chairs arrayed along a long reception hall, and the colonel told the sheikh that his unit had made a mistake in detaining him. By the time the colonel was deployed back to the U.S., he and some of his men had forged genuine friendships with Iraqis.

———————

Every once in a while, no matter how at home I was beginning to feel in Iraq, I realized I didn't know very much at all.

There was the language, and then there was the code: for instance, the questions that, during the sectarian war in 2006 to 2008 and even long afterward, allowed an Iraqi checkpoint officer to determine whether the driver was Sunni or Shi'a without ever directly asking.

As I passed through checkpoints, I constantly had to remind myself not to make eye contact with security guards the way one would do in the West. To do so as an Arab woman would be considered unseemly, and would give away the fact that I was a foreigner. "Just smile a little and look beyond them, as if you're slightly above it all," a female Iraqi colleague instructed me. I found if I followed her instructions, the guards rarely even asked to see my ID.

There were times, though, when I realized there were things I didn't know that I would have never even thought to ask.

Once, when I happened to mention the moon landing in casual conversation, an Iraqi colleague interjected to make sure that I knew it didn't really happen. Stunned, I asked everyone else in the room if they believed the moon landing was faked. They all did, sending me a video explaining the camera angles as proof. Growing up in Canada, I had always been inclined to believe that government officials generally told the truth. But in the kaleidoscope world of Saddam Hussein's Iraq, people had reason to believe the opposite. This skepticism spilled over into a belief that most things were not the way they seemed.

It could be hard to persuade Iraqis of a point of view most Westerners took for granted. Iraqis came to believe that the carnage was what Americans had intended all along—that it was part of a plan to destroy the country. It was difficult to persuade them that the even more frightening alternative was true: that there never was a plan for anything, just assumptions, miscalculations, and the fatal combination of ignorance and arrogance.

When I would try to argue from my Western perspective that, however misguided, the Iraq War wasn't a conspiracy to destroy Iraq, my Arab friends would often look at me with pity.

By 2007, when the U.S. military pumped more forces into Iraq to fight the insurgency, the soldiers had changed. Most were on their second or third tour of duty in a conflict they had originally been told would last six months. Fewer of them believed that a bloody handprint outside a house was a mark of al-Qaeda rather than a traditional blessing in sheep's blood, a common misconception in the early years.

For them, the idea that the war was payback for the attacks of 9/11 or a response to Iraqi weapons of mass destruction—commonly held views at the start of the war—had faded. They were there because they were soldiers; they wanted to keep their buddies safe and get home alive. A lot of them didn't. Most of the ones I knew wanted to help when they could.

One spring morning in 2007, I was with a group of soldiers on the outskirts of Baqubah, where they'd been going from house to house looking for weapons and al-Qaeda fighters since the break of dawn. The twenty-four-year-old lieutenant needed to secure a safe place from which they could keep watch on the street, and settled on the home of a couple with five daughters and a son. I was left to explain to the family that the soldiers would be there for a few hours, and that they wanted the family to stay in the bedroom.

Selma, the mother, was worried the soldiers would put them in danger, but she nonetheless offered the men glasses of tea and apricots from her garden. She was even more worried about her daughters Yasmine and Sabreen, who insisted on walking to school. The school had been closed for several days because of fears that the students would be kidnapped by al-Qaeda or other militant groups. Yasmine's and Sabreen's ambitions were to become teachers, and this was the only opportunity they had to take their high school exams. It was an hour-long walk through streets that could turn violent in an instant, and they weren't even sure the school would be open. But the girls were already dressed in white shirts and long black skirts with matching robin's-egg-blue headscarves, clutching their books in plastic bags.

Selma asked me to ask the soldiers if it would be safe for the girls to go. The platoon commander said he thought it would be okay, and radioed his soldiers to keep an eye out for the two girls walking through the area.

Selma stood in the doorway and watched her daughters walk away, winding through towering date palms, until they were specks on a dusty road. "I'm so afraid for them," she told me.

While editing the story I later wrote about the experience, I looked for a long time at the photo I'd taken of the mother, framed in the doorway. You could see the tension in her shoulders even through the black abaya she was wearing. It was the tension of holding your breath until your loved ones walk through the door again, in a time when going to school or work could get you killed.

PHOTO BY JANE ARRAF.

It's the same sense of suspended time I saw among the families of American soldiers, who were just trying to get through another day at home as they waited to hear whether their father or mother or husband or wife was okay. The tragedy of war, of course, is that no one emerges unscathed.

The U.S. base in Baqubah was darkened at night to avoid mortar attacks. Soldiers so exhausted they looked like they were sleepwalking made their way back from missions, aided by the red glow of infrared flashlights. The sound of helicopters shattered the silence at night. Many of them were "angel flights" transporting the bodies of soldiers killed in combat. It felt like the edge and the end of the world.

I thought back to three years earlier, when I had flown out of Anbar Province with a group of marines who were finally going home after eight months of bitter fighting. As the view of the city gave way to that of the desert, one of the young marines said to me about the people of the country they were leaving, "We hate them and they hate us."

But that wasn't entirely true. Iraqis and Americans were afraid of what they could do to each other.

By 2010, the American military had retreated behind the concrete blast walls of their bases. A year earlier, they had pulled out of Iraqi cities and handed security back over to Iraq. Under an agreement with the Iraqi government, U.S. forces would no longer be out in the streets unless they were accompanied by Iraqi forces. In some areas, Iraqis were reluctant to provide those escorts, keeping the Americans essentially confined to the bases. For the first time since the invasion of Iraq, Iraqi security forces were responsible for keeping Iraqis safe.

U.S. generals still briefed journalists on security in Iraq, but it was difficult for Iraqi journalists to get U.S. security approval to attend those briefings in their own country. In U.S. government terminology, Iraqis weren't Iraqi to the U.S.—they were "local nationals."

I arrived one morning at a U.S. base in Baghdad's heavily fortified "green zone" with an Iraqi colleague I'd invited who had been to the base before. The security briefing seemed to me like something an Iraqi journalist should attend. He was taken away for further investigation, so I waited in front of the trailer he'd been taken into, which was guarded by Ugandan ex-soldiers, now private contractors, and read the warnings posted on the corrugated metal:

> Danger
> Do not stand here!!!
> Do not enter!!!
> Do not knock!!!!

> **LOCAL NATIONALS AND THIRD COUNTRY NATIONALS PROHIBITED ITEMS:**
> Knife blades longer than three inches
> Tape measures longer than six feet
> Pets
> Pictures of genitalia
> Maps of Iraq

The list went on. I never did figure out the risk of tape measures longer than six feet. The ban on Iraqis having maps of Iraq seemed particularly over the top. It was their country, of course, but at the same time, it wasn't exactly their country. Americans were in charge of the rules.

My Iraqi colleague was less upset than I was, though. He was used to the absurdity and the humiliation. As it turned out, he would soon set off to live in the United States under the special visa program for Iraqis who worked with Americans, left to navigate his own way between cultures.

Spin

Natacha Yazbeck

The fact that I
am writing to you
in English
already falsifies what I
wanted to tell you.
My subject:
how to explain to you that I
don't belong to English
though I belong nowhere else,
if not here
in English.
—GUSTAVO PÉREZ FIRMAT, "BILINGUAL BLUES"

If this was the story it should be, I would tell you how sad little Ali looked in his little red T-shirt when he thought of his family. All the others were killed in the Houla massacre. Syria. I would tell you how we stopped and joked about Barcelona and Real Madrid and he cracked a smile and then we cracked a smile, a little too giddy. I would tell you how for a second the room started spinning and little Ali and his little red T-shirt began to fade, because what kind of people grill a kid on how he hid under his brother's body and then chuckle because they made little Ali smile. But this is not the story it should be. So few ever are.

"*Ali habibi?*" (Ali, sweetie?)

He looks up.

"*Ali habibi, shou sar maak?*" (Ali, sweetie, what happened?)

I would tell you how I got to little Ali *habibi*, and who made it happen, and why, and how in fact it was from the safety of Turkey that I spoke to him, and how I followed up once, twice, on Ali and then never spoke to him again. How I don't know where little Ali is now, or if he is still little or still prefers Barca to Real, or if he can sleep at night.

There have been a lot of little Alis since.

I get thanked a lot for my dedication to the little Alis. It is useful when you can talk to them in their own tongue, because it's like you are one of them. It's our capital in English, our brand. Our *raseed* in Arabic. Our capital. We force our own names over little Ali's and call it a byline.

Sometime in the late nineteenth century, the Khourys board a boat for the United States from what is not yet Lebanon. There is hunger, and there are Ottomans. Like a byline, name is everything, and so the village priest begs the family to leave someone behind so that if they all die at sea, at least the name will not die with them somewhere in the cold greenish waters of the Atlantic. They leave behind Jacob, the littlest.

Jacob grows up and begets Benjamin, who begets Judith, who is a little girl when the British and French troops withdraw from what was almost Lebanon. Judith is dead before she hits forty, leaving behind four children.

There is war again, and the four children in turn board boats departing from what is now a disintegrating Lebanon. Then I am born in New Jersey, to one of the four, almost one hundred years after the Khourys first boarded those boats. A little Arab born in New Jersey to parents displaced by war. This is useful, a handy cliché. Like little Ali.

Beydaa', like from the poem we read in high school Arabic class, asks where I was born. We're walking through the Azraq refugee camp in northern Jordan and she's playing with my bracelets. The safest camp for Syrians in the world, donors tell us, and it is. So safe that little Beydaa' clings to my gaudy bracelets like a life raft.

"You, where were you born?" She asks twice.

"Amerka."

"How?" she wants to know. "How were you born in Amerka?" And I do it. I give her false hope, like I'm one of them, because both our mothers named us after great literature even though it's really us kicking her boat back into the very ocean we washed up from.

Jacob's sister died at sea. They threw her body into the Atlantic. No one can remember her name.

My uncle, one of Judith's four orphaned kids, asks if there is something wrong with me. His son is dead, along with his wife and baby boy and their dog. I am belatedly paying my condolences, steely faced, like him, and sitting on temporal fault lines, probably like him, too. I was in Syria when my cousin died, along with his wife and baby boy and their dog, I think. The when is not important. He died in Canada along with his wife and baby boy and dog, suffocated to death trying to escape a fire. A little pile of humans and one dog slumped behind a door.

"My name is on a blacklist at the border," my 'ammo says as I'm paying my condolences, ergo my name, too, and am I crazy to do this to my mother. Everyone asks in their own way how one could brush off an entire family and its collective inherited anxieties. Except my mother, who understands this world and our complicity in it better than all of us combined.

The week before, or two weeks before, on a Friday in Damascus, we're drinking tea near the mosque. Waiting. I don't drink the tea because I am certain I will get sick. I can't be sure they've washed the glasses or boiled the water. This becomes increasingly important as the minutes go by, the small potentially unwashed glass holding the potentially unboiled tea water.

"Drink your tea. It's good," the stringer insists.

I lift the cup and let the steam fog up my glasses. I don't drink. As soon as the bottom of the glass touches the saucer—a clink you could hear distinctly, the square is so quiet—we hear it, me and the stringer who we did not byline, maybe for his own safety and maybe in part also because that's what we do. *Hurriye* (freedom). It sounds like a cliché. Another American motion picture, like Ziad Rahbani would say, before the playwright, too, lost it.

In the months to come, it will be war.

We move, straight across toward the beautiful mosque. My glasses are still slightly fogged. Men in pants and button-down shirts with batons drag a man wearing a red T-shirt, facedown on the concrete, leaving a trail of blood a darker red than his shirt. His black hair is gelled into a deep side part. He got up this morning and took his shower and shaved and gelled his hair to the side. And decided on the red T-shirt.

Then another is being dragged facedown, then two more, then more. I think someone spots us, because the stringer has shoved me into one of the alleys that wind around the mosque and we keep moving.

Days later, near the border, law enforcement politely locks us in a room for the better part of a day for having come to town without "license." They then proceed to beat the crap out of our photographer—another stringer who's a pillar of our bureau—and the driver. I watch. Because that's what we do. We watch. The photographer looks straight at me, silently warning me to keep my mouth shut. I try to say something. I decide instead to keep my mouth shut. They never touch me.

The photographer is religious. A devout Muslim father of two who drags me from my mattress to sleep in his room, closer to him, for my own safety. A brother. The kind we patronize with our benevolent cultural relativism. He doesn't want anyone to know, so we don't tell anyone. We don't tell anyone, and we don't write about it, and we don't byline our stories, and we are driven back to Damascus by the now-silent driver.

In Damascus, around the time my cousin is dying with his wife and baby boy and the dog in Canada, I accidentally call

Michel Samaha, former Lebanese minister and friend of the Assads. There's a number scribbled on a piece of paper on my desk. I assume, wrongly, that my boss has finally secured a Syrian SIM card. I instead dial Michel Samaha. I call my boss to wail about what I've done. He says to meet him and Michel Samaha at 12:30 a.m. in the lobby of a hotel. Shortly before 1:00 a.m. at the hotel, I spot a foreign correspondent for a TV network just leaving a meeting with him, a man with a south-of-Beirut beach club tan and good hair who somehow looks even less human in real life.

Michel Samaha will soon be arrested in Lebanon for plotting bombings, but now, at the hotel, he's just noticed my name and taken a liking to me because he knows my 'ammo, the one whose son has just died, from the party, the Kataeb or Phalange or however you call them in English, back in the day. This is how we get an interview the next day, because he knows my boss. He knows my uncle. I don't say much. I particularly keep my mouth shut on the subject of the party and its history. Our history. My history. Now is not the time, as they say back home. It's never really been the time.

In Bahrain, at the start of the 2011 protests, the imam asks me if I'm related to Sheikh Mohammad Yazbek of the other party, Hezbollah. Lebanon is very small, I say, and we are all family one way or another. The imam takes us to the interview we have been trying to secure, and after a couple of hours of questions— as always, both asking and being asked—I ask for a T-shirt to take home to my friend, a Baghdad correspondent who has asked for the protester T-shirt from Bahrain. A European journalist, who was also at the interview taking notes, looks at me, wide-eyed, and gives a little gasp to indicate, I suppose, that I am not being professional. That it is unprofessional to carry the personal over into the professional. That she has no clue what the man actually said, other than what I or the photographer have translated for her, is lost on her. I've since stopped translating, both voluntarily and/or upon command. I'm told I'm not so collegial anymore. Dictatorships are built on likability. Likability matters.

I told Beydaa' I was born in Amerka. I took a boat once when I was little, going toward war and not away from it. It worked out fine. Safe passage, as they say. I don't remember any of it, no matter how hard I try, but it was the summer of 1985. The question of what in New Jersey would make war seem the better option for a twentysomething-year-old woman and her child remains unanswered. I've stopped asking.

I think we docked at the same port Judith's kids had departed from. We spent the summer in the mountains up north, where Jacob begot Judith and Assad's troops would later burn their home—my home, maybe—to the ground. Sometime later in 1985, my mother and I drove through the mountains of Lebanon, across the border to Syria, Assad's Syria, and waited there. Then we flew back to Newark. I don't know the details. I don't remember it ever happening. I didn't see Syria again for more than two decades.

Aylan Kurdi was wearing a red T-shirt when he washed up dead on a beach in Turkey. The world saw Aylan Kurdi, age three, after he was dead. Only for a moment, but still, we saw. And we felt good about ourselves for having seen Aylan Kurdi, Syrian, Kurdish, age three. Aylan was kind of light skinned and not uncomfortably skinny. Also, you couldn't see his face, which is always useful, to not see the eyes. Yemenis are generally very skinny and generally, although not exclusively, browner and therefore much more difficult to see. Perhaps it's not that no one sees them so much as no one really looks at them, with their skinny dead babies.

Another Yemeni baby died today. More than one, and in this case "baby" is inaccurate. This one was either a fetus or a preemie, but you couldn't tell for sure from the picture. It might have been expelled from its mother's womb. We really try to figure it out but we can't tell. Do you call a body an "it," anyway? We do, in our air-conditioned newsroom.

The photo was deemed too graphic to publish, so I will describe it here. There's no need for a graphic-content warning because it's just words. Nice and linear and concise and in English. I don't know the baby's name, because the baby might not have had a name because the baby might not have been born, and anyway it's bad luck to say the name before birth.

The baby is as small as the medic's outstretched hands. It fits neatly into the palms of his outstretched hands, except for the nubby little arms, which flap down from the fleshy part of his palms. The baby is burned to what would be described as a crisp. The little burned arm nubs are exceptionally flappy. It is a burned, flappy little Yemeni almost-human, small enough to fit in the outstretched palms of the medic's hands. The nubs flap behind my eyelids every night for a week.

We don't publish the picture. It's too graphic, and people are too sensitive. Those of us who count as people, with sensibilities.

At a bar in Beirut once, right after the war—the 2006 one—a photographer is tacking his pictures of a burning Eiffel Tower to the wall. Torino, the tiny bar with the red lights. He tells me about hostile environment training, and about how it's not whether you make the right decision, it's how fast you can make decisions. Good journalists decide on the spot. I can't decide anything on the spot. What's real and what's not real and what this story is actually about, and what's mine and what's been forced into me and what my tongue is and if I even have one. Outside the field, I can't decide anything at all, on the spot or in hindsight. If I am in love and whether I hate my work and should I explode or just give up. The photographer writes the name of a woman down on the back of one of his burning Eiffel Tower Polaroids. Two years later, that woman becomes my first bureau chief, through no connection to the photographer. Life is strange that way.

The bartender at Torino begs me to make peace with my father, whom no one has seen in years. He is handsome, and intelligent, and patient, the bartender with the messenger bag. He brings levity to life. Connection to a city, a world, that was never really mine. Years spent coming to accept that I don't know what it's like to sleep in the *malja'* (bomb shelter), and I don't know what it's like to get stuck at school for a week because your parents can't cross over, and I don't know what it's like to pee in a Nido can, are soon over. I can't stomach the powdered milk or the sight of the red Nido can. All it takes is fifteen minutes as a journalist in Syria for the narrative to shift. Now I know more. Fifteen minutes for their entire childhoods.

The bartender is part Syrian, long estranged from an abusive Lebanese father. When his father died, he cried for days at his grave. He asked him out loud for forgiveness.

"Don't wait until you're at his grave."

I buried my father a long time ago, I remind him, and I don't need forgiveness. But I do. I need forgiveness. Every day. Because complicit does not begin to describe it. To write from, and in, that same pipeline that disfigured my people, my history, my land, my family, to write in the very language and for the very people who did it, which is also your language and who are also your people, and to do it so that you are liked, so that you are tagged, to be popular because your brand is your currency. To sell out every minute of every day, and to be thanked for your part in our very disfiguration. To be willingly complicit in this, in the fact that my tax dollars fund the wheels on the planes bombing the babies of my people. I need forgiveness every day. I need it, from little Ali and Beydaa', because this job is really ultimately all about us and our needs. Because when I stepped away for a minute, to leave our world and go back to school, it was like someone had turned the lights out and I was just standing there, in the dark, waiting for an end to something that was already dead.

The blue-eyed photographer and I are in Riyadh, backstage at the 2018 Arab Fashion Week. It's my increasingly not-so-secret ambition to ditch journalism, ditch academia, and become an aesthetician like my aunt, the youngest of the four whom Judith left behind. Except I hate social media, which apparently is career suicide for both journalists and makeup artists.

Cameras are banned at this fashion week. We've smuggled our cameras in beneath the abayas, and in one large backpack, thanks to the Italian charm of the blue-eyed photographer. Blue eyes go a long, long way where we're from. Toni said it all in 1969, and there's not much to add.

My sister gifts me a bracelet engraved by hand with a line from *Beloved*, but I cannot wear it and I never wear it, and I make no secret of it. "Grown don't mean nothing to a mother," it reads, which is what I always tell her, but I'm old, not grown, and not a mother. I cannot bear the sight of the beautiful silver words. So I leave it on the nightstand at my mother's house for her to wear, except she doesn't because my sister had it made especially for me. So it just sits there, looking at me every time I spend the night in my childhood bed, acutely aware that I'm nowhere near motherhood.

"Did you check your phone?" The photographer's blue eyes look up from the lens, red with anger. Grief. I've seen that look. I check my phone. Abdullah al-Qadry is dead. Our stringer. Husband, son, father of a baby. Nearly decapitated in Yemen. Thankfully, someone later says, not on assignment for us. Thankfully.

In Philly, years earlier, my cousin calls me one January afternoon and asks if I've checked my Facebook. I never want to check my Facebook. "Did you at least read the *Times* today?" But I stopped reading the English news the minute I stepped away from the field. Exasperated, she tells me Leila is dead, Leila

Alaoui, an al-Qaeda bullet in Burkina Faso. Two weeks after I last saw her in Beirut.

I left the field once, for almost five years, because I didn't understand anything anymore, and because at heart I have always suspected I'm not really a journalist. I can't remember most of the five years. The fog hasn't really ever lifted. I try to explain to my therapist that it's not trauma, or post-trauma, or post-traumatic stress, although it's probably a disorder, that the mind can actually bear this world. Maybe we are always a little bit depressed. Maybe sometimes it's not just war. It's the rest of the world that leaves you traumatized.

And maybe there is no possible way to tell the stories we should. To pretend they are something other than stories. I am waiting to go to Yemen, but you don't have to go anywhere anymore to be covering your beat. Plenty of great work gets done from a distance, my boss reminds me, and we need that distance. Because we're not far enough away.

Ali Abdullah Saleh is killed and Sana'a collapses, again. Our stringers are trapped. Again.

I call a contact, a dear friend, to make sure she is okay. For the first time in a year, she loses it. She saw a child scoop water up from the side of the road and drink it because people can't afford to buy water. A camp for the internally displaced—who, if their ports weren't under blockade, would have boarded boats and turned into refugees, but for now they are IDPs, internally displaced persons—is bombed. A boat of Ethiopian and Somali refugees is spotted by the Yemeni coast guard, so the smugglers throw people into the water, and probably stomp on their heads to keep them down. Another boat capsizes. She loses it. The next month, when we meet in person, she thanks me for my dedication, which took the form of using my phone, paid for by my company, from an air-conditioned flat in a high-rise in Dubai. She thanks me for my stories.

I don't know where little Ali and Beydaa' are now, but Mazhar is dead and Abdullah is dead and Leila is dead and Baraa is dead. My cousin Joe is dead, and Ramzi is also my cousin and he is also dead. Mohammed has no eyes or left arm anymore, and the other Mohammed is in jail.

I am in Dubai now, and my business card says I cover Yemen. I am in Dubai now, being thanked for caring, and six years after little Ali put on his little red T-shirt that morning, the room starts its lilting, comforting spin again.

Bint el-Balad

Nour Malas

At first, they were just black shadows cast across the desert expanse. As they drew nearer, they came into focus as a trudging mass of humanity.

Syrians.

Women in loose robes dragged toddlers, babies propped up on their hips. Men carrying parents and grandparents on their shoulders stepped ahead, calling back for assurances as women collapsed in the heat. Flimsy plastic bags, crammed with clothes and other belongings, dangled off shoulders and wrists. In the midday glaze, as light shimmered off the desert like water droplets, the scene at the Syrian-Iraqi border seemed almost biblical. My Iraqi colleague Ali, who had already tasted the wrath of displacement from his own country, squatted in the shade of our car and cried.

I, too, had watched this scene many times already, in Syria and on its borders. Recently, at another crossing into Iraq, thousands of Syrians had trampled over a bridge that all but collapsed into a river, capturing the media's waning attention of the then three-year-old refugee crisis. From Iraq, I went to Lebanon, Jordan, and Turkey, aiming to report on the refugee crisis from every border of Syria that I could. I was determined to see every dimension of this war so that I could better understand it. But not just for my reporting. This was a deeply personal assignment for me, and yet one that never quite felt personal enough.

Syria: never the country I called home, but certainly my homeland. I would untangle the many shades of this identity at the very moment the country was coming undone. Through my reporting, I would learn more about the people of Syria—Syrians, like me—from cities I knew, towns I had never heard of, and faraway villages I wouldn't think to visit if it weren't for my job.

My parents are from Damascus, Syria, but my siblings and I were raised in other countries in the Middle East and in the United States. Home was a place we created for ourselves over and over in places that never felt as though they were indisputably our own. Still, growing up, we always knew where we were from—Syria—even if we didn't live there.

In Saudi Arabia, for example, where my father built a career in the construction industry, we weren't quite as foreign as the Western expats, but we weren't Saudi either. Life felt temporary, even after many years. In Lebanon, one of our latest adopted homes, it took only a couple of words for new neighbors and friends to identify our Syrian accents.

We spent summers in Damascus, at the apartment my parents bought specifically to keep roots in Syria. And though it seemed fickle to declare this was the place *I was from* based on yearly visits, nothing else came as close to making as much sense. After ten years in Lebanon, my Lebanese friends would jokingly ask, "But how do you still sound *so Syrian*?" I found it a condescending expectation—that my words and mannerisms would meld into the mainstream around me—but it was also a fair question: how do you retain so strongly strands of somewhere or something you have never lived?

I would grapple with that question subtly, slowly, over my formative years—and then sharply, suddenly, in my job.

MIN WEIN? (WHERE ARE YOU FROM?)

I particularly never identified with the straddle that comes with being a hyphenated American: Syrian American, in my case. But because I worked for a U.S. newspaper, I found that not only was that duality an accurate and apt description of me throughout my reporting in the Middle East, it was also a helpful one that I could use to my advantage in certain situations. Still, it was always a little awkward explaining I had never lived in Syria. Sometimes this conveyed a social class barrier—of someone with the means to live abroad—or else a woman so Westernized that I might as well have not been of Syrian origin at all.

But remembrances of Syria over many cups of tea, and even a meal or two scraped together from meager ingredients, eventually diluted the differences. After all, it wasn't just that I spoke Arabic but my specifically Syrian accent that eased me into the small, intimate quarters of refugees and helped me get reporting done, for the most part, with ease and trust.

I learned to navigate the corners of my family identity and history, and use my experiences as a native reporter in the region, to see and access deep or difficult parts of the story. Instead of dreading the question *"Min wein, anseh?"* (Where are you from, miss?), which I was asked in every conversation and interview, I came to cherish the mutual exploration that would follow. What bound us was always more obvious, in the moment, than what made us different.

At least for the first few years of the war, this was true.

I never anticipated that I would cover this kind of war in my homeland. I told family and friends often how lucky I considered myself to have *this* job, *this* assignment, at *this* very moment. It was like an elevator pitch I perfected: It wasn't just that it was a huge story, I would say, a skill-building and name-making experience. It was a privilege to get to know my country, whatever the circumstances.

Privately, I felt guilty that it took the Arab Spring and a night-marish descent into war to accidentally spark this personal journey. As a college student in Lebanon, where I also first started to work as a journalist, I learned more about that country than my own. This felt like a betrayal, however inextricably linked the two nations' histories were. Soon I had more Lebanese friends than Syrian. Beirut, with its beachside bars and an American university we liked to call "Harvard of the Middle East," was a cooler place for twentysomethings than Damascus, where a semisocialist economy made the city feel like it lagged a decade or two behind.

When the early rumbles of the Arab Spring started, and my editor at the *Wall Street Journal* asked me to look into what was happening in Syria, I was mortified. Sure, I was Syrian, but I didn't know the country nearly as well as he might have assumed. And I predicted—mostly correctly—that few people I personally knew would be willing to talk to me in my capacity as a foreign correspondent for an American newspaper.

But as with any assignment, I worked away until I had contacts and sources I trusted and who trusted me, people offering snippets of life in a country fragmenting faster than we could document. Eventually, I even began to excel at the part of the job I found the most difficult: pressing traumatized and vulnerable people to recall experiences and details they couldn't, or didn't want to, in order to explain the suffering of Syrians in our stories. In moments of great synergy, it felt like I was drawing on a special power that helped me glide into people's lives, even at times of horror or tragedy.

TASHREED (DISPLACEMENT)

For a while, my job was a welcome safety net. It gave me an excuse to dissect and report a convoluted war with the aimed precision of a lab investigator, or a fact-finding mission, while dueling narratives swirled all around. My focus on deadlines and news cycles left no room for personal reflection or outrage, or the debates and conspiracy theories consuming the Arab world. I thought it was better that way, as week after week, and then year after year, the war killed, injured, depressed, or polarized everyone around me. Everyone knew someone who stopped talking to a brother or aunt on the opposite side. Relatives trickled out of Syria, packing up homes they doubted they would ever return to. My mother wept every time she watched the news.

Whether they're taking shelter from barrel bombs in the caves of Idlib or Aleppo or in the relative safety of Beirut or Berlin, Syrians everywhere will talk about *tashreed*—literally, displacement. *"Tsharadna, ikhtee"* (We've been displaced, sister), people would say to me over and over. The word meant so much more than simple physical displacement. *Tsharadna* meant we were ripped apart, made dispossessed—evicted, even. Over time, it began to reflect the complete shattering of the nation and the people it had encompassed.

Throughout the war, I downplayed my own feelings. What an inappropriate indulgence it felt like to recognize that somehow I had a small connection to this mass tragedy, beyond my job. I felt unentitled to this pain. I was, after all, a longtime expat—not a born-and-bred Syrian. I was experiencing this primarily as a journalist. My family was safe. Colleagues and friends praised my reporting as brave, but what was momentary courage driven by professional purpose when millions of people—my people—had no choice but to face violence every day? I pushed those thoughts aside and planned the next story, the next trip.

Still, my accent, my name, and ultimately my feelings always betrayed me. To myself and others, I was undeniably Syrian. And as the war got more violent, *"Min wein?"*—Where are you from?—became a more pointed question, demanding an answer with significant specificity: Which neighborhood, what sect? Here, too, I used my reporter's role as a veneer to protect myself from the type of probing often faced by journalists related to the places they are covering. "I'm just a reporter" was an easy, and honest, answer to "What side are you on?"

By the time the conflict had been raging for a few years, Syrians had perfected the coy game of finding out strangers' political views without asking. Only a straight-up rebel supporter, some would say, would still refer to the conflict as a "revolution." Regime backers tended to call it "the war," while those in the hazy area between the regime and its opponents reverted to the conspicuously broad term "the events."

I watched people do this verbal dance often, only to realize later that I was walking a similar tightrope in my own reporting and writing. I was so aware—even paranoid—of my personal connection to the story that I strained to project unreasonable neutrality, sometimes to the point of pretending I had no sympathy for any tragedy, on any side. I compartmentalized the suffering and made it my job to cut through it, to write clearly and straightforwardly. Interviewing a former prisoner, I asked minute details—and asked again and again, for accuracy of order and verification—about a torture tactic called "the chair." It felt cruel, but necessary. With every mass killing, I seemed to raise the bar for what I thought constituted enough information to piece together an account. In short, I nearly stopped believing anyone. I would probe all sides for answers, unflinching when fathers described rolling their dead babies into tiny shrouds and nodding mechanically as families talked about eating soil to stave off starvation.

I made it clear to Syrian officials in Damascus that I was on no side, even though they constantly invoked my being Syrian, and gave trite explanations about the job of journalists—a funny thing to explain in a state without independent media. When I traveled around the country with rebels, I didn't comment on the regime's actions or praise the rebel movement: I wanted it known I was there as a reporter, not as a sympathizer or an activist.

TA'TEER (DESTITUTION)

As a reporter, I tried to explore Damascus as I would have on summer vacations or visits to aunts, uncles, and cousins in the past. I was curious, and apprehensive, to see how the beloved hometown of my parents and grandparents was coping with the war. I felt this was my prerogative as a native, even though I was there as an American journalist. I wanted to steal any moment that would revive the Damascus in my memory with a determination to prove, to perhaps nobody but myself, that this was Syria: breezy balconies wrapped in jasmine vines, walks to the neighborhood cassette store for the latest mixtape, and crowded family dinners—not the divided nation showing its new faces in my notebooks.

Most of my close relatives had left the city by then. A few had stayed on, living stalled lives with little or no work, refusing to leave home unless violence came to the doorstep. One invited me for a home-cooked meal. She seemed enthusiastic to reconnect and offer familiarity and care in an otherwise electrified environment. The neighbors and some other relatives would join, too, she said. I couldn't wait to sit with people I knew and trusted, to take a breath and shed some of the paranoia I carried around with me in wartime Syria. Maybe we would even smile and laugh.

When I arrived, the table was set for six, but my relative and I were the only two there. The others had realized I was a journalist on assignment and, assuming my every movement would be tracked by the government, got cold feet.

"I wasn't going to talk about work or anything about politics!" I fumed, embarrassed to have ruined the dinner, but also feeling frustrated that a simple meal with family had become an undertaking of risks and calculations.

"I know," my relative said bashfully. "But this is Syria." She promised to gather us all another time.

Syria. The more I reported on it, the farther away it began to seem, like a receding goal that had become so distant that none of us—Syrians as a whole—could remember what it was originally about.

The war contorted and dragged on, and my own ability to contort my Syrian-ness in ways that served my reporting—my special power—began to fade, becoming instead an unshakable burden. I struggled to use the fly-on-the-wall perch I sometimes secured, feeling like it could breach the trust of the people allowing me into their lives, even though they always knew I was a journalist.

At a refugee camp in the Jordanian desert one late summer day, that struggle smacked me straight in the face.

Abu Nawras, a retired Syrian army intelligence officer, was said to be the first refugee to have registered at the camp. He was impatient. There I was, trying to get him to revive the details of his earliest moments at the refugee camp, when two days earlier, a fresh disaster had struck his—our—country: the first large-scale chemical-weapons attack outside Damascus. I covered the aftermath of the attacks remotely from my reporting trip in Jordan. A small television screen in his trailer looped images of gagging children and lifeless bodies. The former American president Barack Obama had called the action a "red line." Syrians, within the country and across the Middle East, were holding a collective breath to see what would happen next.

Abu Nawras paced the length of his new home, a caravan of a couple of yards. His eyes were bloodshot with anger. We had talked for hours by then, first courteously, then profoundly, on the course of the uprising-turned-war, life in Syria before, and what could come next. I remember offering my view as a reporter covering the conflict and its many players. This was something Syrians frequently and frantically looked to journalists for: insight into what the great powers of the world were doing with their country. It was as if we held a crystal ball or could some-how make the levers churn to produce a more favorable out-come, or at least less bloodshed.

Displaced Syrians often say it is even worse to watch their country crumbling from afar, helpless and detached, even if their displacement means they are alive. The word *ta'teer*, many would say, describes this surreal fate that has enraptured the Syrian people: destitution. *T'atarna*—we have become destitute. Syrians who shake their heads and cry at the *ta'teer* they and their coun-try have endured are reflecting grief so deep it has barely begun to surface.

My notes from the end of my day with Abu Nawras are a scribble. But a few quotes are well formed:

"So we have a rainbow now. Great. Why does America like to give a red line, a blue line, what's next, a green line?"

"Why did this happen to us in Syria? Why?"

"If I doubt America, I will doubt every journalist who works for America."

I made the argument that the U.S. was less involved, less stra-tegically calculating, in Syria than many Syrians assumed. "They're not as powerful in this war as you think they are, sir," I said. I remember using an Arabic idiom, "like a deaf person at a wedding processional," to describe what I had seen of American policy in Syria so far—meaning the U.S. was often struggling to catch up in the chaos or to get a full picture of what was happen-ing on the ground. In other instances, this analysis would usually prompt a sigh, even a chuckle. But Abu Nawras was silent, look-ing at the floor. Suddenly, he said: "Carry this message back to President Obama." I saw my camera tripod hurled at me first, and then my scarf.

I had encountered plenty of rude people on the job before, but never once among the displaced and desperate families of Syria or Iraq, some of the greatest hosts I have ever known. His reac-tion was more surprising because I was *bint el-balad*—literally, a "daughter of the country"—and I thought we were talking on some kind of common ground. Abu Nawras said the interview was over and chucked my notebook at me next. I stood in the gravel-covered desert outside the caravan, stunned.

NASSEEB (FATE)

It had been two years since I had reported daily on Syria when my editors sent me to Germany to help track an unfolding migrant crisis. Those two years of reprieve had given me distance and replenished my resolve. I had moved to a new post in Baghdad, from which I had already reported on Iraqi migrants joining the fray, pawning belongings, and gathering life savings to get to the Turkish coast and, eventually, Greece and beyond. Dozens were already lost at sea, which is how the Iraqi mothers I interviewed described their missing sons, unable to process the eventuality that they could have died trying to make the crossing. It was a deeply miserable story, but I was excited to cover it in Germany, eager to learn the circumstances leading to this latest mass rush to sea. Syrians had been trickling into Europe for years; some kind of dam had broken for others seeking safety and better lives, too.

In Berlin, I visited a registration center that was the first stop for some migrants and refugees coming into Germany. On the sidewalks and under trees, they laid out on blankets, segregated into families and by the nations they fled. There was an Afghan corner, and one where Ethiopians and Eritreans gathered. Children played and cried. Young mothers propped babies on their hips. My mind flashed back to the impromptu refugee camps of northern Syria and the exodus at the country's borders, although that parallel was inaccurate. Here we were in the safety of a European nation, yet it didn't quite feel that way. The vulnerabilities and uncertainties of war seemed to trail the people trying to escape it.

I was talking to a young couple from Mosul in Iraq, Omar and Nadia, when a small crowd began to gather. Some assumed I was an aid worker, or perhaps an Arabic-speaking German bureaucrat. "We waited in line five hours yesterday but didn't make it to the counter," shouted an Egyptian man. Hala and Mahmoud, from Aleppo in Syria, had been sitting quietly on a patch of grass with their baby. Mahmoud stood up to join the group. "It's been twenty-eight days and we haven't registered yet," he said softly. "*Nasseeb*" (fate), he said, shrugging. It's just our fate, many Syrians say, giving in to what they describe as God's designs for their lives. "We've been here for three months!" someone else yelled. They begged, one another and me, for answers: "What comes next?"

There should have been nothing unusual or unexpected about that scene, but it felt surreal, and sudden. I had watched and written stories as Syrians were displaced from their homes, then their cities. Then they scattered across provinces within Syria. And finally, they moved through borders and rivers to neighboring countries, where they struggled to adjust even in places where they shared the same language and history. They picked up and moved, starting anew again and again, landing now in Europe and pulling a much larger wave with them. Their arrival in Berlin could have marked a moment of hope and renewal, a breakthrough to a place of safety and perhaps stability. But all I saw at the registration center was sorrow and, mostly, overwhelming exhaustion.

Side by side with people from Afghanistan and parts of Africa who have been fleeing their own civil conflicts for decades, Syrians finally saw their future. There was a new sense of permanence to this exile, an inevitability to giving up on home. I hadn't sensed this kind of complete resignation from Syrians before—or perhaps I had forgotten it, as I became distracted from my own distress by covering other stories. How did we get here? What had happened to my country? I cried as I left the registration center, and every night for a while.

In the next several weeks, two colleagues and I rode trains back and forth between Austria and Germany, meeting and interviewing refugees and migrants and following their paths. I focused on meeting Syrians, whom I thought I could spot even before they clambered onto the train, and easily by their accents once on board. The train was a cross-section of the Syrian conflict. Rebels who had given up on the fight shared compartments with army conscripts—quiet deserters, not defectors—who had once been their opponents in battle. Pharmacists and law school students sat near illiterate farmers and handymen. On the EuroCity train, they were equal in fate—*nasseeb*—and on the same precarious brink of an uncertain future.

One of the subjects of the story my colleagues and I eventually wrote was a Syrian man named Samer Kabab and his five-year-old son, Amer. I hadn't planned to write about this particular family, but their journey kept unfolding in gripping ways. I also became wrapped up in it, resurfacing my struggle over how to cover the story without coming too close.

We had ridden the train several times by the time I met Samer and Amer, and still the anticipation of what was to come once we crossed the border into Germany was sickening. Most refugees and migrants hoping to reach farther destinations in Germany, or even other countries, weren't aware of the regulations requiring them to declare themselves upon entry. German police would board the train and pull off migrants as commuters and tourists watched with heads hung low or covering their faces in concern. This particular time, I was also forced off the train by the policemen, who were arguing that journalists were not allowed to be there. That was when I ended up hand in hand with small Amer. I had seen him with his father on the train, and now he was alone on the platform. When his father, Samer, resurfaced, he asked politely if he could borrow my cell phone to make a call before he and Amer marched away in line with the rest of the group. In the chaos, we didn't talk any more or exchange numbers.

The next day, I received a WhatsApp message from a Syrian number. "My husband and son, a small boy with long hair, do you know where they are?" It was Samer's wife, Amina, who was still in Damascus with their baby boy. I learned from her that Samer had used my phone to call his brother, who had arrived before him in Germany. The brother passed on my number to her. I had no idea where her husband and son had ended up. But I promised to try to find out and let her know. "Bless you, darling," she wrote back. "Forgive me for the inconvenience. I am worried about my son."

I tracked down Samer and Amer, who had settled into a temporary migrant center on the outskirts of Frankfurt. It was a community gym that had been turned into a holding and registration center. Syrians, accustomed to refugee camps, called it "the camp." Until Samer managed to get a cell phone, I was his link to his wife back in Damascus. I would call other Syrians at the gymnasium, other families I had met on the train, to relay messages back and forth between Amina in Damascus, who was texting and sending me voice messages, and her husband.

"Thank you, dear, you are now like my daughter," she once said. "You have entered our lives and my heart and I am grateful for you."

I visited Samer and Amer at the center, discreetly. No reporters were allowed there, but no one asked me any questions on my repeated visits, during which I must have seemed like a relative or friend. Samer showed me his notebooks from German language class, and Amer introduced me to his new friends. He had become a handful for his father, who joked that he left the manual for raising his son back in Syria and hid the painful details of their life at the cramped gymnasium from his wife.

In Damascus, Amina was growing frustrated, and it showed

in her messages to me. "Did you visit today? How are they doing?" She missed her little boy and wanted to join them in Germany, but wasn't sure she could brave the trip on her own with a baby. Samer's plan, meanwhile, was to better gauge the asylum process and settle in before planning to bring over the rest of the family. The waiting game was weighing on Samer and Amina. They stopped talking for three weeks. "We keep arguing over nothing," Samer told me. "Sometimes it's simpler not to talk." He had given up everything back in Syria—a business and two homes—for a better life for his family, and now he worried he had torn it apart forever. "*Nasseeb*," he said: fate.

ALHAMDILLAH (THANK GOD)

I was conscious of Amina's discomfort at watching a reporter spend time with her child when for her, he was so far out of reach. One afternoon, Samer, Amer, and I went apple picking with a few other Syrian families, walking along the side of a highway and under a bridge to reach a vast field that had been first discovered by Afghan families at the camp. Parents were improvising to keep their children entertained, and the landscape outside Frankfurt was a delight. Amer crawled out of a cornfield, his long bangs shading his eyes, and climbed up my back.

"Auntie Nour," he said, "will you live with us in the camp?"

The boy, missing his mother, was growing attached to me. I juggled the rest of my reporting on this story according to instinct and my best judgment. I started to spend just enough time with them as was necessary for the reporting. I sent Amina, back in Damascus, updates when she asked. I checked in with both Samer and Amina periodically on her plans to leave Syria, but didn't probe.

When I left Germany, my communication with both of them trailed off. I turned to other stories and talked to Samer from time to time, but for a while, he didn't respond to me. When

PHOTO BY ELLEN EMMERENTZE THOMMESSEN JERVELL.

our story featuring his family was published, I sent him a link and pasted the text and images, writing a note for him to make sure to flip through the beautiful photos—portraits of father and son. He didn't reply. I felt sheepish, but hoped to hear from them soon.

Amina messaged me two months later. She had decided to join her husband and son, and was texting me from the Turkish coast, where she said she was stranded after having been robbed by a smuggler. She wasn't asking for money, she said, just a copy of my passport so she could receive a money transfer, but the desperation in her voice made clear she needed all the help she could get. Part of the ethical conduct of journalists is not to curry favors or buy gifts for the people you are covering; they should want to tell their stories for the sake of the historical record. These rules are smudged in reporting among vulnerable communities, when it is considered good practice to show appreciation to hosts who often offer journalists shelter and food—for example, donations of warm clothing or a meal.

In this case, I didn't know what to do. Could I help Amina reunite with her husband and child? Would I be seen as overly sympathetic, or even unethical? Wary once again of my Syrianness on the job, I decided not to, and apologized to Amina for being unable to help. I didn't hear back. Months passed by. It was the end of the year and I was spending the holidays with my family. I couldn't stop thinking of Amina and her family. Why had I taken that stand? Why didn't I ask an editor what was appropriate? What happened to her? Did she make it to Germany?

I wondered whether Samer and Amer were ever moved out of that smelly gymnasium. I wondered if Amer would see his mother and brother again. They had dropped off the map. How could this be, after I followed them so closely, that I could lose touch with them like this? I felt like a vulture—a journalist who swooped in, got my story, and flew out.

Another two months later, a voice message on WhatsApp

from a German number I didn't recognize confirmed my deep sense of guilt.

"Hello, old friend," Samer said. "Amina and I wanted to let you know she made it here. We are waiting for your visit."

I called immediately, and in between tears and apologies, Amina and I reconciled a problem we had never acknowledged. I apologized for not helping her. She, astonishingly, apologized for asking for a favor. "It's just that you felt so familiar," she said. "I didn't know what to do or who to turn to."

They had been moved into a small home and have a new baby girl. The boys were settling into school in Germany. Amer tells his parents he barely remembers me, which is a relief. When I ask how things are, they say, *"Alhamdillah"*—thanks be to God—though many pieces of a stable life, including work for Samer, are still missing.

I keep in touch with several families from the EuroCity trains, but not all, and not as consistently as I would like. I think of them and the many others still in Turkey, Lebanon, Jordan, Iraq, and, of course, Syria: Syrians with no other recourse but to be Syrian and live by the rules of *tashreed*, and the consequences of what that means in each adopted home. I think of our divergent paths and *nasseeb*, and of their grace and resignation to God's will.

And I'm humbled by how these people, thankful for their own uncertain circumstances, are worried about mine: Where am I right now? Am I still traveling so much? Have I seen my parents lately? When will I get married? They ask after me with diligence and care, as if I am one of them—as if I am the one left behind. "See you back in the homeland," we say sometimes as good-byes, mutually unwilling to set a date or define what that even means.

Hull & Hawija

Hind Hassan

When I was about sixteen, my father had some Iraqi friends over for dinner at our home in England. I walked into the living room, greeted the men, and shook their hands. When they left, I was severely scolded by my parents. Their insinuation was that a woman—especially a young, unmarried woman—shouldn't offer her hand to a group of men. My behavior was the antithesis of what was culturally expected of me in such an environment: I was to be feminine, soft-spoken, and reserved.

This was a typical scene from my youth. I had spent years rebelling against certain aspects of my parents' interpretation of the Iraqi Muslim identity that I was supposed to inherit. I didn't want to shoulder the burden of my family's expectations. But to them, what I had done was yet another example of how I'd lost touch with my religion, culture, and identity.

We left Iraq when I was just three years old, in the midst of the Iran-Iraq War. My parents never intended to stay abroad: my dad had planned to finish his doctorate in England, after which we'd return to Iraq, where he and my mother would take up teaching jobs. In their ideal world, I'd study to become a doctor before marrying relatively young, preferably another doctor, and so would my brothers and sisters. But the conflicts ran into each other, back-to-back, without a breath in between. The United Nations imposed economic sanctions on our home country, crippling the economy. The then-strong Iraqi dinar crashed, and my father's scholarship money ran out.

We lived in Hull at the time, a predominantly white working-class city in the north of England with a population of just over three hundred thousand. There were now five children, most of us were in school, and the aspirational dreams my parents had arrived at the shores of the UK with were drifting away. Instead, they worked anywhere they could to keep the family afloat: in the back of restaurants washing dishes; behind the till at news-stands; and on the floors at local clothing shops. In their spare time, they'd track the situation in Iraq by watching the news. When they had guests over, or visited friends, they'd watch to-gether. For most of my formative years, news was very much a permanent fixture.

One of my earliest childhood memories is of my mother cry-ing as she watched the bodies of Iraqis who had died in Iran during the war be returned to Iraq. In the years that followed, she cried often, particularly for her soldier brother, whose letters from an Iranian prison eventually stopped arriving in the mail. She cried again when news reached her that, after ten years, he was alive, and had returned home in a prisoner exchange deal. She shed tears during the Gulf War, followed by the 2003 U.S.-led invasion, and for the guilt she felt over not having been able to see her father before he died. The more distant she was from everything she knew, the more rigid she became at home, and the more I rebelled.

I didn't want to pray, go to the mosque, learn Arabic, or wear a headscarf. I wanted to wear makeup, go to parties, and look like everyone else. But my unibrow, brown skin, and afternoon curfew made that difficult. At primary school, I and other peo-ple of color were used to racial slurs such as "Paki." I spent the bulk of my teens hiding my life at home from my friends. I had two distinct identities that I couldn't quite reconcile: at home I was an Iraqi Muslim, while at school I was a northern Brit.

The first time I returned to Iraq—at the age of seventeen,

fourteen years after we'd fled—came as a shock. My mother cried again, this time from happiness. She was reunited with female family members, who ululated; she embraced my uncle who had been held in Iran, and they both cried. She said incarceration had changed the way he looked: he was now frail and old. Iraq, meanwhile, remained stuck in time, fraying at its dilapidated edges following years of war. I finally met girls my age who looked like me, but I still felt like a foreigner. My Arabic was broken, my reference points weren't the same as theirs, and my outlook was different. My mother had started to float the idea of marriage; during the trip, she arranged a visit to the family home of an Iraqi doctor who lived in Hull in the hopes that I'd be tempted by their affluent and relatively liberal lifestyle. One uncle told me he looked forward to my next visit to the country—when I'd be wearing a headscarf.

In March 2003, the United States invaded Iraq. A million antiwar demonstrators in the United Kingdom marched against the conflict. Unlike for the other Iraq wars, politicians, UN officials, and ordinary people came together to oppose the invasion. There was even an antiwar protest in Hull, a city that wasn't exactly known for its international political activism.

It had been twelve years since the Gulf War. The country appearing on every news channel and covering the front of every newspaper was the country I was from: I knew it, I'd visited it, I'd resented it. In that context, at eighteen, I started to watch the news by choice. For the first time, I listened closely to my parents' heated discussions with their friends. The same dread I felt as a child watching the news flashes had returned, but it wasn't because the developments saddened my parents—this time they saddened me, too. I read everything I could about Iraq, its history and its culture, and then I'd watch the bombs drop on television with the rest of the country.

This immersion in politics turned out not to be a phase, as my parents had hoped. Shortly after beginning my undergraduate studies at Leeds University, I discovered the campus was a hub for political debates, activism, and journalism. My chemistry degree took a backseat: I wrote for the student paper, took part in campus elections, and was a member of the student union. By the time I completed my degree, I'd decided to change direction and quit chemistry for journalism. Much to my parents' disappointment, and with the help of a scholarship, I moved to London to begin a graduate degree in broadcast journalism.

Growing up in Hull, I wasn't able to fully grasp what it meant to be Iraqi. I hadn't suffered in the way Iraqis who remained in the country had, so while I was outraged by that suffering, I still felt disconnected from it.

It wasn't until I joined *Vice News Tonight* on HBO in September 2016 that I traveled to Iraq to report from the ground for the first time. Before joining *Vice News Tonight*, I had worked for Al Jazeera International and Sky News, where I had dealt extensively with politics in the Middle East, in particular the rise of the Islamic State in Iraq and Syria. Iraqi and Middle Eastern politics had naturally become a journalistic passion, although I was producing reports from the UK. I felt I had a unique understanding of part of the region's culture and was eager to get on the field. Iraqi forces were about to begin a military offensive against the Islamic State in Iraq, so I pushed my new managers at *Vice News Tonight* to let me report on the imminent humanitarian crisis.

In October of that year, a few of my coworkers and I traveled to Qayyarah, an Iraqi town roughly thirty-five miles from Mosul, to report on the aftermath of the battle against ISIS. The violent militant group had been pushed out about two months earlier, but not before they'd set the area's oil fields alight. Big black clouds of smoke had been billowing over the town for months, creating a thick film of soot that blanketed the area like black snow; we wanted to investigate the impact the pollution was having on residents, especially children, who still lived there. I had felt that my basic grasp of Arabic and my Iraqi identity would help us deliver an authentic story.

At first, many of the male residents we encountered in Qay-yarah were eager to share their experiences, but the women were cautious to speak—unless it was just with me. (Some Iraqis would guess my background right away from my name, while others would think I was a foreigner until they heard my local dialect. They would then ask me about my family, my tribe, and where in Iraq I was from.)

One mother who lived dangerously close to the blazing fires told me she could not clean the black soot off her children, no matter how hard she tried, and that they were vomiting and coughing because of the thick fumes that they were inhaling. "I'm only speaking to you because you're my daughter," she said. Every morning the woman would wake up at the break of dawn to clean her humble home, but by midday, the black soot would engulf the curtains, chairs, and floors yet again. The sheep, cows, and chickens also turned to black from the soot, contaminating the main source of food in the town; water, too, had reportedly been polluted.

For hours, we watched children carelessly playing football under the plumes of smoke and hanging around the burning wells. Doctors we spoke to had told us they were concerned about the long-term effects the fumes would have on the children; the United Nations had said that millions may have been exposed to the soot and gases from the smoke. At the time, the local hospital had closed. The clinic we visited was bare, the beds and equipment were stained black, and the doctors told us they didn't have enough medicine to treat the residents. Person after person complained of difficulty breathing and coughing until they became sick. They'd stopped going to the clinic to seek medical help because they were tired of being sent away without treatment.

Health problems weren't the only concerns the town's residents faced. One mother told me that when her sons played together, they would pretend to shoot one another. She was exasperated: how could they have any hope at all when ISIS glorified violence and hung dead bodies in the street to taunt the town? What were the children to make of such atrocities? Young men approached me and asked if I wanted to see barbaric ISIS videos they had been sent. Most of the children hadn't been to school for years.

Buraq, a little girl who must have been about eight, caught my attention. She was sharp and cheeky, asking to have her photo taken with the other children. I didn't quite catch her name, having never heard it before, so I asked her how to spell it. She froze and smiled nervously at me, but stayed silent. A boy who stood next to her laughed at me as he said Buraq hadn't been to school for three years, so she couldn't read or write. I was surprised by my own ignorance.

I was born in a village near the south of Iraq. Chasing chickens in the backyard of a relative's house with my brother and cousins remains one of the strongest memories I have of the few years I lived there. Buraq and her friends reminded me of that time, before we fled the country, and of the young cousins I'd met when I'd returned briefly at seventeen. Like them, Buraq spoke with an air of authority, wise beyond her years, mimicking the language and hand gestures of adults. They loved to play and tease one another, but war, crippling sanctions, and the threat of violence had simultaneously accelerated and stunted their childhood.

I had been spared Buraq's experiences of conflict. Instead, as a child, I had watched catastrophic events unfold from the safety of my living room in Hull. It was a curious feeling: merging archived memories of the news stories I'd witnessed as a child with heartbreaking real-life testimonies in Iraq. While my Iraqi background helped me navigate the story, it also made me realize how far removed I had been.

By October 2017, a year following my initial reporting trip, ISIS had all but completely been defeated in Iraq. Hawija, however, remained under the group's control. All routes in and out of the town had been blocked by the Iraqi army in an attempt to stop ISIS from seizing weapons and supplies. Two male colleagues from *Vice News Tonight* and I returned to the country to report from the front lines of the battle, where we conducted a number of interviews with federal police officers.

We had planned to make our way back to the Qayyarah airbase at sundown, but Captain Hussein Majid—who was in charge of a group of men defending one of the Hawija city front lines and who had been tasked with looking after us—cautioned that it was too dangerous for us to travel so far so late in the day. He suggested that we accompany him and a soldier to a nearby safe house that belonged to one of the soldier's relatives instead. The mud-brick house sat in front of a large yard that was scattered with cages holding chickens and ducks. An elderly man lived there with members of his immediate and extended family. The women of the household had moved to the second house, which was located just behind the one we were staying in, for the night.

After we washed up and changed our clothes, we were led to a room that had been filled with mattresses for the men to sleep on. I was to sleep in a separate room. Moments later, the elderly man walked in with the soldier, bringing with him fresh bread and plates of food. We said thank you, apologized for the inconvenience, and joined them to eat what they'd prepared: duck stew, fried potato, and egg. After dinner, we moved out onto the porch, where a number of other men joined us, including the host's son, who looked more like a boy than a man. I joked that he was too young to be smoking, and his father chuckled and told us that he was seventeen, married, and expecting a child. (This surprised my colleagues more than it did me—one of my aunts had gotten married at the age of fifteen, and it isn't uncommon for Iraqi women in more traditional households to marry in their late teens.)

The son brought us a tray of chai. Our host drew a victorious breath after taking a sip, exclaiming, "Ah, how we missed this tea!"

Without thinking, I asked why he'd gone so long without tea.

"Because of ISIS," he replied, explaining that after the security forces had blocked the routes in and out of the area, tea prices had spiked.

It hadn't fully dawned on me that the area, which was situated several miles from Hawija city, had been under the control of ISIS until just days earlier.

We talked for hours with the men about life under ISIS. Family and friends would periodically disappear, the children of the town had been out of school for months, livelihoods were put on hold, and food prices soared. They had been living on meager quantities of bread and rice for a year, and yet there they were, hosting a group of strangers—British and Irish journalists they had never met before. They had gone above and beyond, slaughtering a duck for us, letting us drink their precious tea, and allowing us to shower and sleep in their home.

Hospitality is an important social custom in Iraq and its neighboring countries. As such, generosity can be a competitive sport among members of the Iraqi community in Hull. Adults loudly and aggressively argue over who has the privilege of paying the bill at restaurants. At dinner parties, there's often enough food and drink to feed three times the number of people in attendance. When a family friend heard that my mother was experiencing complications during the birth of my younger brother, she snuck into our house by climbing through a back window that had been left ajar, cleaned the entire home, and cooked a meal for the family before leaving the same way.

I had witnessed many moments of Iraqi hospitality over the years, but none of them compared with those I experienced with the family in that safe house. The simple act of drinking tea and sharing stories with these strangers who had suffered so much under ISIS was one of my most memorable reporting experiences.

The morning after that dinner, we made our way to another village on the outskirts of Hawija that had been liberated mere days before our arrival. We visited the home of a family who told us more gruesome details about life under ISIS, and how their day-to-day existence had drastically changed following the Iraqi military offensive. The house next door had belonged to an ISIS fighter, and his family had fled days before the insurgency. Due to that proximity, the family, who were constantly watched by their neighbors, lived in perpetual fear of being reported for breaking strict Islamic rules. One male member of the family had been kidnapped by ISIS and tortured for months after they discovered he'd once served as a soldier. Those who crossed ISIS and its stringent laws were executed in a nearby area.

One of the women we spoke to was wearing a purple abaya. The color was so bold that I complimented her on it. She said that after ISIS had seized control of the village she was allowed to wear only dark colors. "Today is Eid," she exclaimed. "We're celebrating!" Her excitement was palpable. Her two-year-old daughter, Amani, burst into tears upon meeting me: the only world she knew was one in which ISIS fighters were in control, and she probably wasn't sure what to make of me—an unveiled woman wearing a black T-shirt and combats. Our fixer, who was handling our logistics, calmed her down by giving her a small chocolate bar, which she devoured with a quizzical look on her face. This was, her mother said, the first time she'd ever tasted chocolate.

We interviewed the family members just outside the guest house. In the backdrop were clouds of smoke hovering over Hawija from the ongoing military offensive. After the interview, they brought chairs to the yard and we drank tea together. The local journalist and I translated for the other crew members, who had acquired a taste for chai. As we left, we apologized for taking up so much of their time. They told us that it had been so long since they'd had guests that our company was a relief.

We made our way to the nearby spot where ISIS routinely executed locals, accompanied by one of the men we'd just interviewed. The shift in settings was jarring. After a five-minute drive, we passed a former ISIS checkpoint that was covered in pro-ISIS graffiti. The man from the interview told us that the last execution he had witnessed was of two young Shi'a boys whose religious views contradicted those of ISIS. They were forced to kneel in the public space before being decapitated. Their heads were placed on their chests and their corpses left in the square; locals were told that they, too, would be executed if they chose to move the bodies. After the execution, ISIS fighters kicked the heads around like they were footballs.

Meeting this family, the people we had stayed with the night before, Buraq, and many others was humbling. My strict upbringing, identity crisis, and experiences with racism had made me feel like a victim. But here, my privilege was striking, and the sense of shame I felt as a result was overwhelming. These were proud people—abundant in generosity. I couldn't shake the feeling of immense guilt that it was down to pure luck that I lived in England, and that these families had lived under the control of a death cult.

The following day, we returned to the front lines of the battle in Hawija, accompanied by two federal police officers. Upon arriving at a village in the district, a convoy of army vehicles slowed us down. We were forced to stop as dozens of villagers surrounded the vehicles, cheering and chanting. Moments earlier, they had been liberated from ISIS. Many men were holding razor blades, shaving off one another's beards. One jubilant man had two lit cigarettes in his mouth: he excitedly told us that he would have been punished days earlier, as smoking was forbidden under ISIS rule.

As we moved farther north, we reached the Hashd, a mostly Shi'a paramilitary umbrella group, some of whose militias are supported by Iran. The Hashd was pushing farther into the few areas of Hawija that were still controlled by ISIS, alongside the federal police. Many of these men were from the south of Iraq. When they learned that I was also born in the south, some were perplexed, asking why I would want to go to a war zone. I laughed awkwardly, not so sure myself. Nevertheless, they brought anyone they could find from the same region to me, saying they'd found "another member of my family" and demanding that we take pictures together.

Two days later, Hawija was declared fully liberated.

While reporting from Iraq, I often messaged my father, sending him photos and asking for help with niche politics and translations. After initially opposing my career in journalism, he'd accepted that he was never going to change my mind. Now he was even engaging with it, never fazed or impressed—Iraq was nothing new to him, after all. But he was interested, and happy that journalism had at least allowed me to understand the place we were born a little bit better.

And I, for the first time, wanted to know more about the details of his life. I was learning that his culture, the one he had imposed upon me, was a key part of his identity and his experiences. My parents' anger and frustration with how I lived my life were products of their own identity crises.

The next time I visited my father in Hull, I showed him pictures of the soldiers and locals we had met, recounting the stories they'd told us. My father had served in the army for two years in Iraq—conscription was compulsory for all men under Saddam Hussein's regime. As I told him stories of the soldiers, he shared memories of the bases he'd covered and the places he'd visited. He'd lived under the Saddam regime and through the start of the Iran-Iraq War, and worried for his family during the Gulf War and 2003 invasion. Some of his friends had been killed, family members threatened, and relatives locked up in foreign prisons.

But in all of our conversations, he never looked for sympathy. He and my mother had sacrificed their careers, families, and dreams in order to allow their children to live a different life than their own.

Years of studying and multiple degrees hadn't stopped my father from washing dishes in take-out joints and running a newsstand in order to pay for our education. The only life I knew was the one I'd lived in Hull, among a community that had long felt alien to me. In returning to Iraq, I saw a snapshot of the struggles he'd faced—more profound than anything I'd ever experienced—and the obstacles he had to overcome to do what he thought was best for his family.

After pursuing a career that would allow me to report on the stories of those affected by conflict, I finally came to realize that for years I'd glossed over the most obvious one.

RESILIENCE

Just Stop

Eman Helal

Eighteen years ago, on my first day of secondary school, I crossed a road by myself for the very first time. As a girl, I was forbidden by my mother from doing even the most basic things. Simple pastimes like hanging out with classmates after final exams were a distant, unattainable dream. These strict laws were nonnegotiable. When my mother said no, a frequent occurrence, she didn't explain why. I had to accept her demands, no questions asked.

Even though my mother had struggled against her own strict mother when she was younger—she went to an all-women's college instead of her first choice, Cairo University, which she was forbidden to attend because it was coed—she still inflicted that same strictness on me.

The logic behind this sort of parenting is, of course, that it will protect us, as women, from damage to our "honor" and "reputation" in a society that tends to judge us far more harshly than members of the opposite sex. In Egypt, women are often viewed with suspicion if they lead lives that are too liberal or place the demands of their careers above their families.

Meanwhile, I watched men enjoy the sort of freedom I longed for—freedom that they then abused by judging and harassing women, making it less safe for those women to lead lives free from restriction. It was a vicious cycle that proved to be my biggest obstacle in my career as a female photojournalist.

———————

After graduating from journalism school in Cairo in 2006, I found work at a local newspaper as a photojournalist. I threw myself into the job and often worked long hours that meant I'd come home to the house I shared with my family well after sundown. But my older brother was unhappy with my choice of career, and our relationship deteriorated. The tension came to a head when he issued me an ultimatum: I had to "respect" the rules of the house and come home earlier, or I'd have to move out. (He was not subject to the same rules; he was the only man in the family, as my father died in January 2007, and therefore wielded considerable power.)

This was the first time I clashed with my brother so severely. I struggled to come to terms with the fact that he refused to support me. I persisted, regardless, continuing to stay at the office as late as I needed to finish my work. But the tension between me and my mother and brother lingered. With time, my mother became more understanding and supportive of my career. My brother, however, never altered his views. We had to stop talking about the situation entirely to maintain our relationship.

As a woman, I was breaking rules not only within my family but also within society. Photojournalism, for many years, was considered a "man's job"—you can probably count the number of female photojournalists in Egypt on one hand.

Between 2008 and 2015, I worked for four different local daily newspapers. Even though they had hired me as a photojournalist, I still had to prove that I was capable of covering the same assignments—hard news, such as clashes and protests—that men were handed without a second thought. I plowed away, working overtime and during my days off. Safe working environments, such as large, overly air-conditioned conference rooms, were not for me. I didn't want to attend conferences or photograph interviews with public figures. I was looking for the street. That was the only form of journalism I was passionate about.

Editors at the local newspapers generally preferred sending male photographers on important assignments. In 2012, I wanted to cover the funeral of sixteen army officers who had been killed in a terrorist attack on the Sinai Peninsula, but my boss asked my male colleague to go instead. Realizing I, too, wanted to go, my colleague took me with him. When my boss found out later that day that I'd gone, he was furious and refused to even look at my photos. Though I was not surprised, I thought it was selfish and sexist of him and my other editors to prevent me from documenting crucial moments in my country's history.

Over those seven long years as a photojournalist at various local newspapers, I was sent on assignment outside of Egypt just once. Being handed the assignment was a small victory for me. Because I had worked so hard, I was able to gain my boss's trust, or at least enough of it that she didn't find the idea of my covering instability of some sort or getting on a plane entirely ridiculous. My male colleagues were against my boss's vote of confidence, and they even sought to discourage her from discussing the idea with our editor in chief. But finally, I was allowed to take on a challenge that would illustrate my capabilities and determination.

It was December 2010, and the assignment was in Juba: I was to cover the referendum on the secession of South Sudan. The experience was a complicated one. It was the first time I'd traveled outside of Egypt, ever, and I had no practical training in how to work abroad or in unsafe environments.

As it turned out, the biggest threat of the trip was a colleague. He had arrived days before me and promised to pick me up from the airport, but he didn't show up. It was nighttime and too dangerous to be in the streets after sunset. Nonetheless, I had no choice but to make my way to the hotel by cab, along with another female Egyptian journalist.

When I finally arrived, the reporter was there. He harassed me—he was drunk and touched me inappropriately.

The situation was nothing short of a nightmare, but I didn't want to tell my boss or colleagues about it. This was the first time that the newspaper had agreed to send a female photographer abroad. Telling them might justify their initial reasoning for not allowing a female reporter to travel. They might use my experience to prevent other women photographers or reporters from traveling under similar circumstances, due to the risks associated with being a female crossing borders without a companion. I was shouldering the hefty responsibility of proving that as a woman, I was professional and capable of dealing with the pressures of working in a foreign country. I was also frightened that if I told them, they wouldn't believe me.

Instead, I avoided the reporter who'd harassed me for the rest of the trip and focused on my work. I was lucky that a crew from BBC Arabic was staying at the same hotel—they accompanied me during reporting trips, helping me feel a little less isolated.

The irony of being held back from covering "hard" news and forced to work in an office for my own safety was that I sometimes didn't even feel safe in my place of work, when I took public transport, or when I walked on the streets. I have found that most Egyptian men do not respect women. They treat us as if we were their possessions, and therefore have the right to do whatever they please with us. This way of thinking starts and is cultivated at home, where men are taught—even by their mothers—that they are in charge and they are protectors of women. Their power goes unchecked.

In Egypt, the simple act of deciding what to wear every morning is a laborious game of calculations for me. It depends on what kind of transportation I'll take, whom I'll be meeting, and which part of the city I'll be shooting in. Should I put makeup on? What color clothing should I wear? Is my blouse long enough?

It doesn't end there. As I walk to the subway, my mission is almost always to avoid eliciting lewd or sexual comments, even though it's impossible for me to control what men say to me. I try to avoid walking near men, and I'm extra careful if a man walks behind me: I walk quickly, but I also try not to attract unnecessary attention to myself.

When I travel on the subway, if I'm alone, I get into the women-only car. (I get into the "mixed" cars only if I'm traveling with a man.) The car is always congested—women prefer to take it to avoid potential harassment.

And then, of course, when I finally get to work and find that all the major assignments have already been given to my

Ramses metro station, Cairo, Egypt; January 2015. Many incidents of sexual harassment have been reported at this crowded train station. Women usually prefer to use the cars designated for women for fear of being harassed in the cars crowded with men. PHOTO BY EMAN HELAL.

male colleagues—meaning I'm confined to my desk instead of being on the field—I'm still exposed to sexism and misogyny, even inside the office. More than once, I have seen male colleagues leering at female anchors as they watch television. Their discussion revolves not around the news the woman is delivering but instead around how short her dress is, or how many buttons are left undone on her blouse. They look away from the TV only to stare at the derrieres of their female colleagues as they pass by. The sole safe space for women in the entire office is the restroom, where they convene to talk about harassment that they have faced from their colleagues and even bosses.

Harassment, whether sexual or physical, is commonplace in Egypt. The prevailing attitude is that men are going to harass women no matter what, so women are perpetually unsafe and require protection.

This way of thinking also became a tool for the government during the 2011 revolution as they sought to control antigovernment protesters—particularly female ones. Surely, they thought, if a woman was protesting, she should expect to be harassed. During the demonstrations, there were reports of women being groped and stripped; the military conducted forced virginity tests on some female protesters.

The attempts to thus control female protesters failed, and women still demonstrated alongside men, playing an equal role in the revolution.

When the revolution had first broken out, my family was on edge, as was the rest of the country. The situation had quickly become unstable: antigovernment activists had been calling for a nationwide uprising, demonstrating in large numbers against corruption, unemployment, poverty, and, most important, the rule of President Hosni Mubarak, who'd clutched onto his power with impunity for thirty years. The Day of Rage on

Tahrir Square, Cairo, Egypt; March 2011. An Egyptian woman sits on the ground after being assaulted during a march marking International Women's Day. Some of the men surrounding her are her harassers, while others are trying to help her. PHOTO BY EMAN HELAL.

January 25, 2011, marked the beginning of the revolution, as people courageously poured into Tahrir Square, symbolizing an end to years of fear that had prevented widespread mobilization of any kind.

January 28, dubbed the Friday of Anger, was earmarked as a potential turning point in the uprisings. Hundreds of thousands of protesters flooded Cairo and other Egyptian cities following Friday prayers. Prisons were opened and set alight—some accused the interior ministry of facilitating the outbreak to justify unleashing force on protesters—and the military was deployed onto the streets. (Mubarak did indeed address the nation that day, not to step down, but to pledge to form a new government.) The government-controlled media announced that the state would confront any citizen who opposed Egypt with violence and asked parents to stop their children from leaving their homes. My mother panicked, locked us up in the house, and hid the keys to prevent me from going outside.

This was the first significant fallout I'd ever had with her. I was fuming. "No one will stop me from doing my job," I recall saying. I demanded that she give me the keys, and stormed out, slamming the door behind me.

When I arrived at my office, I had time and the headspace to calm down and compose myself. I felt guilty for raising my voice at my own mother and worried about how she was feeling. The government had cut all cell phone activity to prevent communication between protesters and disrupt further mobilization on the streets. The only way to contact anyone was by landline. I called home, not knowing who would answer. My sister picked up promptly, telling me that my mother had broken down into tears and was praying that I would return home safely.

Conflict journalists can be selfish. We follow our ambitions ruthlessly, often putting ourselves in danger without caring about how our friends, family, and lovers may feel about the fragility of our safety. My mother wasn't trying to block my ambitions, I thought. She was merely worried something terrible might happen to me. That fear was a real, legitimate one.

I realized that day that not only was I responsible for documenting what I saw, I was also responsible for coming home safely. At various points during that stressful day, I believed I would die and never return home or see my mother, sister, and brother again. But I was not scared. I felt it was my duty to tell the truth for my country. I had to challenge the system that would have preferred me to be holed up at home. I was also overwhelmed by a feeling of awe and admiration—I was proud of everyone who had participated in the protests that day. They, too, had risked their lives.

The following day, I showed up at the protests with my camera in hand and joined a march to take photos. We were soon attacked by a police tank shooting tear gas at us. The police descended on the protesters to arrest them and an officer ran toward me. I tried to escape but wasn't quick enough. Time stopped. The officer grabbed me, broke my camera, and punched me in the face.

After that incident, which left me rattled and with a black eye, my family once again refused to let me leave the house. This time around, I couldn't wrangle my way out of the situation. They decided we would head to our home in the countryside for safety and to prevent me from covering the revolution. I was forced to go along· if it had been my choice, I would have gone back to the streets to continue reporting.

I spent four days in the countryside, possibly the worst four days of my adult life. Watching the demonstrations at Tahrir Square on television from the comfort of a couch rather than being there with my camera made me feel helpless and useless. I nagged at my mother relentlessly and eventually decided the only way I could return to Cairo would be by lying to her. I made up a story that sounded believable, telling her that the newspaper had threatened to fire me if I remained absent for an extended period without good reason.

We eventually returned to the city. Thankfully, by the time we got back, I still had my job. I did my best to make my mother feel better about my return to work, keeping her informed of my whereabouts and hiding from my family the true extent of the violence I had witnessed and experienced. Some days, I would hide in my room as soon as I got home from work so that I could change my bloodied clothes before anyone saw me. I didn't speak to my siblings or my mother about what I saw for months because I knew that if I did, I would face even more pressure from them to stay home.

Two months later—on March 8, a few weeks after Mubarak stepped down—I joined hundreds of Egyptian women gathered at Tahrir Square to celebrate International Women's Day. Many of the women held flowers; some of them gave several to soldiers who were patrolling the area. After a short march, we formed small groups along the sidewalks, holding hands and chanting slogans in support of women's rights. Those few moments were magical, but they did not last. A group of men suddenly approached us, saying we needed to go home because "we didn't belong outside." "You're disrupting the streets," they shouted. The women attempted to refute the men's claims and insults to get them to stop, but to no avail.

Then some of the men started to physically attack us. We screamed and began running toward the army officers, hoping they would protect us. I was terrified, but managed to take a few pictures in those few seconds before breaking into a run along with the other women. I was a target, just like them. An army officer opened fire into the air to scare off the harassers, who then fled the scene within minutes.

That day, I came to a stark realization: I was afraid of men, and the harder I fought, the more intense the fear became. I can't think of an experience that is more harrowing than a woman being sexually harassed or assaulted by a man.

I decided to use my work to expose the inherently misogynistic nature of some men's behavior, committing three years to a photography project called "Just Stop" about sexual harassment in Egypt. While the idea for the project had been lingering in my mind for months, I hadn't decided to pursue it until I'd witnessed and learned of numerous organized attacks by misogynists on innocent Egyptian women. Many of the women I'd spoken to told the same story: a group of men would surround the woman before trying to rip her clothes off and touch her body. They would then pretend they were trying to help her, so that passersby wouldn't notice what was happening. I channeled my anger about increasing attacks of this nature into my project, which I'd decided would feature images depicting the difficulties Egyptian women face when it comes to sexual harassment. I started searching the streets, looking for potential images that would convey the extent of the daily harassment that Egyptian women face, as well as the pressure to hide and protect their bodies.

Few people in the newsroom supported my project. In fact, many of my male colleagues mocked me for it. Sometimes they would suggest deridingly that I take on assignments related to sexual harassment, saying things like "Eman should cover the assignment, as she's the professional on this issue." Their behavior both depressed and infuriated me.

One day, after I had filed several photos that illustrated sexual harassment of varying forms on the streets of Cairo, I heard some of my male colleagues making fun of my work. They were

Qasr el Nil Bridge, Cairo, Egypt; January 2015. Two young women are harassed by a group of men while walking along the bridge, where boat rides on the Nile offer cheap outings for tourists and Egyptians. The bridge leads to Tahrir Square and the downtown area, where the youth congregate.
PHOTO BY EMAN HELAL.

laughing as they discussed one of my photos, which depicted a teenager touching his crotch area with one hand while crudely imitating the motions of fellatio with his other. Instead of condemning the boy's behavior, my colleagues condemned my own, saying that it had been rude and indecent of me to photograph the boy in that situation.

I had taken the picture during another International Women's Day protest, in March 2013, exactly two years following the march that took place weeks after Mubarak stepped down. I was shaking when I took it, but felt empowered by the women who surrounded me in protest. The world needs to see this, I thought, and took out my camera. When I took the photo, the boy didn't even realize that I was taking a shot of him. He looked behind him, to see if there was anything happening in the vicinity that I wanted to capture.

Talaat Harb Square, Cairo, Egypt; March 2013. Boys make lewd gestures during an antiharassment protest at a march marking International Women's Day. PHOTO BY EMAN HELAL.

The newspaper, of course, did not publish the picture. (While I worked closely with a photo editor who supported my vision, a senior editor ultimately refused to sign off on it.) But I wanted to disseminate my work as best as I could, so I submitted some of my photos to workshops, and others to various photography programs, one of which was entitled Reporting Change in Arab Spring Countries. Some of them were published by World Press Photo Foundation, the *New York Times Lens* blog, and *Polka* magazine.

A male colleague once told me during one of my night shifts that I would never get married. "Eman, who would marry you?" he asked. "Who would marry a woman who works this late around her male colleagues, and who spends most of her time in the streets?" I will never, ever forget those words. I felt like he was trying to break not only my determination but also my soul.

It's painful and demeaning to be surrounded by men who don't respect career-focused and ambitious women. Many Egyptian men prefer to marry women who will stay at home to serve them, or at least women who limit their work and outings so that they can be home early enough to prepare food and take care of children. To these men, everything domestic is the woman's responsibility. This way of thinking leaves women like me in an impossible situation. The price I have to pay for pursuing a career is singledom. It's as if I don't have the right to marry and build a family as my male colleagues do, just because I "chose" a career.

As I write, I'm thirty-three and living in Denmark, where I'm studying for a year. This is the first time I've ever been away from home for such a long time. And it's the first time I've ever lived alone. Living alone and abroad, without my mother—as tricky as she was—and without my friends is not easy. Some nights, I feel lonely and depressed. But I never regret my choices. If I could turn time back to when I was a girl who'd just graduated from university with a journalism degree, I'd do nothing differently. Becoming a photographer in Egypt, despite facing adversity from my mother, workplace, men, and society, was the best choice I've ever made.

Living in Egypt during this extremely complicated, hostile, and volatile political era is overwhelming, particularly if you're a journalist, and even more so if you're a woman journalist. There is no such thing as freedom of speech in Egypt. Working on simple assignments put me in situations of great danger. Police have been known to crack down on journalists and to imprison them. I consider my current experience in Denmark as something of a reprieve from all of those difficulties, a break from all of that stress. I'm also now able to focus on improving my photography, instead of battling harassment, my struggles with male colleagues, and other societal pressures.

This is a crucial chapter in my long journey of self-discovery. Even though I've put a pause on my work on Egypt, it is always on my mind. I intend to continue focusing on women who have been abused, because I hope my work will empower other women who are struggling with harassment and assault—any obstacle that prevents them from moving around freely, whether that's crossing the street by themselves or pursuing the job of their dreams.

Three Girls from Morocco

Aida Alami ◆

Dear Muslims, Immigrants, Women, Disabled,
LGBTQ folk, and All People of Color,
I love you, boldly and proudly.
We will endure
We will not break.
—SHAUN KING, CIVIL RIGHTS ACTIVIST

I grew up in Marrakesh daydreaming about two things: becoming a reporter and moving to New York. At the age of eighteen, I set out to do both, leaving Morocco to pursue a journalism degree at Hunter College in Manhattan. I was determined to build a life in the United States and had no intention of ever moving back. I didn't feel I had any business to do in my home country. To my mind, Morocco wasn't a particularly exciting place for an aspiring journalist. And the region seemed to me like it was stuck in time, crushed by dictators who were supported by the West.

But as the years passed and the political climate in the Arab world deteriorated, becoming more and more hostile to freedom and human rights, I experienced a sudden urge to return home. Life in New York, where I was finishing up a master's degree at Columbia Journalism School, had become predictable. I needed a challenge. The U.S. economy had faltered and journalism jobs had dried up. Scores of American journalists were moving to the Middle East to become foreign reporters. With little to do in the U.S. thanks to the barren job market, I decided to relocate to

Morocco in late 2009, even though I was uncertain of what I'd do and how I'd feel about moving back to a place that had so often suffocated me.

One year after my return, a Tunisian street vendor self-immolated, triggering the Arab Spring.

The protests spread rapidly, and freedom from decades of brutal dictatorship finally felt within reach. I was elated. For the first time, I was proud to be Arab. The Tunisian revolution marked a new chapter in the region and in my life. I decided then to report solely on the Arab world. I was hopeful that I could present an authentic narrative to the Western media outlets I eagerly wished to work for. In hindsight, though, my professional mission had already become a personal one.

Five years later, I was living in Paris, having followed the wave of refugees who were making the perilous journey to Europe, and found myself again in a personal and professional rut. I had recently experienced a period of grief and loss after a close friend of mine had died. I was also exhausted by the prospect of continually covering the ills of the Arab world half a decade after the start of the Arab Spring. I felt that my reporting had become redundant. I was no longer inspired by my work. And on top of that, terrorism had come close to my new home several months before, when the Islamic State had slaughtered 130 people in an attack that left France reeling.

Fortunately, right around that time, I had a meeting that saved my creativity and maybe even my soul.

I had stumbled on the story of a woman named Amal Bentounsi, an Arab French activist who was fighting police brutality. I wanted to know more about her, but because the French national media pay little attention to activists and movements considered "radical," there wasn't much information readily available to the public.

It was Ramadan, which fell during the months of June and July in 2016. Amal Bentounsi was nearly impossible to reach.

For days, I contacted her incessantly. The checkmarks indicating she'd received and read the texts I'd sent her piled up. (I later learned Amal is constantly solicited by journalists, activists, families of victims of police brutality, and so on.) Finally, she called back and agreed to meet. As it was Ramadan, Amal told me she was entertaining guests and could come to the city only after *iftar*, the evening meal for fasting Muslims, no earlier than ten p.m.

I didn't know what to expect from my meeting with this mother of four who'd left her children in the care of her husband to drive from a Parisian suburb into the capital to meet me—a journalist and stranger—late at night. All I knew about Amal was that her twenty-eight-year-old brother, Amine, had been shot in the back by a French police officer, and that she'd vowed to get justice for his murder.

From what I'd read about him, I learned that life had never been easy for Amine. At thirteen, he had been expelled from school. In the weeks that followed his expulsion, he loitered in the streets, mixing with delinquents. Soon after, he started a fire in a trash can that ended up burning down an entire day-care facility. Luckily, it was the weekend, so the building was empty and nobody was hurt. But Amine was imprisoned for arson in Fleury-Mérogis—the country's notorious high-security prison—becoming the youngest prisoner in the republic at the time. Amid all these troubles, Amine adopted a French name, Jean-Pierre, in the hope that it would help him integrate into French society, with no success.

When I left to go meet Amal, it was almost midnight. The streets were alive with the buzz of young Arabs mingling with post-*iftar* energy. (I love Ramadan in Paris. When I spend the holy month back home in Morocco, I'm suffocated by the heavy weight of state law, which strictly forbids citizens from breaking fast in public. But in Paris, Ramadan unites an entire community. Walking around Parisian neighborhoods that are home to Muslims floods me with a sense of comfort and familiarity. I smile at the men and they call me *ma soeur*—sister—offering me dates. I'm not religious or nostalgic, but in these moments, I feel distinctly Moroccan.)

I made my way to Place de La République, the main square, where protesters had been camping for weeks, demonstrating against a labor bill. I paused at the Bataclan concert hall, one of the sites of the terrorist attacks several months before. Passersby were still paying their respects to the dead with flowers and candles. I sent my own warm thoughts to the victims and their families—some of whom I'd interviewed when I reported on the attacks for *Foreign Policy*. Life had begun to feel very fragile to me. The neighborhood that I called home—I lived a mere ten blocks from the Bataclan at the time—had been shaken.

When I got to Place de La République, where we'd agreed to meet, dozens of protesters were camping near the statue of Marianne. I wondered what the Goddess of Liberty, proudly holding a torch and watching over her country and its liberal values, was thinking during these strange and trying times. I didn't know it yet, but Amal was about to become my Marianne. Our encounter would shift my perspective and propel my career into a new direction.

The Bataclan hadn't been my only close brush with terrorism. In January 2016, just two months after the Paris attacks and six months before I met Amal, my dear friend Leila—a French-Moroccan photographer who had been on assignment in Burkina Faso—was shot several times at close range by al-Qaeda terrorists, in an attack that left twenty-nine others dead. She was thirty-three when she was gunned down, two years older than me.

Three days after she was shot, Leila's brother Soulaimane finally called me. I didn't want to pick up the phone. I was paralyzed by an awful intuition that the unthinkable had happened. As I stood alone in my cramped Parisian apartment, where I'd been pacing for three very long days, I knew that the longer I waited, the longer I could find refuge in a comfortable state of denial, even if it were for another few seconds. When I did answer the call, in just four words, those final glimpses of hope were gone forever: "She didn't make it." It struck me that Soulaimane spoke in English before he broke down into tears, probably using a foreign language to tone down the cruelty of the sentence. Words—on which I have built my whole career—failed me. I grieved in silence.

When she died, Leila had been in Ouagadougou with Amnesty International, taking photographs of women who'd survived violence and abuse. Projects like these were what she thrived on: she'd devoted her entire adult life to raising awareness of the plight of victims of war, terrorism, and poverty through her images. The essence of Leila's work was to empower, rather than to victimize, her subjects. I tried doing the same with my own career in journalism, through writing and reporting on terrorism in the Arab world and beyond for mainstream Western publications like the *New York Times*.

Leila did not know fear. She used to say that positivity generated positive events. That belief, she explained, assured her that "good karma" would continue to protect her as she traveled to unstable countries. She glided through them, as if guarded by a shield of luck. Leila fought aggressively for her life during those three grueling days after she was shot. Even though I was aware her body had been riddled with bullets at close range, I was convinced her good karma would save her. The day Leila Alaoui died, I took some consolation in just one thing: she hadn't wanted an ordinary life, and in a cruel twist of fate, both her life and her death were anything but ordinary.

My job over the past few years has required me to interview people who have lost loved ones to war and terrorism. In the Arab world, such tragedies are commonplace. For years, I'd managed to distance myself from those interviews. In some cases, I found myself speaking to family members of terrorists. Even then, I kept my emotions and judgment at bay. I made sure I prioritized the importance of documenting what I saw over any visceral reaction to the disturbing events that swirled around me.

But when acts of terrorism reached Paris, and then Leila, my capacity to feel isolated from them started to diminish. France was no longer a neutral home base where I could pause to reflect on and write about the atrocities of the Arab world. The attacks on the Bataclan showed that the country had become a key target for the Islamic State and its sympathizers. The Arab world and its baggage, it seemed, were chasing me. It became hard to compartmentalize. Leila's death forced me onto the receiving end of the fallout from terrorist attacks. I was the one being called by journalists who wanted comments about Leila and her death. I was both the one consoling and the one being consoled.

I finally spotted Amal at Place de la République. She was engaged in an intense discussion with a group of young activists who were gathered around a projector screening *Who Killed Ali Ziri?*, a documentary about the death of an elderly Arab man at the hands of French police in 2009.

She was dressed in sweatpants and I felt a pang of guilt for pulling a busy mother away from her young children. We awkwardly said hello and sat at the terrace of one of the many cafés facing the square. Like me, Amal was born in Morocco. Her parents moved to France when she was still a baby. While there isn't a social etiquette rule book, you generally never ask a Moroccan you've just met if they observe Ramadan or if they drink alcohol. When I meet other Muslims, particularly in reporting situations, I let them take the lead. So when Amal ordered a virgin mojito, so did I.

At that point, I wasn't sure exactly why I was interviewing Amal, other than a personal desire to meet her. I had a vague idea of directing a documentary about second- and third-generation immigrants in France and the integration challenges they faced.

The nation had yet to address its major assimilation problem, sparked by several waves of postcolonial migration. Mounting terrorist acts deepened an already palpable divide, enabling persecution of the Muslim population by the state and a spike in Islamophobia. I wanted to find activists who were part of what I believed to be the racial awakening of an entire generation, inspired by African American movements and their own struggle for equality.

When Amal started telling me Amine's story, I sensed her hesitation and reluctance to divulge. The last time Amal had seen her brother was two years before he died, when she had driven him to the Gare du Nord train station in Paris. Amine was on a furlough from prison, where he was serving an eight-year sentence for robbery, on top of the time he'd already served for arson. He had completed most of that term, which had been reduced to six years, and had only a few months left. Amine was supposed to return to prison that same day. Instead, he decided to make a run for it. His escape attempt was successful until two years later, when he was caught by the police. They asked him for his ID and he began running away from them. One of the officers then shot him in the back—an injury that would prove fatal.

Amal is a beautiful woman. Her warmth struck me within seconds of us meeting. She smiled genuinely and seemed to trust me immediately. But despite this, her big brown eyes shifted away from mine and darted around the square as she told me about Amine's past. She rushed through key details about what had happened to him. I'd later come to understand this was because to many, Amine's problematic record meant his death at the hands of a police officer wasn't really tragic, because he had been on the wrong side of the law.

We both let our guards down while discussing Amal's aspiration to get justice for her brother. As a self-imposed rule, I never speak about myself with sources during interviews. But I opened up to Amal about Leila's death just six months earlier, a loss that had destabilized me and still sometimes kept me awake at night. Amal and I understood each other. While drinking virgin mojitos in the middle of a bustling square in Paris, we—two Moroccan strangers—connected over something as abstract as death. Her brother, a child of immigrants and victim of police brutality in a political environment that enabled Islamophobia; my dear friend, a victim of terrorism and Islamic extremism.

Despite attending a French high school, I had rejected the French education system. I wanted to free myself from French colonialism, the remnants of which lingered, even after the liberation of my country on paper. (Morocco had been under the rule of the French Protectorate from 1912 to 1956.) I was still a high school student in Marrakesh when the September 11 terror attacks rattled New York in 2001. Bereft of so many innocent civilians, America was grieving for its dead while also preparing to avenge them by striking the Muslim world. It was in this charged environment that I started to apply to universities abroad. I was, at the time, oblivious to world events, despite my interest in journalism. In fact, I wasn't particularly concerned about what was happening in the Middle East. This might have been because I was still young, or simply because I didn't feel much solidarity with the Muslim world—if anything, I felt like "the other" in my own country.

In December of that year, I went to a party where I ran into Leila, who was home in Marrakesh for the winter break. At the time, she was studying sociology and film at Hofstra University in New York. I hadn't seen her in a while, and back then, we weren't very close. She'd always intimidated me—I thought she was far too cool to be my friend.

I stood in a corner at the party, alone; I used to be quite shy, especially in crowded social settings. (In retrospect, it's surprising that I pursued a career that involves having to speak to people I don't know on a daily basis.) Leila spotted and approached me and we started a conversation. I was curious to hear more about her experiences in New York, so I bombarded her with questions. She was in love with her new life. I confided in her my concerns about how I was going to pay for college in the city. School in France was free, so the United States was a tough sell to my parents. Convinced that I'd "blossom" in New York, Leila said I shouldn't be deterred. She suggested that I attend Hunter, an inexpensive city college in Manhattan, and worry only about finding funding to pay for grad school. Thirteen months later, I was a student at Hunter; seven years later, I went to grad school at Columbia.

Leila and I grew closer in New York. She introduced me to her community of friends, helping me make New York my home. We spent some of the happiest years of our friendship in the city. In 2008, Leila moved back to Morocco because she felt it would kick-start her photography career. Coincidentally, I moved back a year later. We embarked on different paths—she was a photographer and I was a news reporter. But we focused on the same issues, and eventually worked together on the plight of sub-Saharan migrants in Morocco. We attended street protests in 2011, galvanized by the energy of the people. One of my dearest memories with Leila was when we stood side by side on a truck as she photographed young Moroccans with their fists up in the air, screaming for freedom.

Soon after I moved to France in 2012, Leila started dividing her time between Beirut and Paris. In 2014, she started working on a project about first-generation immigrants who had lost their jobs after dedicating years of their professional lives to the Renault factory in a Parisian suburb. Leila wanted to document how these immigrants had left their countries and devoted themselves to France without receiving much recognition in return. She interviewed the immigrants tirelessly for months, riding her bike to their suburb to meet them, bonding with them in ways that left them distraught by her absence when she was gone. That was Leila's last major artistic project before she passed away.

Moving to France opened up old wounds—the wounds of colonial history, but also the wounds of resentment against Muslims, which was still rising. This particular move was different from when I'd left to go to the United States in 2002: I was finally paying attention to how Muslims were being treated in the wake of tragedies perpetrated by extremists. Instead of feeling bitter about or hiding from it, I decided to seek out those who were positively reacting to discrimination. While Leila focused on the North Africans who had given everything to France after leaving their homes behind them, I focused on their children. The different generations were fighting with the same sense of pride and desire to reclaim their religious and national identities.

Leila and I always felt out of place. We shared a fascination with other outcasts—individuals who reminded us of how privileged we were and who inspired us to give them a voice. We were overwhelmed and humbled by their struggles. When Leila died, I repeatedly asked myself what she would have done had it been I who'd perished instead. The answer is easy: she would have continued pouring her energy into her work.

I still find myself dwelling on the irony of Leila being killed by terrorists after having spent years of her short life working to dispel racism and challenge stereotypes. I wonder what she would have made of today's political realities, as the demonization of the "other" accelerates at a disturbing pace. The United States has elected a president whose discriminatory policies have already had a concrete impact on refugees and immigrants from predominantly Muslim countries and beyond. His rhetoric has further inflamed the Islamophobia that already saturates Europe, emboldening ultra-right-wing movements everywhere. Meanwhile, the dream of a prosperous, free Middle East is no more. The Arab Spring has in many ways disappointed us.

But these failures and disappointments have, at the same time, reinvigorated Arabs, Muslims, and other minorities. In 2015, I wrote a profile for the *New York Times* on two young French Muslims who work for a media platform called *Le Bondy*

Blog. The news site piqued my interest as all of its contributors hailed from Parisian projects, or *banlieues*, and reported on minority communities they knew inside and out. The platform gave the members of these little-known and misunderstood communities an authentic voice, allowing them to contest the stories that reporters who had "parachuted" in had already told. I continue to learn from these activists, particularly their rejection of victimization and their desire to make a difference and to gain equal rights and respect.

On the same evening that Leila was gunned down in front of a café as she stepped out of a car to buy a salad in Ouagadougou, another story made the headlines in France. Newscasts that night showed a shattered Amal emerging from the Bobigny courthouse in the suburbs of Paris. Damien Saboundjian, the police officer who'd killed her brother, had just been acquitted of all charges. "They took away his right to live," she told journalists who were present at the verdict. The setback didn't stop Amal from continuing her fight. She filed for an appeal. A year later, Saboundjian was found guilty of murder without the intention to kill.

In the months leading up to the appeal trial, I chronicled Amal's struggle for justice and we grew closer. Amal's personal life had been plagued by tragedy and hardship. She'd never received a college education (though she's now pursuing a law degree). She'd fought to marry a Portuguese man she'd met when she was just thirteen. She'd lost her brother. And yet she managed, in the span of a few years, to become the face of the fight against police brutality. She alone can gather crowds of thousands in the French capital to protest against institutional racism—a concept that remains absent from the mainstream conversation in France.

I tried hard while working with Amal to not let my strong admiration for her cloud my judgment as a reporter. Instead, I found strength in her hope and determination. I channel that strength into *France's Children*, a documentary feature I'm currently working on about Muslim empowerment and activism in the country. As part of my work, I'm closely following the lives of Arab and Muslim millennial immigrants who are mobilizing, inspired by the fascinating example set by the American Black Power movement. Amal is the film's main protagonist. I spent weeks with her and other inspiring activists, building their trust as I filmed them.

Working on *France's Children*, difficult as it has been, has finally brought me some peace. I know I'm doing something meaningful. And I know Leila would be proud.

Words, Not Weapons

Shamael Elnoor ◆

I faced my first moral dilemma as a journalist in September 2013, when I was working for a Sudanese national broadcaster called Al Shorooq whose editorial views reflected those of the ruling party.

Up until that point in my career at Al Shorooq, my reporting had been free from political influence. Today, Sudan is one of the least free countries in the world when it comes to freedom of the press, but this wasn't always the case. My formative years in journalism, from 2007 to 2011, came after the end of a brutal twenty-two-year-long civil war; those postwar years witnessed a remarkable surge in political activity and, by extension, journalistic activity. The situation was constantly changing, and there was much to report on.

But when South Sudan seceded in 2011, the political situation deteriorated, taking civil liberties, including relative journalistic freedoms, along with it. There was talk of enforcing Sharia law on Sudan's entire population, since South Sudan was largely Christian, and its secession meant that the population of Sudan was now majority Muslim. What's more, much of Sudan's oil revenue had come from the south, and the loss of that source of income triggered multiple economic shocks across the country. Economic growth slowed and inflation surged.

Amid those economic strains, the Sudanese government

decided to cut fuel subsidies. In September 2013, people took to the streets to protest the decision. It was a disaster. There was chaos everywhere, and fuel prices were intolerable. I was in Nairobi at the time attending a workshop; news of street protests had started spreading beyond borders. Demonstrations unfolded in Khartoum as well as in other cities. What an unbelievable mess it was! The streets were boiling, covered with the blood of young protesters.

Upon returning from Nairobi, I quickly learned that our managers at Al Shorooq wanted us to turn a blind eye to the reality of what was unraveling on the ground. The station was funded by Sudan's ruling party—National Congress Party, or NCP. Although initially NCP had wanted Al Shorooq to operate independently, after the secession in 2011, it gradually tightened its grip on the network, ousting the previous administration and starting the process of its "Sudanization." The state's increased control meant that when the street protests erupted in 2013, Al Shorooq had no choice but to give in to the pressure to further NCP's agenda—an infuriating sequence of events, but in hindsight, not an unusual one. News organizations in Sudan are often coerced into toeing the ruling party's lines.

Our youth were being shot dead by the ruling militia, and the police were calling them "vandals and criminals." As an editor and producer at the channel, I was instructed to repeat those expressions and inject them into my news reports, with no regard to ethics. What an unbearable moral crisis! It was as if our independent editorial policies had evaporated.

It wasn't just the channel that I worked for that took this editorial line. The freedom of every other station in the country was at stake. One media outlet published the headline TABBAT YAD AL MOUKHARIBEEN (damned are the thugs). The very use of those words underscored how harsh the press was on those who opposed the status quo: the phrase is used in the Qur'an to condemn sinners. Many journalists went on strike, but publishers continued to produce and distribute newspapers under the control of the government and security forces. No words can describe the moral and mental anguish other journalists and I suffered back then.

I was adamant that I didn't want to be forced to write false or warped truths, and sought the advice of some of my colleagues. Although they initially agreed to a mass resignation to exert pressure on the administration, they subsequently backed down. After some thought, I opted to quit, but at first the administration rejected my resignation. I wasn't able to leave the station for good until twelve months after the protests first broke out.

I learned from this experience that there was only one way for me to be a journalist. What value does journalism really have if it doesn't accurately serve the people and reflect the street as it is? My resolve was strengthened, and my experience underscored that the word can shake despots in a way that weapons can't.

It was this resolution to not shy away from taking risks in my reporting that led me to take an unfathomable one about six months later, in March 2015, when I traveled to Darfur to interview a man depicted by the media as a murderer and rapist.

Darfur, a region in western Sudan, has long been home to clashes between Arabs and the indigenous Africans. The conflict came to a head in 2003, when two non-Arab groups began fighting the Sudanese government, which they had charged with mistreating and oppressing the non-Arab population of Darfur.

Complicating matters was the involvement of the Janjaweed, a militia made up of Arab tribes. When the war in Darfur broke out, the Sudanese government provided the Janjaweed with weapons with which to fight the Africans. (While the government has denied that this ever occurred, Human Rights Watch and other aid organizations maintain there is "irrefutable evidence" of state support for the Janjaweed at the time. The government, it has been said, distrusted its own armed forces because many of its soldiers hailed from Darfur. As a result, it turned to the Janjaweed for its counterinsurgency.)

The Janjaweed had an infamous reputation in local and Western media: they were known for being responsible for atrocities against the Africans, including looting, burning, forced displacement, and rape. The war in Darfur was categorized by some as a genocide; the United Nations estimates that it has left up to three hundred thousand civilians dead.

The man I was going to interview was the spiritual leader and chief of the Janjaweed, Musa Hilal—an Arab fighting Africans in systematic operations bearing alarming similarities to ethnic cleansing. An interview with him would have been a tremendous opportunity for any reporter, and so I reached out to my contacts, hoping to gain access. From there, things moved quickly. Some local fixers I knew managed to arrange a meeting for me with an official of the Janjaweed.

One of those fixers was a prominent African fighter. As he knew the area well, I asked him how we'd be navigating the territory that was under the control of the leader of the Janjaweed, his enemy, and if we'd be safe. He said he had open lines of communication with Hilal himself and that he could set up an interview without difficulty. I was astonished—the two were supposed to be enemies! Hilal was meant to be fighting the Africans. It was unbelievable; the sides were at opposite ends of the conflict, and yet there seemed to be a veneer of mutual trust.

My fixer gave me the number of Hilal's personal assistant, a young man. I called him, and after we briefly exchanged greetings, he put me through to the sheikh, as they like to refer to him. How surreal! There came a quiet, barely audible voice. Hilal told me I was welcome to come meet him and said he trusted and respected the individual who had arranged the meeting—otherwise, he wouldn't have agreed to it. "We asked about you and looked into what you have written," he said. "You're really good!"

When I arrived for the first time in the war-ridden province of Darfur, the fighting between the various African movements and the government had eased, but tribal clashes were rife, on top of tensions within the ranks of the state's Arab allies. The area I visited didn't fall under state jurisdiction; the tribes and their militias had full autonomy, and I was at their mercy. Moving from place to place as a journalist, especially on missions like these, constitutes a grave risk. You must coordinate with a person who has the authority to guarantee your personal safety and to facilitate your movements. After I arrived at Geneina Airport, to the west of Darfur, a four-by-four that was to drive me to our agreed-upon meeting place was waiting for me. The vehicle was full of men with their faces covered carrying Kalashnikovs. This was the first time I'd traveled in a military vehicle. Mixed feelings washed over me: fear and anxiety, but also excitement and adrenaline.

It was a long journey from the airport. When we finally arrived, I was escorted to a tent in which Hilal was waiting. I'd only ever imagined him to be the violent, bloodthirsty man I had seen in the news. In real life, he seemed remarkably calm, his complexion youthful and supple—like that of a movie star, not that of a desert bush fighter. He wore tinted glasses and kept a piece of candy in his mouth during our entire meeting. His mustache was perfectly trimmed.

The talk went smoothly. We discussed what the militia's relationship with the state was—after Darfur, the government and the Janjaweed had clashed—and whether he was interested in breaking into politics. For the first time ever, Hilal explicitly said he had political ambitions. His exact words were "I'd like to rule Sudan one day."

That piece sparked extensive controversy when it was published, for I was the first journalist to write about Hilal as a political figure rather than the leader of a militia. The attention it garnered gave me more confidence and courage to face danger while reporting from the ground. It dawned upon me afterward what I'd accomplished: a distinguished feat of journalism, the result of a life-altering risk.

The consequences of writing that piece proved weighty, particularly considering the government's contentious relationship with Hilal. A few months later, when I was on my way back from a trip to Uganda with two colleagues, we were detained at the Khartoum airport. It was about two a.m., and an officer asked us to step aside during a routine security check. It was clear that we were going to be questioned about some security matter.

We waited anxiously before being escorted to a security office. I was perhaps optimistic: I expected at worst we'd be delayed for a few hours, and that the officers were simply going to ask us about our participation in the workshop on corruption that we'd just been attending in Uganda—a country deemed an enemy of Sudan. But after an officer took away my money and phone and led us out of the building to the street, where a Toyota with four armed soldiers in fatigues was waiting for us, it hit me that we were most certainly being arrested.

We got into the vehicle and sat among the heavily armed soldiers. No one told us where we were headed, but as the car reached Khartoum University and made its way toward the bridge leading to Bahri city, I realized we were en route to the political security facility, the most violent division of the security forces. What did we, as journalists, have to do with political security? Upon our arrival at the large, depressing building, we were taken to filthy corridors, where we were made to wait until sunrise. The soldiers guarding us prevented us from speaking to one another. No one volunteered any information, and none of us dared to ask for any. I was anxious that my family would be concerned about where I was. I know how overly worried my mother can be about everything: the idea that she could be staying up late waiting for my arrival bothered me immensely.

When dawn broke, several officers arrived, and I was taken to an office where I was interrogated about the workshop I'd attended. One officer was adamant that the workshop was a front for some armed opposition activity and accused me of being a

member of the communist party. I told them I was just a journalist and had nothing to do with the party, but of course they
didn't believe a word I said.

After they stopped interrogating me about the workshop and
my suspected political activity, they moved on to my reporting,
asking me what my problem with the regime was, accusing me
and the colleagues who had also attended the workshop of
wanting anarchy, and suggesting that we "liked" what had happened to the countries involved in the Arab Spring. They questioned me persistently about my interview with Hilal. This went
on for hours. The officer who had arrested us at the airport
would periodically enter the room and violently beat the chair
to scare me into confessing things that were not true. At the
end, I told the officers I would sign whatever they wanted me to
sign, but they could be sure that the contents of the report would
be false.

When the interrogation finally ended, we were sent back to
those filthy, miserable corridors. The long journey, the waiting,
and the lack of food and sleep all started to take a toll on me.
Hours passed, and with no signs of an imminent release, and no
answers to any of our questions, I started to feel my heartbeat
quicken. My body began to shake uncontrollably as my blood
pressure dropped. The officer took me to an office, and I lay
down on a dreadful bed, where I remained for hours, feeling
steadily worse. Finally, the officer ordered a car to take me to a
hospital owned and operated by the security forces, where a
young doctor gave me a little blue pill and hooked me to an in-
travenous drip. The pill worked like magic; I gave in and slept
like a log in that room with the officer guarding me.

We left the hospital in the afternoon and I was taken back to
that dismal security building. Finally, we were released, but the
officers kept our identification papers. We had to return to
the building three separate times after our release before we
were able to retrieve them. On those return trips, every time
someone at the security building heard my name, they'd do a

double-take, whispering to each other, "Is that Shamael Elnoor?" It seemed they perceived me as ill-mannered and violent.

Even though the security forces had ultimately released me, they weren't convinced that I wasn't a member of the communist party. Maybe they wanted to fabricate a story to strip me of my press status: they clearly felt threatened by me, an independent journalist who had interviewed the leader of a deadly militia. They simply couldn't believe a reporter could be independent, and those were the lengths that they would go to in order to scare me into silence, even though they had no proof of wrongdoing.

All the same, I returned to Darfur less than two years later to investigate the conflict between Arab tribes over the gold-laden mountain of Jabal Amir. After the secession of South Sudan and subsequent loss of oil revenue, gold had become a key commodity in Sudan. Unregulated small-scale mines produced gold revenue for the state, but armed militias had begun to take a share of some of those revenues. Hilal effectively controlled parts of Jabal Amir; he had allegedly made millions of dollars from the gold (a charge he has denied). The state seemingly had no control in the area. Corporations worked directly with various Arab tribes; the metals ministry was completely absent.

My mission was to try to prove or disprove an allegation recently made by the Sudanese interior minister that three thousand foreign fighters were patrolling a section of the mountain, trying to get a cut for themselves. Fighting among rival tribes over the gold had resulted in hundreds of deaths, while foreign mercenaries were allegedly aiming for their own share of the commodity. Because artisanal gold mining had emerged as a crucial source of revenue for some of the militias, the interior minister's allegation caused a huge stir politically, and journalists were scrambling to get the story. I was risking my safety and even my life by traveling to this unregulated no-man's-land, controlled only by tribal men with guns.

I arrived at Geneina Airport by plane and was taken to a village close to the mountain. My fixer got to work right away, arranging for bodyguards and an armed vehicle to take us to the mountain that had sparked so much controversy. As we inched closer to our destination, surrounded by armed men, a number of scenarios started to play out in my head, including the possibility of a violent kidnapping.

As soon as we arrived at the mountain, I noticed that it reeked of alcohol. The smell was unbearably pungent. Drug dealing and arms dealing were also rife in this lawless area; they took place openly. The hard labor and high temperatures were too difficult to handle without drugs and alcohol, it seemed. I walked along the mountain scanning for the alleged foreign armed forces, flanked by militiamen. The place was pure anarchy.

Contrary to the interior minister's allegations, I discovered that the foreigners—mostly from Chad—roaming the mountain were traders and metal miners, not fighters. They were still trying to get a cut for themselves, however. I spoke to these men, as well as men from the Rizeigat tribe, which had seized portions of the mountain. The assignment confirmed to me that Arab fighters had built a state within a state, and that, as suspected, the government had no control over the mountain. We headed back to the village peacefully in the afternoon. The road was open and safe.

My fixer and I got a ride from the village to the airport the next morning with a Janjaweed field commander who struck up a vulgar conversation in a mix of Sudanese and Libyan Arabic. He talked incessantly about marriage, and how he had wed several women at once. This sort of bragging wasn't uncommon during my reporting trips, particularly those in Darfur. Men I interviewed would sometimes boast about their sexual abilities. They even had the audacity to repeatedly ask me about my sex life and were surprised to hear that I wasn't married.

Despite these disturbing conversations, I was not at all afraid during the trip to Jabal Amir. I was merely worried that state security would stop me from doing my job, considering their disdain and suspicion toward me and other independent journalists, and that my reporting mission would be aborted before I would be able to complete it.

On our way to the airport in Geneina, we saw an Abbala on his mule carrying a weapon. (The Abbala tribe is an Arab ethnic group that herds camels on long winter and summer journeys.) I was seated in between the driver and my escort; the Abbala looked at me strangely from behind his traditionally designed sunglasses. He had a quick conversation with the driver, but I couldn't hear what was said. The driver then told me that the man had offered to buy me from them. When I asked if he would sell me to the man, he said, "Why not, if he pays a good price?" adding that he cared only for money.

Even though the tone of the conversation teetered between serious and humorous, I felt nervous. Incidents of kidnapping and hostage taking are normal occurrences in Darfur. I composed myself and said a transaction of that sort would embarrass the tribe's chief. The man drove on.

In February 2017, Sudan's most prominent extremist and the uncle of the president, Al-Tayyib Mustafa, wrote a rebuttal to an article I had published ten days earlier criticizing political Islam in the country. In my piece, "Obsession with Virtue," I lambasted Islamist parties' preoccupation with form and righteousness at the expense of focusing on public health and building an educated society. "Islamic regimes are concerned about matters of virtue, women's dress, and appearance more than health and education issues," I wrote.

Mustafa's response wasn't merely a defense. It was a smear campaign. He referred to me as a "worm," and called on people to prevent me and "the likes of me" from corrupting the virtues of the country. "This vain woman thinks that her animosity toward the ruling regime allows her to cross red lines and be brazen toward God, his messenger, and his religion," he wrote, conflating my criticism of the regime with criticism of Islam.

Days later, the abuse started. The newspapers were full of articles that advocated skinning, lashing, and branding me an infidel. The harassment culminated when an imam known to support Daesh in Sudan announced that his Friday sermon would be called "Shamael's journalism and silliness." As the jihadi usually consults his social media followers on sermon topics, Facebook and Twitter lit up with fury.

This was clearly an organized campaign against me. Shifting these toxic opinions from paper to pulpit was like playing with fire. On Friday, I livestreamed the sermon from home. The feeling was strange. The young man got on his podium and delivered his sermon, mentioning my name at the end of every sentence and paragraph as if he wanted people to be wary and to remember it. He accused me of heresy, blasphemy, and apostasy, which is punishable by death in Sudan. By the end of the sermon, I was literally branded an infidel.

I was shaken. My safety had been thrown into jeopardy, and my phone wouldn't stop ringing; friends urged me to head to the nearest embassy and ask for asylum. Various organizations that had been following the situation also called me to offer assistance. At the time, I felt like there was nothing to say. It was too late; I had already been defamed.

I soon learned that the jihadis formed a WhatsApp group specifically to coordinate the campaign that had been waged against me. For about a month, the newspaper articles kept coming. *Al-Tayyar*, the newspaper I was working for, responded by forming a task force to manage the crisis. We called the police and asked for protection because the entire staff was unquestionably in danger. The police sent out a special patrol unit. I had to limit my movements and lost a great deal of personal freedom. I couldn't go out in public alone. I missed going to my favorite restaurant. Some people even advised me to carry a gun.

The campaign's objective was obviously to drag me into some sort of a journalistic war of words. I decided to take the legal route, filing lawsuits instead of responding directly by writing a rebuttal piece, but they were useless. Every time I filed a claim, my detractors filed one against me, accusing me of insulting the faith. (Although Mustafa's relationship with the government has soured in recent years, he has enjoyed a form of invisible protection from the state, both because he is related to the president and because he is something of an icon to jihadis.)

I tried to keep the matter from my family, but after the sermon I had to tell them what was going on. They wouldn't stop checking up on me when I wasn't at home. Between their overbearing phone calls and interview requests from the media, my phone literally would not stop ringing. It wasn't just that my personal security was threatened: my personal life was disrupted, too.

A human rights division at the United Nations contacted the Sudanese government and asked what measures were being taken to protect the journalist who had been threatened by extremists. When that specific piece of news came to light, the president's uncle resumed his smear campaign even more viciously.

I was so weighed down by an entire month of intense anxiety that I traveled to the United Arab Emirates for a two-week break to pull myself together and find my inner strength again. By the time I returned to Khartoum, the tension had subsided, but I still felt unsettled.

That said, today, I continue along my journalistic path in Sudan, and my beliefs and commitments remain unshaken. I didn't fully understand the value of my choices until after I faced all this danger and harassment—from the state, from tribesmen, and from Islamists. I have been a journalist for a decade now, and let me tell you what I have learned: this is what journalism should be, or else it shouldn't *be*, at all. Though these experiences have had high prices, they haven't weakened or deterred me. I have no other option but to move forward, like the many brave journalists who face persecution.

This is our destiny, and we remain ever devoted to it.

TRANSLATED FROM ARABIC BY
MARIAM ANTAR

Yemeni Women with Fighting Spirits

Amira Al-Sharif ◆

I discovered photography at age eight, and have never looked back. At the time, my father was building a home for our family in Saudi Arabia, where we lived before the Gulf War forced us to flee to Yemen. I was so fascinated by the process that I decided to document the stages of construction with his Polaroid camera. There are very few photographs of me as a child, and my parents say it's because I always had control of the family's camera—if anyone took it away from me, I would throw a fit, as if someone had deprived me of my favorite toy.

Although I was born in Saudi Arabia, I've spent most of my life in Yemen, a tiny, poor country at the very edge of the Arabian Peninsula. My father is an imam—a Muslim preacher—so I was raised in a conservative household along with my two brothers and five sisters. (Yemenis tend to have rather large families.) I wear the hijab when I'm in some public places, but when I'm out on the actual streets of Yemen, I wear a burqa.

Today, at thirty-five, I don't have a husband, but I do have my camera. Mine is an unusual situation for a woman in this country, as Yemenis usually get married in their teens. Women often depend on men for the most basic of tasks, particularly moving around from place to place. Had I gotten married as a younger woman, I would have been expected to rely on my husband and to focus on raising a family, not on pursuing a career. I defied those societal expectations. Being unwed is the price I have paid for my professional life.

When I decided to become a photographer at the age of twenty-two, I had to grapple with how my family might react, and how I would logistically be able to pursue a career in the industry when it is so difficult for women to move around freely in Yemen.

I had secretly started working for a local English-language newspaper, the *Yemen Observer*, while at university. The university's administration quickly detained me for covering a student strike: women were not meant to attend such demonstrations, let alone publicize them. The university penalized me by registering me as absent for a term. With the help of a friend, I pushed back, and the decision was overturned.

At first, I kept my ambitions a secret, in part to protect my parents. I didn't want to burden them with my desire to break free from the many rules imposed upon Yemeni women. But soon after the incident with my university, my father learned from a relative that I had been taking photographs in Hayeil—a local souk. I would start my days in the old town: it was my favorite place to take photographs and one of the few where I could move around without limitations.

My father was upset and accused me of taking advantage of the trust he'd granted me. I'd been sent to university to learn, and to then come home, he said, not to take photos in the streets. His final decision was to forbid me from returning to university.

This came as a shock to me, but I knew it was a spur-of-the-moment reaction. Baba had always been supportive of my ambitions; when I was a child, he had encouraged me to work hard so I could reach the top of my class. He had also bought me my first camera as a gift. He was clearly just worried about how society would react to my roaming around town with a camera.

I apologized, knowing that I had to calm him down in order

to win over his trust again. After a few days of silence, I worked up the courage to negotiate with him, pointing out that my work at the *Yemen Observer* was strengthening my linguistic skills because I had to translate reports written by local journalists from Arabic into English. He relented and eventually allowed me to return to school.

A year later, I graduated from university. I was the first woman in the Al-Sharif family to do so. Even though he accepted my career choice, my father could not bring himself to attend my graduation. My accomplishment had set a precedent for the entire family, however. A year later, my sister graduated from Arhab University, and our father attended the ceremony. Another relative of mine has since allowed both his daughters to attend Sana'a University. Over time, my father has grown proud of me, although he still worries for my safety; now, he even suggests subjects for me to photograph.

Photography is perceived as a "man's job" in Yemen. I am probably one of a handful of professional women photographers in a nation of 28 million people.

In Yemen, men and women interact completely differently from the way they do in the U.S. or other Western countries. Women must limit their interactions with the opposite sex, unless the man is a close relative. In public, women dress conservatively—more conservatively than in many other Muslim countries, with most wearing burqas.

From a logistical perspective, this conservatism means it's extremely difficult to be a woman photographer in Yemen. As a female, it's nearly impossible for me to capture images in places where women are simply not allowed to be, like the main areas of mosques, social gatherings with men, and sporting events. What's more, we also can't take photographs at night, as women rarely leave their homes in the evening in Yemen. (I usually take photos from seven a.m. till the sun begins to set and it is time for *mughrib*—evening prayers.)

At one newspaper where I worked, I had to convince my manager to allow me to cover the funeral of a Yemeni Jewish teacher who had been murdered—even though I had already been assigned to cover the trial of the murderer—because the event was in the public sphere. Eventually, my manager agreed to give me a chance, with the caveat that the newspaper would not cover my travel expenses. Accepting the terms, I paid for my own taxi and bus rides, finished my work, and submitted my photos. The next day, a front-page story on the teacher's funeral appeared in the newspaper, along with five of my photos.

Despite that front-page success, I wasn't able to secure jobs I applied for afterward at several different newspapers. It was clear that the various publications did not want a female photographer on staff. Why bring a woman on board to do a job that would require her to be able to move about without restrictions?

I had very few choices—I could have given up photography altogether, or worked as a freelancer, which would have offered me very little stability. Fortunately, I found work as a fixer for U.S. journalists, which has allowed me to continue working as a photographer in my spare time.

For nearly a decade, I have been photographing Yemeni women in prisons, in their homes, in the desert, and in rural and urban areas. There are indeed advantages to being a woman photojournalist, particularly with assignments involving women and family. I have been able to access the most personal and private of spaces for women, in which they can express themselves comfortably. I have photographed a number of young women who had been married off at a very young age, for example, and they felt comfortable working with me simply because I am a Yemeni woman, too. They would never have allowed a man, or a foreigner, to capture images of them. I consider the intimate access I have to women's lives and thoughts to be a gift.

In my photography, I try to evoke the nuances of how these women care for all those who surround them—their partners, parents, children, relatives, neighbors. I have photographed weddings, engagements, baby showers, family gatherings, and religious celebrations. I had to develop intimate friendships with these women before they lowered their guards. Sometimes, they allow me to take photographs of their faces, but then ask me not to publish them for fear of reprisals from their families.

It was this access that led me to put together a project called "Yemeni Women with Fighting Spirits," featuring pioneering and resilient women who have taken fate into their own hands despite the odds stacked against them.

Saadiya Eissa Soliman Abdullah is one of those women. I met her in the summer of 2014 during a reporting trip to the Yemeni island of Socotra. Thanks to Socotra's location—it's about four hundred miles from the mainland—the island had mostly remained shielded from decades of conflict in Yemen. (Since 2004, the Iran-backed Houthi rebels have been locked in conflict with the Yemeni military.)

As conflict rages on in mainland Yemen, Saadiya has been fighting her own little war. She and her seven children live off the land, just as her parents and grandparents did before her. But for fourteen years she has been struggling to keep that land from a local tribe whose members claim they're the rightful owners. The tribe has attacked Saadiya repeatedly because she and her family host tourists as guests, therefore benefiting from ecotourism. She was once assaulted by tribesmen who broke into her home and threw rocks at her, leaving her head with a gaping cut. She was also held in a male prison for fifty days. But she never gave up.

During my trip to Socotra, I woke up with Saadiya at four a.m. to follow her throughout her day as she tended to her goats and sheep and fed her family fish she'd caught with her own hands. On the island, she was able to move around freely, and so was I. While spending time with Saadiya, I was inside a world even Yemenis themselves do not see. People on the island don't follow the same customs as Yemenis on the mainland. Socotrans greet each other by shaking hands, looking into each other's eyes, and then touching noses.

There is something particularly whimsical and otherworldly about Saadiya and her surroundings. She loves her trees—which she planted herself—and her birds as much as she loves her children. "See all those birds?" Saadiya asked me as I observed her working. "I give them bread, dates, and many other things. I am a bird queen." Saadiya built her two homes with palm trees, one for the warmer months and one for the winter. She collects seashells, and dislikes anything that taints the beauty of her surroundings.

Detwah Lagoon, Socotra, Yemen; May 30, 2014. Saadiya Eissa Suliman Abdullah has an early dinner with her children after a day of clearing land on the hill above her home. PHOTO BY AMIRA AL-SHARIF.

"I have a fighting spirit, which is why I have encountered many obstacles and hardships in my life," Saadiya told me. "Whatever happens, I am not leaving my land. The land belongs to those who were born and live on it. I fear nobody." Facing adversity from women and men alike, Saadiya called herself "strong and independent."

Saadiya breaks every possible stereotype about Yemeni women. She is dominant, cunning, and watchful. She takes control of her fate and her surroundings with a vigor for survival. Saadiya is also ambitious—she plans to build a restaurant to serve tourists. I do not feel sorry for Saadiya because she endures hardships. Instead, I admire and honor her for taking her own path despite those hardships, and for staying wise and hospitable even when all those around her seek to bring her down.

At the time of our interview, Saadiya had just received official papers from a local court declaring that she had the right to the land.

In March 2015, a mere nine months after I'd photographed Saadiya, the conflict on the mainland between the Houthis and the Yemeni military escalated into a full-scale civil war. Soon afterward, Saudi Arabia, along with an alliance of more than ten countries, declared a military intervention in Yemen. The kingdom's goal was to halt the progress of the Houthis, who allegedly receive military support from Saudi Arabia's regional enemy, Iran.

Since that godforsaken month, more than ten thousand Yemenis have been killed, and millions have been pushed toward famine. Historical monuments in the old city of Sana'a have been destroyed. Weddings, refugee camps, hospitals, residential areas, mosques, schools, food-storage warehouses, and other essential civilian infrastructure have been targeted. Today, Yemenis have limited or no access to clean water, electricity, health care, or security.

Of course, this war has affected me both personally and professionally. My sisters' neighborhood was among those bombed, and although they were fortunately able to escape with their families, all of their neighbors perished in the bombing; they witnessed this loss of life with their own eyes. They now live in nearby villages, still fearful. Their trauma has seeped through to the rest of the family, touching us almost as if we were there with them that night. I sometimes even have nightmares about my family's starving cats, who have also suffered tremendously during the war—occasionally, they would roam the streets to search for food, and end up eating garbage before heading home again. (One of the cats in particular, Asel, was a source of great peace for me during the bombings. My nightmare turned to reality when she left home with a broken leg and didn't return; we feared for her life while she was away for a year. She recently somehow managed to make her way back to my sisters. Even animals have the strong will to stay alive.)

But despite death, famine, and misery, life continues in Yemen. This bittersweet reality of maimed and starved bodies coexisting with the most routine aspects of daily life has defined my approach to imagery. Western photographers tend to be drawn to the carnage, but I have continued to seek out the other part of Yemen that is full of life, love, and hope.

In part, this is because photographing scenes of war would be tremendously difficult, if not impossible, for me as a woman. War has exacerbated the soul-crushing limitations on our movements. Night or day, Saudi Arabia's bombardments of Sana'a make it dangerous to walk on what is left of the streets. Limited access between and in cities, particularly Aden and Sana'a, means that it's virtually impossible for me to follow people I'm photographing. Internet access is sporadic. Before taking any pictures, I have to obtain permission from the Houthis in the north of the country and from security authorities, including the Saudi coalition, in the south. Even leaving the country for conferences or educational trips poses a challenge—the cost of travel is extremely high, and the visa application process cumbersome.

I did, at first, take photographs of the destruction Saudi bombs had unleashed on Yemeni people, albeit from a distance and sometimes weeks or months after the actual bombings. I went to the Al-Fulaihi area in the old city of Sana'a in December 2016, fourteen months after it had been destroyed by Saudi air strikes. I visited a garden that was part of a twenty-five-hundred-year-old protected UNESCO World Heritage site; I understood this strike in particular to have been an attempt to erase Yemeni history.

I was drawn to the nearby home of a vegetable seller who lived with his wife and eight children, curious as to how they'd got on in the aftermath of the bombing. There, I spotted colorful laundry hung on tree branches just outside the ramshackle home. *You can destroy our homes, but the Yemenis will still do laundry*, I thought.

Sana'a, Yemen; December 20, 2016. The home of a vegetable seller, his wife, and their eight children fourteen months after the Saudi-led coalition bombarded the Al-Fulaihi area of the UNESCO World Heritage site in the old city of Sana'a. PHOTO BY AMIRA AL-SHARIF.

I want to show the side of war that very few people see: the laundry hung up on tree branches to dry; the children playing at the beach; the women preparing food for their families; the little sisters who look after one another when their mother is busy and their father is away fighting. I also want to show what life is like in remote villages and islands that are safe from the bombs but not from poverty. There is a special kind of resilience and beauty in those tucked-away spots of life. I want you all to see the true beauty of my suffering country. With my camera, I strive to empower, not victimize, the people in my images.

In February 2017, I met a mother who had recently had her third child. She had told me that she was about to host a party. It is Yemeni tradition to celebrate the good health of a newborn forty days after his or her birth. I was moved by the idea of a

Al-Sheikh Othman, Aden, south of Yemen; February 2, 2017. A girl takes care of her younger sister while their mother prepares to host a party marking the birth of her third child. Children are among the most vulnerable groups affected by the Yemeni war. One Yemeni child dies every ten minutes, the latest UN data show. PHOTO BY AMIRA AL-SHARIF.

party. To me, it marked a celebration not only of the newborn but also of youth and the future.

While the mother prepared the food for her guests, I spent some time with her two playful daughters. One of them had henna tattooed onto her arms and was wearing a glimmering pastel-yellow dress. Her innocence struck me, and I took a photo of her.

As I was taking the photo, I thought of the photographs of the male Yemeni fighters and of the children dying of malnutrition that had started to make it into mainstream press coverage. The image that I captured of the baby girls showed the other side of that tragic story. I wish I could flood the internet with these types of images.

A month after the party, I decided to travel to Al-Qurai'e, a village in the directorate of Al-Boriqah controlled by the Saudi coalition forces, to document the effect pollution was having on the roughly eighty Yemeni families who lived there. The town suffers from an illiteracy rate of more than 98 percent, and its people live well below the poverty line. As a direct consequence of the civil war, Al-Qurai'e has effectively become a dump. Basic services including water, health, education, and electricity are unavailable, and there's virtually no infrastructure to speak of. Al-Qurai'e is today an environmental hazard zone in which the burning of industrial waste has created toxic gases, putting local children at risk.

A trusted friend traveled with me to help me with statistics and data collection; we had to pretend that he was my father, even though he was only eleven years older than me. We couldn't move around freely in the area as it was guarded by United Arab Emirates forces and Saudi-backed mercenaries. The local "guide" who accompanied us during our reporting trip directed our movements, allowing us to film only what he saw fit. We had been informed by the local leader that the area surrounding the garbage dump in the village, known as the Ostrich Well, was under strict surveillance by the coalition forces, who were on the lookout for al-Qaeda militants; nearby movements were allegedly monitored via sensor devices. As we made our way to the dump, we were acutely aware that we were being watched. Despite the fact that we had a permit, the local leader told us to leave. Before we left Al-Qurai'e, I took photos of the harm it was wreaking on the people in the village.

As we made our way back home, already feeling ill due to our exposure to the pollution, my colleague and I were harassed by members of the Security Belt militia in Aden. The director demanded to see the photographs I'd taken. We later learned through media reports that the coalition forces had been running prisons in the area. They were so preoccupied with the idea of my stumbling upon and photographing those secret prisons that they had completely overlooked the photos I'd taken showing the effects of burning industrial waste near people's homes.

Al-Boriqah, south of Yemen; March 9, 2017. In the small community of Al-Qurai'e, at the edge of Aden, some 450 inhabitants live below the poverty line. PHOTO BY AMIRA AL-SHARIF.

In January 2018, three of my male colleagues and I decided to visit the Arabian jasmine farms of Bayt Al-Faqih in the province of Hodeidah. The weather was pleasant and we rolled our windows down to enjoy the mild breeze. This was the first time I'd driven my car outside of Sana'a. I'd wanted to take images of the jasmine farms: a photo essay of blooming white flowers during the darkness of war. I also had plans to move to Hodeidah to start a year-long project photographing women.

I did not realize at the time how risky it was to be traveling without a *mahram* (a close male relative); perhaps I hadn't thought the trip through to the extent that I should have. The twisty roads of the mountains flattened out into a highway dotted with checkpoints. An officer at the first one we stopped at in Bajel looked at us suspiciously and asked me to park the car. We were then questioned by six separate police officers for almost three hours.

They asked for our identification papers and confiscated our cell phones as they questioned us. I had two phones with me, and I gave the officers only one. When the officer asked me to unlock it, I did so without flinching: I had deleted all of its data the day before, as I sometimes do when preparing for my reporting trips. "You're going to pay for deleting the messages," the officer said, realizing that I'd outsmarted him.

My colleagues and I had not committed a crime, but we were treated as if we were criminals, simply because we were unrelated and traveling together. I explained to the officers that I needed them with me to help me navigate the mountains—it was too risky for me to do so on my own—and they were like family. We had departed from my family home in Sana'a, I added, so my parents knew who I was with and had no problem with my travel plans.

My explanations went unheard. Two hours later, I was asked to sign a document (by stamping it with my finger) that stipulated that my colleagues and I were engaged in an illegal, shameful act when we were found. I refused, saying that being found in bed with a lover might be considered shameful, but driving through a checkpoint with three loyal colleagues was not. The officer screamed at me and said he'd take me to a place "where I'd be forced to stamp the document." My colleagues also refused, but they were beaten until they gave in. We were taken to a nearby "investigative office" where I was questioned by no fewer than eight officers and instructed to stamp documents I wasn't allowed to read. I was too overwhelmed to resist. I was then taken to a women's prison.

When I arrived at the facility, all I could do was think about how a few years prior, I'd photographed several women's prisons in Yemen for a project I'd worked on with an organization in London. I never thought I would be a prisoner in one of those jail cells. But the fact that I had been on that particular assignment at those prisons might have saved me: as soon as I entered the facility, I came across a female police officer who recognized me. A few hours later, thanks to her intervention, I was released from the prison and sent back to the investigations department.

A friend put me in touch with a relative of hers who was a deputy in the department. He apologized for my detention, and even invited me to his nearby home for dinner. I initially refused—I was worried he would take me to a torture cell, not to his home—but my friend advised me to go. He did, thankfully, take me to his home just as he had promised, which was within walking distance of the investigations department. There, I met his sick mother and his beautiful young wife. She seemed suspicious of me, but she served me a falafel sandwich and orange juice all the same. The woman eventually opened up, confiding in me that she had fought with her husband earlier that day and that she had no one to talk to. I spent the night at the deputy's house but could not sleep. I was terrified about what would happen if I had to go to court.

The following morning, the officer took me back to the investigations department. On our way there, I ran to my car and retrieved my camera, laptop, and external hard drives, even though I wasn't allowed to. The police shouted at me as I hurried away. I took the items back to the house of the officer, gave them to his wife, and said, "Hide these bags, even from your husband. These items contain my livelihood; without them, I have no future."

She listened to me carefully and promised to hide them for me. I realized that I had become friends with this woman, literally overnight. I was finally released without charge. But my colleagues were not as lucky; one of them was tortured before his release. All this because I wanted to take photos of flowers at the jasmine farms.

After that incident, I continued on my journey to Hodeidah to move closer to the types of stories I wanted to cover. I had been thinking about the move for a long while, but had to build up the courage to see it through. Yemeni women rarely live alone, so I struggled to find a place to stay. For weeks, I stayed with a friend in the city as I searched for a landlord who would accept a single female tenant, without any success. But then, unexpectedly, the wife of the officer whose home I had stayed at while in detention—the woman who had become my friend— called me, asking me how I was and if I had found a place to live. When I told her I was still looking, she said her family in Hodeidah had an extra room in their home that her parents could temporarily rent out to me. I was touched by her offer, and agreed. We'd barely had time together, but the woman wanted to help me, despite the knowledge that my lifestyle is somewhat unorthodox by Yemeni standards.

Today I am living in Al-Hoseiniya, in a health clinic with a friend of mine who is a dentist. Although I do not live with my family, and am able to focus primarily on my work, I would not say I feel independent. This town is particularly closed-minded, more so than the average Yemeni town. Women can't drive cars or go to the market on their own. Because this is a rebel-held area, there are ongoing clashes nearby. But I have still managed to take beautiful photographs of women and children and of daily life, and for that reason, I am content.

I have hope in this darkness. We can't bring back the dead, or restore the disabled, the disfigured, and the limbless. We can't bring back the ruins of ancient Yemen, our historical Paradise Lost. But we can hope and we can fight. Yemen will one day once again be known for its cinema, its mocha coffee, its clothes, its Jewish musicians, its islands, and its caves. It will be a tourist destination. The youth who have fled the country with their families will return.

I haven't yet come to terms with how the war has affected me personally, but I know that while it has killed so many innocent people, it has galvanized me to tell unexpected, heartwarming stories. I am committed to being the best photographer I can be. Whenever I think of giving up—I have indeed thought of giving up—I remember I cannot because many girls are relying on me to show the world what fighting spirits they are.

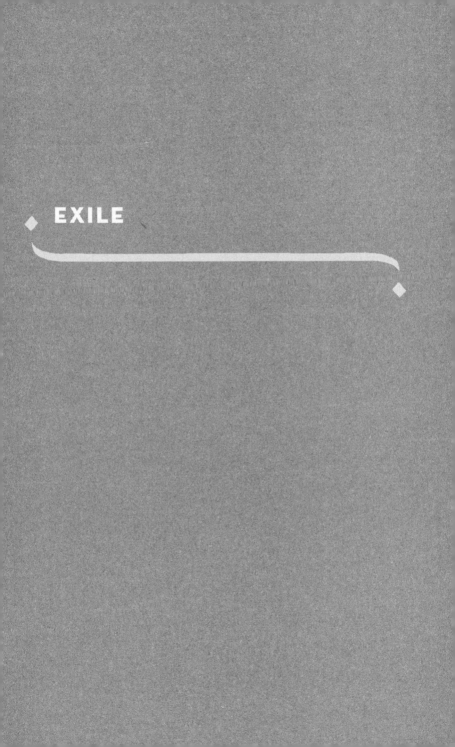

EXILE

Between the Explosions

Asmaa al-Ghoul

*"Our memory is far from an ideal instrument;
it is not only arbitrary and capricious, it is also chained
to time, like a dog."*
—SVETLANA ALEXIEVICH

There's one question that always seems to nag at me, whether I'm cooking for my children, walking home in the freezing French winter after dropping my daughter, Zeina, off at school, or even buying a baguette: *Is this what I want?* Do I really want to be the "ordinary mother" I dreamed of being all those years while I was working as a journalist in the Gaza Strip?

I won't deny that when I come across pictures of former colleagues on social media, I feel a rush of nostalgia for the breaking news, the interviews, the travels, and the conferences that are part of a journalist's life. Occasionally, I yearn to be back on the field and in the editing room. But then I'll remember what I endured during those long years when my job as a journalist took priority over the literary career I longed for and over raising my son and daughter. I feel guilty about never having written down all the short stories and novels I constructed in my head, as journalism had stripped me of language and feelings, and for having missed my son's childhood because I was so focused on my career. I'm keen to avoid repeating the mistake with my daughter.

My ex-husband worked in the same field as me. I often wonder if our marriage would have survived had I dedicated myself to our life together, rather than focusing solely on my journalistic ambitions. I increasingly felt useless, and the gap between us grew larger. As it did, other problems started to emerge.

What has journalism done to me? I'm thirty-five, twice divorced, and a single mother of two. I willingly left behind all my journalistic achievements in Gaza, my hometown, and came to a foreign country to start anew. What and who am I here?

In the middle of war, you investigate and you write story after story after story. But you lose your own story in between the explosions. Somewhere amid the reporting, the rapid political changes, and the writing, you find yourself in an existence you never chose, an existence dictated by the political situation around you. Even if you find strength and success in that existence, you can never choose what you truly want.

In 2003, I got married for the first time, leaving my journalistic career in Palestine behind to move to the United Arab Emirates with my husband. In the hopes that I would continue my career in the UAE, I sent my CV to media outlets all over the country, but to no avail. I chose instead to immerse myself in literature.

In fact, I had first entered the world of writing through literature, not journalism: as a young girl and aspiring author, I wrote poetry and short stories. I was enamored with literature. I had also come to discover that journalism drains your energy, while literature can save your soul. In the UAE, I found myself resorting to literature as a distraction from my pain and loneliness.

My husband had a large and rich library filled with books and DVDs that he hardly ever touched. That space became my life, so much so that each book I read or film I watched haunted me. After watching the film *The Others*, I spent the night terrified. After reading *Perfume* by Patrick Süskind, I felt depressed (even more depressed than I already was). And after reading *Love in the Time of Cholera* by Gabriel García Márquez, I felt like my heart was skipping with joy, even though I was cooped up in a small apartment in an Abu Dhabi high-rise that I barely ever left.

Sometimes I paced the apartment, which in reality was no more than a prison. One day I opened the front door, walked out, and never came back. I got a divorce and took my clipped wings and my son back home to Gaza in 2005, having realized that I couldn't truly fly anywhere but there.

I eventually found work as a reporter for the Palestinian newspaper *Al-Ayyam*. I'd been wanting to work there since high school, so this was nothing short of a dream for me. I also volunteered for a human rights organization, helping them launch their own magazine. The work, though unpaid, energized me and allowed me to visit areas all over the Gaza Strip. The time I spent at *Al-Ayyam* helped me hone my journalistic and linguistic skills.

Still, I very much felt that literature was an entire body of language, while journalism was just the leftovers. Literature and writing nourished me, while journalism was a sacrifice. Every time I wrote as a journalist, I felt like I was losing my ability to write literary prose. Journalism also caused me to lose my sense of self, as I was focused on external things—people and wartime—instead of internal ones.

I tried to merge the two worlds. One of the first pieces I wrote for *Al-Ayyam* was a review of *Gate of the Sun*, a film based on a book by novelist Elias Khoury, which was published in the arts section of the newspaper. I was proud of it, but shortly thereafter, the editor on the local desk delivered a message to me from the editor in chief of the newspaper: he needed journalists, not critics.

Despite the obstacles, I continued pursuing my literary ambitions. Soon after I joined *Al-Ayyam* in 2005, I was awarded grants from external organizations for my writing. Thanks to these grants, I traveled to the United States twice and to South Korea once. Each time I traveled, *Al-Ayyam* froze my salary, even though I wrote cultural dispatches for them from wherever I was.

My editors did not approve of how long it took me to write and research stories. I didn't want to rush, but they wanted me to file articles daily. Some of them seemed to measure news by quantity and word count, not by quality.

This was my depressing world, but I learned to carve my own niche. For example, if my editors asked me to report on an ordinary conference, I would find an extraordinary moment in that conference to write about.

By the time Israel invaded northern Gaza in 2006, I had put my literary writing on hold and become a full-fledged conflict reporter.

I went straight to the front lines, where bullets whizzed by my ears, without a bulletproof vest or any other form of protection afforded to foreign news crews. Nothing would deter me. There were moments of sheer terror, but there were also moments of liberation: I enjoyed the fact that I was finally at the front lines, just like my peers who worked for foreign news outlets.

Those of us covering the events were all cheating death, or playing with it. I played that game multiple times during my reporting career out of my own free will, until I learned what real fear was. Looking back, it's hard for me to internalize how courageous I was with my pen. It was as if I were a different woman. It's unclear where I left that particular self. At which door, in which city, with which war?

I was, of course, scared for my child. But I never felt for a moment that I had to sacrifice my job because of my role as a mother. Why should women have to make those kinds of choices? I behaved like any career-focused journalist would. And during war, there is no time to think about whether or not you love your job. You simply do what you have to do, fueled by a desire to tell the truth. Perhaps this sounds like a cliché, but in reality, it is dangerously true.

Just over two years later, I feared for my child again when war broke out in Gaza; it was as if the gates of hell had opened. The situation was so chaotic at the beginning that it took us a few days to gauge what was actually happening.

On the first day of the war, a huge explosion rocked the city at 11:15 a.m. My first instinct was to rush to my son's school in the Tal Al-Hawa neighborhood. People everywhere were running and screaming. The area was engulfed in smoke, buildings had been destroyed, and I could hear a series of explosions in the distance. A car stopped for me and the driver gave me a lift to the school.

As soon as I arrived, I rushed to my son's classroom and saw shards of glass on his seat. I panicked and looked for him among the crying children. He was sitting on the floor with the others, but he wasn't crying, just flushed. I took him home.

Others were not as lucky. People everywhere were desperately looking for their children or siblings. All of the schools were in the Tal Al-Hawa district in central Gaza, not too far from the security headquarters run by Hamas—most of which were bombed out by Israel. One of the bombs struck an officers' graduation ceremony; several dozen were martyred. During the first two days of the war, no one left their homes. We hadn't truly experienced war before then—this kind of terror was new to us. It wasn't an invasion, or an isolated incident of shelling, or an assassination. It was all-out war: planes, tanks, and warships, all striking Gaza at the same time.

I wrote about the events as they happened for *Al-Ayyam* while also writing about the dangers journalists were facing and violations against freedom of speech for the SKeyes Center for Media and Cultural Freedom, an institution founded in 2007 following the assassination of Lebanese journalist and historian Samir Kassir. On top of that, I was also freelancing for *Al-Quds Al-Arabi*, a London-based newspaper run by Palestinian expats.

Throughout the war, danger kept us company. Every minute

of every day was terrifying. I was playing with death on one hand and defending my womanhood to society on the other, trying to prove that women can cover a war alongside men while keeping their so-called honor intact. I sometimes felt as though danger and death were very distant and my strength would protect me. I got so used to writing about death that I felt it could not possibly make me its victim.

I resigned from *Al-Ayyam* in 2009, after it became clear that I would no longer be allowed to remain neutral in my reporting. Divisions between Fatah and Hamas, the two main Palestinian political parties, had started to emerge. Hamas had swept to victory in the January 2006 elections for the Palestinian Legislative Council, drawing the ire of Western powers and Israel, who imposed sanctions on the Palestinian territories in response. Hamas wrested control of the Gaza Strip in a civil war in 2007, while Fatah kept control of the West Bank, effectively splitting Palestinian territory into two. There have been flare-ups between the parties for years.

Not one newspaper or broadcaster, including *Al-Ayyam*, escaped the polarization. My pen was expected to take sides. Amid those divisions, Hamas started a campaign to Islamize the Gaza Strip. In July 2009, I had my own confrontation with them while I was at the beach. I was sitting with friends at a public café when an armed group of men in civilian clothing began hurling insults and untruths at us, claiming that we were "partying" and going swimming in indecent clothing. We defended ourselves with words and reason. It was a conflict over virtue. Who had the moral high ground? What did it mean to be honorable? Imposing morals with the force of arms, or giving people the freedom to choose?

The Hamas operatives arrested the young men who were with us that evening, but I refused to go along with them, so they seized my passport. When they asked if I had a *mahram* with me, I said I was in my late twenties—why would I need one? They continued to exert pressure on me, so I called my father, who told them he knew exactly where I was. After one of the Hamas men received several calls demanding he back down, he reluctantly returned the passport to me. As he left, he warned me: "I'll be following you."

"And I, you," I replied.

The following day, the story of what happened to me and my friends at the beach reached various media outlets and human rights organizations. Islamists tend to count on the fact that incidents having to do with women and their reputation or "honor" get swept under the rug. But my brave friends and I wouldn't let that happen. The war between the truth and so-called virtue lasted all summer. Rumors started circling about the event, twisting the reality of what happened; some people implied that we were caught in some sort of a "shameful" situation.

When my friends were released, they told us they were asked all sorts of absurd questions during the investigation, among them: "Have you slept with X?" "How would you feel if your sister hung out with your friends?" "Would you approve if your sister had a relationship with a friend of yours?" What a terrifying perception of sexuality. Male promiscuity is allowed, for a man's honor is untouchable.

This is how a group of fellow activists and I came to form the youth movements Is-ha (wake up) and the Secular Youth Congregation. We started organizing protests and issuing press releases that challenged how Islam and Gaza were portrayed. We protested the closure of Sharik, a youth organization. We organized our first sit-in during the election period of 2010, just before the Arab Spring erupted in Tunisia (the elections never actually transpired).

I had stepped away from both journalism and literature, becoming instead a political activist. I stopped working for the printed press, but stayed on as a reporter with SKeyes, and also began a blog about current events that was soon frequented by thousands of visitors. I took to the streets to demand change because I didn't want to simply champion certain values from an ivory tower, leaving the people to bear the brunt of carrying out those demands. I wanted to be honest. I didn't want my words to contradict my actions.

Just over a year later, the Arab Spring was upon us. We started to believe in our ability to inspire change. The toppling of Tunisian president Zine el-Abidine Ben Ali lifted our hopes further. The events galvanized newly formed youth movements across the Gaza Strip and the West Bank. Activists organized protests in solidarity with the revolutionaries in Egypt.

But there were certainly moments when I was engaging in this sort of political activism that I started to miss journalism and its objectivity. I grew tired of the constant confrontation, of having to fight to defend our dreams. I was arrested in the midst of these protests, on January 31, 2011. It was a difficult experience. I was beaten, insulted, and intimidated by both male and female members of Hamas. And of course, we also had to deal with infiltrators—people who were planted into our youth movements by political parties.

Still, the majority of us had only one motive: liberating Gaza from its prison and its pain. We didn't think the Palestinian Authority's president, Mahmoud Abbas, was a viable solution. His movement, Fatah, was guilty of bastardizing the Palestinian cause, turning it into an investment opportunity and benefiting only a small group of brokers whose homeland was money, not the land itself. We wanted unity among Palestinians.

Less than two months after my first arrest, I was arrested again. It was March 15, 2011, a date that would mark Gaza's attempt at the Arab Spring. We demonstrated, calling for an end to the political polarization among the Palestinians. Perhaps our slogan should have specifically called for the fall of the ruling parties—it would have been a stronger and more pointed message. Supporters of Fatah in the West Bank and Hamas in Gaza took to the streets to oppose our demonstrations. In Gaza, men in tracksuits and pajamas—since they weren't in uniform, no one could accuse them of being part of Hamas—attacked us with knives and sticks and hurled profanities at us. Some of the protesters got into skirmishes, and, sure enough, by the end of the day, a number of activists, including me, had been arrested in both Gaza and the West Bank. While I was in jail, I saw those same men in the tracksuits and pajamas handing cameras and other items they had confiscated from protesters, journalists, and street vendors to the authorities.

That was the same day the revolution in Syria started. We even shared the same hashtag, #mar15, leading an electronic stampede in cyberspace, but their struggle went on for years, whereas ours quickly dissipated. Those in power defamed, interrogated, and beat the family members of activists in an attempt to pressure us into backing down. My father was among those targeted. I began to lose hope.

The tension escalated to the point that by the end of March 2011, I felt I had to leave. I moved to Cairo, Egypt. While living there, I traveled to attend workshops and conferences in various European cities, meeting young activists from all over the Arab world. I soon met an Egyptian journalist in Cairo, and we got married in October. I continued to blog, but I was starting to miss the neutrality of journalism even more.

I grew tired of traveling and longed for Gaza. Over a period of three years, from 2011 to 2013, I moved between Egypt and Gaza. Every time my family traveled to or from the strip, we suffered enormously at the Rafah Border Crossing. That suffering weighed on my marriage, which by that point had already become fragile.

Eventually, I gave up on adapting to Egypt and boldly made my way back to Gaza to stay. I was pregnant with my daughter then and had to start from zero yet again. I continued reporting on breaches against journalists for SKeyes and worked on research papers about the youth and the Arab Spring. I began reading again, engaged less and less in politics, and didn't go to demonstrations.

My husband came back to Gaza for the birth of baby Zeina.

Her arrival lessened the rift between us ever so slightly. The lingering tensions became more obvious after the start of the fall of the Arab Spring in 2012, however. It was as if our personal project were intractably linked to the Arab Spring project.

Despite our marital troubles, my husband and I traveled together that year to Los Angeles, where I was to receive the Courage in Journalism Award from the International Women's Media Foundation. While we were there, I sensed a new war was creeping up on Gaza. I feared for my family and my son, whom I had left there. My husband remained in America, while I returned to Gaza with my infant daughter.

A week later, the 2012 war erupted. The air strikes were ferocious. I left the house during the bombings to take photos. I posted them on my Facebook page, which was even more popular than my blog. I also continued to report for SKeyes, the only organization I remained committed to throughout.

During the war, I wondered how life might have been different had I been a regular mother who wasn't living and working in a war zone. I watched my daughter, Zeina, recoil in fear for the first time at the noise of the shelling. My son, daughter, nephew, and I all slept in the foyer of the house. The war brought us ever closer—we were scared together, and we laughed together. We didn't leave home for UNRWA (United Nations Relief and Works Agency for Palestine Refugees) schools, like hundreds of families did. We sometimes argued over what was better: to stay or to leave. But we stayed.

I decided after that 2012 eight-day war to stay away from politics, and also to stop believing in change. It was hard to admit that I hated what I used to love. I took off my political and social hats, and focused again on journalism. I didn't just *want* to be a journalist again—I needed it. Despair was eating me up.

But after my protests against the government in Gaza, no one wanted to employ me. I had been labeled a troublemaker and a rebel.

Eventually, I found a job with *Al-Monitor*, a U.S.-based news website. I trained myself to be objective again. Journalism forced me to focus on what was right in front of me. I wrote daring reports. I was still fighting the Palestinian divisions, mind you, but this time with investigations, not protests. I also secured a book deal for my book, *A Rebel in Gaza*.

Even though I'd occasionally felt as though the only things I knew I wanted in life were to write and to become a mother, and at this point I had done both, my moments of doubt were constant. After my book was published, people sent me letters of appreciation and admiration, but I often felt like I couldn't see what they described as my accomplishments.

My husband returned from the U.S. to settle with us in Gaza, but the professional jealousy between us, both in literature and in journalism, peaked. It's difficult for a woman who has succeeded in one particular field to live with a man looking to succeed in the same field. This certainly was not the sole cause of the escalating tension between us, but it was definitely one of them. Our relationship came to an end and we separated in early 2014. Love came to an end and the Arab Spring came to an end and dreams came crumbling down.

When Facebook reminds me of what I posted back then, I laugh at my illusions. We thought that we were going to change the world. Where did I get all that confidence from? How did I come to think I was so influential, and that my thoughts, and the thoughts of my generation, would make a difference in the world? Our entire generation believed in change. We were out on the streets protesting. We resisted and we insisted. Perhaps it was our youth and our first loves that gave us such hope. But then everything stopped moving. Politics became filthier than ever before. We were the victims of a whirlwind of emotions, social media, and the people we met in this revolutionary environment. How I pity the generation that will have to go out to do it all over again.

We were delusional. *That* is why we woke up and found our

lives in complete chaos. What our revolutionaries lacked was not ideology but practical means. Life is not built on nor does it change through Facebook or social media. Those changes come through streets, schools, colleges, and other educational institutions.

My personal pain was indeed immense. Little did I know that a bigger pain was around the corner, waiting for me.

The 2014 war lasted for fifty-one days. It was like nothing before. I had experienced fear, danger, death, and sadness in the previous two wars, but in this war, we experienced a fear of everything and a fear for everything. We didn't eat, sleep, or walk without a lump in our throats and a knot in our hearts.

I chased death; I even felt like I was looking for it. I took risks. I traveled all over Gaza, both alone and with other journalists, in taxis whose drivers would call their families and say their good-byes before setting off on the journey to dangerous places. I didn't contact anyone. My family didn't even know where I was sometimes. My friends learned of my whereabouts only when my stories were published on *Al-Monitor*. My mother would get angry because she was so worried; she would even cry. I've always left a trail of tears behind me, like when I left tears in my son's eyes during the first war, which I now regret deeply.

I wanted to gather the pain of the war's wounds into my arms so it could join my old wounds, but the war had burned the air in my chest. I couldn't breathe or protect my son and daughter. My son, Nasser, lost his speech when the tower next to our house was bombed repeatedly. During that bombing, I was wounded by shrapnel and stones when I rushed to bring my father into safety from the balcony.

Israeli forces attacked Rafah on August 1, 2014. I was flooded with dozens of messages telling me that it was my duty to cover the invasion since it was my hometown. I was the only journalist from Gaza to visit Rafah, along with three reporters from the *New York Times* whom I'd convinced to join me, despite the fact that any car traveling to or from the area was a target for the Israel Defense Forces. Our driver gave me his bulletproof vest and helmet to wear. It was the first time I wore a bulletproof vest in the three wars that I covered.

As soon as we entered Rafah, we watched a plane shelling the home of a local family, the Abu Tahas. We went to the Kuwaiti hospital straightaway, where we witnessed some family members carry in the dead and wounded. Among them was a tiny baby, dressed in pink.

I went into a room and saw people lining up the dead bodies. Everything in that scene pointed to the fact that those corpses had been alive just moments earlier: their clothes, the position of their bodies, and their white feet. I thought that if I talked to them, they would talk back. I recognized the baby from moments earlier. He was dead. His name was Rizk Abu Taha.

I went into another room, where a distraught and hysterical mother was wailing. She asked if I had come across a baby dressed in pink—the dead baby on the floor that I had just seen. She didn't know he was dead, and everyone was hiding the tragedy from her intentionally. She held me as if she knew I wouldn't lie to her, begging me to tell her the truth as she sobbed. I couldn't lie, because if it were me, I wouldn't want to be lied to. When I told her that her child was among the dead, the woman collapsed, and so, too, did my role as a journalist—in those very moments, I acted beyond my role as a journalist. I acted like a mother.

The woman held me tight, not believing what I had just said, screaming and asking me again and again if it was true. The child was her firstborn. She held her breasts and wailed: "What will I do with these now?"—referring to her breast milk.

I returned to Gaza with my father, who had been visiting my grandma in the south during a ceasefire. He warned me about the risk of being bombed, so I distracted him with family stories until I looked out the window and realized that we were safely out of Rafah. But Rafah wouldn't leave us.

The next morning, Sunday, August 3, 2014, I woke up to a phone call from a journalist who had called to inform me that my uncle's family home had been hit in a missile attack. Their house had been built by my grandfather when he moved to Rafah in 1948 after the Israelis occupied his home village, Sarafand Al-Ammar. I was born and grew up in that house.

Two missiles fired by an F-16 aircraft hit the house at 6:20 a.m. that fateful morning. Those two missiles killed my uncle, Ismail al-Ghoul; his wife, Khadra al-Ghoul; their two sons, Wael and Mohammad; their two daughters, Hanadi and Asmaa; and my cousin Wael's three children, Mustafa, Malak, and Ismail. All nine of my family members were martyred by that Israeli bombing.

I saw their pictures on social media. My youngest cousin's corpse was placed in an ice-cream freezer, the only available freezer in the entire hospital.

I was lucky that I had been able to say my farewells to all the victims before they passed away. On the fifth day of the war, I had taken a risk and gone to Rafah to write about the bombing that killed the Ghannam family. While I was there, I visited my uncle's family and took pictures. Amal, my cousin's wife, had just given birth to twin baby boys, Mustafa and Ibrahim. They were tiny, much like two angels. When I saw them, I felt they were a window of hope and light.

I didn't know then that that would be the last time I would ever see some of them. We laughed and talked about the coincidence that had allowed us to meet. How I wished I'd stayed longer and talked more. The picture I took of the twins is now priceless, since one twin, Mustafa, was martyred while the other twin, Ibrahim, survived, along with his mother.

Life is full of surprises, and so, too, is writing. When we look at the past, it seems like it's begotten by today—like it happened to facilitate everything that's happening at this moment. As

Svetlana Alexievich says: "We look at the past from today. We cannot look at it from anywhere else."

Looking back, it's hard to believe that all those experiences were mine. I moved to France in the summer of 2016, perhaps in part due to the stress and pressure I had endured while on the field.

I constantly wavered between my job and my family—wanting to ensure my family's safety on one hand, and wanting to cover conflict in a distinguished way on the other. I was caught between being a mother soothing a son's and a daughter's fears and, at the same time, writing about other women's children who were being killed by the hundreds. That struggle never went away, and I would face it in all three conflicts that I covered. Those strong memories persist. My family and I often speak about them; they have become a part of our personal history.

What I do know for certain is that exceptional circumstances have put me in many different situations. Often, the choices I made in those situations were out of my hands—I probably wouldn't have made the same decisions had I been living under "normal" circumstances. Back then, the exceptional was often "normal," although the "normal" now feels like it's a terrible exception that I'm not as good at handling.

Starting anew is daunting. It's more than I can bear. There are questions I carry with me every second, when I'm asleep and when I'm awake, regarding war and peace, literature and journalism, blogging or writing: Is this me? Am I doing what others want from me, or what I want? I still don't know the answer.

TRANSLATED FROM ARABIC BY
MARIAM ANTAR

Fight or Flight

Heba Shibani

I never set out to become a journalist, and I certainly didn't anticipate that one evening in 2012 I would be pulled over by thugs while driving home from my job at a private TV station. The incident happened in the Gergaresh district of Tripoli, of all places, one of the city's most prominent and posh neighborhoods. I'd just finished a long day of work at the station. It was early in the evening, on the cusp of sunset, and the main streets were busy. Those were the good old days, before the Libya Dawn party—a grouping of pro-Islamist militias—took over the capital, when Libyans still felt safe enough to go out after dark.

I had decided to take the back roads to avoid traffic, not noticing that I'd been followed by two cars with black-tinted windows that pulled over in front of me, blocking my path and barricading the narrow road. Two men dressed in military-style clothing with long hair and large beards got out and rushed to my car. In shock, I froze. The thugs—who wielded machine guns—went straight for my SUV's doors. They screamed at me and pounded the car with their fists, saying they'd shoot unless I opened the doors. Luckily, I always keep my doors locked when driving. I clenched the steering wheel, thinking that I might never see my loved ones again. The men started shooting into the air.

In the seconds that followed, a mystical force came over me. (Whatever it was, I'm thankful for it.) I snapped out of my frozen state, putting my car in reverse and flooring the accelerator. I'd never focused on anything as intensely as I did in those few minutes. I drove quickly along the winding streets, cutting through traffic and coming dangerously close to causing multiple accidents as I made my way back to the office—not to the police, not to my apartment, but to the office, where I knew I could summon the help of armed security guards. All I could think was that I needed protection from men with guns as big as the ones that were pointed at me.

The locked car doors probably saved me that night. The next day, when my fear and shock had subsided, I wondered why the men hadn't shot me, given that I was in plain sight. My husband theorized that the thugs must have wanted either to scare me or to steal the car, which is why no physical harm was done to me or the vehicle, apart from a broken window. (The window had been broken at some point during the attack, although I'm not sure exactly when, as I was so traumatized by the entire experience.) We both knew, however, that due to my reporting choices, I had enemies who wanted to hurt me; some probably wanted me dead.

I had intended to file a police report the night that I was attacked, but friends advised my husband and me not to, for several reasons that mostly seemed understandable at the time. I was fine; the police had no actual power over militias or thugs; and if they opened an investigation into the incident, they would have to question potential witnesses, meaning the armed men would likely find out and plan to retaliate. Besides all that, as a woman, I should not be seen at a police station. That point, in particular, infuriated me; male-dominated spaces like prisons are often considered off-limits to women in Libya, even if a woman is a victim of a crime and wishes to report it. Everyone around me thought silence was the best course of action, so I agreed.

I didn't want my family to find out about the threats I faced as a reporter, so I didn't speak about the situation publicly until Human Rights Watch approached me for a report on Libyan journalists who had come under attack during and after the revolution. Had my family found out, they would surely have told me to quit my job. To this day, they still don't know about the incident—they haven't seen the report, and I haven't ever mentioned it to them.

My first job was as a teacher. I studied English literature at university and started teaching the language while I was still a student. My family harbored the hope that I would ultimately become a university professor—being a teacher was deemed a socially acceptable job for a woman in a conservative society. It didn't take me long to realize I wasn't passionate about what I was doing, and that I didn't want to settle into a career just because it was considered woman-friendly.

When friends who had set up a private TV station approached me in 2011 to ask me to join as a presenter, I was both nervous and thrilled. Before joining Alassema, I had no practical experience in journalism. But I took to being on air quickly, learning and honing my reporting skills along the way.

Earlier that year, protests had erupted against President Muammar Gaddafi, who had ruled the country with impunity for more than forty years. The protests were met with brutal force from the regime. A NATO alliance enforced a no-fly zone on the country as a violent civil war broke out, leading to the ousting and then the murder of Gaddafi. With the fall of the regime, which had suppressed free speech, journalism in Libya flourished.

After years of self- and state-imposed censorship, Libyan journalists could now report the news freely as well as express their opinions publicly. This was an unprecedented moment in Libya's media landscape: the number of Libyan TV stations surged from two to more than twenty. Newspapers exploded by the dozens. Suddenly, Tripoli was filled with newly minted journalists. That there were so many new media outlets didn't mean these reporters weren't subject to abuse, particularly when covering sensitive, taboo topics and when militiamen started to take over the country.

Alassema, which was set up by some friends of mine who were opposed to the Gaddafi regime, was one of the new stations. But as I became a seasoned reporter there, something began to feel off. Some of the stories I covered were deeply unpopular, particularly those that highlighted the abuses that anti-Gaddafi "revolutionary" groups (as they were then known) were inflicting upon pro-Gaddafi loyalists whom they were keeping captive in illegal prisons. Upon taking a closer look, it became increasingly clear to me that some of these prisons' occupants were unarmed, innocent civilians who had been caught in the wrong place at the wrong time, detained for merely defending their ideas.

To report on post-Gaddafi realities that depicted the revolutionary groups in a negative light, it seemed, was unacceptable to viewers, even though these stories needed to be covered. When I told the stories of these people on air, even coworkers and friends accused me of being a political pawn for the Gaddafi loyalists. In reality, I was criticizing all parties, and defending the idea that *everyone* should have a say in Libya's political life. Perhaps I shouldn't have been taken aback, considering the unforgiving and volatile situation in Tripoli, but I firmly believed that violence would only beget further violence, and that the vicious cycle needed to be stopped. The only way I felt I could uphold that view and advocate for peace as a journalist was by telling stories that were being ignored.

The situation became so toxic and polarizing that I started receiving hate mail almost daily, from both February 17 loyalists (meaning the members of the Gaddafi opposition, who declared a Day of Rage on February 17, 2011; the date also marked the beginning of the civil war) and Gaddafi supporters. Even though I tried to be as neutral as possible in my reporting, I couldn't please both sides, nor did I feel I belonged to either; each one branded me an enemy.

After one of my reports, which exposed atrocious forms of torture at the prisons that had been mainly ignored by the local press, some of my social media followers sent me vile and threatening messages demanding that I stop chasing the story. My opponents also criticized me for appearing on TV without a hijab, demanding that I "cover up." As most of the threats were posted online by individuals who had fake usernames, we had no concrete evidence against them and couldn't take any action. If people recognized me on the streets—thanks to the power of makeup, they often did not—they would give me angry looks or hurl insults at me.

I tried to ignore them, but one incident in particular will forever stay with me. It was 2012, and I was at a supermarket doing some grocery shopping when a well-dressed older woman approached me. I didn't feel threatened by her, so when she asked me if I was the "girl who appears on TV every other night," I said yes without flinching. As soon as I confirmed my identity, the woman started verbally attacking me. She was hysterical. At some point, she began repeating that I "should be raped" so that I would know "how families and women feel when it happens to them." Those were the words that stung the most. The insults then escalated into a full-on threat: the woman asked why I "defended" pro-Gaddafi loyalists, adding that she'd make sure "bad things" would come my way, and that I'd deserve whatever I'd get. I was so shocked by her vicious behavior that I started to feel like the entire incident was happening to someone else. People started gathering around us. Some tried to make her stop, but she persisted, so everyone watched in silence.

The feeling of being attacked was a familiar one, but when I heard the word "rape," I froze, just like I'd frozen in the car when the thugs harassed me. I didn't talk; I didn't move. I wanted to walk away, but I was in so much shock that I couldn't do anything at all. I felt powerless and confused. I didn't understand the woman's anger, or where it came from.

It was probably at that point that any hope I had in Libya started to fade. What kind of optimism could we have, I thought, if this respectable-looking woman, who didn't even know me, threatened and cursed me just because she didn't like my reporting?

Looking back on that incident years later—as horrible as it was—I understand why she behaved the way that she did. The country was imploding, and as a result, many people had been brainwashed by the media, politicians, militias, and so-called religious leaders who practically instructed Libyans to hate and attack one another. The tension was so intense and so palpable that the idea of healthy dialogue was nonexistent, despite the fact that the media had become freer since the revolution. The woman who attacked me was reacting to that toxic environment. To her, I represented the viewpoint of "the other," and she hated me because of it. As far as she was concerned, I was her enemy. I can now reflect on that experience with a little more empathy, and I do not blame the woman for the horrible things she said to me. I blame the sorry state of the country.

By the end of 2012, things were becoming increasingly difficult for me at Alassema. My managers instructed me to keep my news coverage away from "the world of militias"; they wanted me to focus strictly on low-key social and political events rather than criminal activities or human rights abuses. When I criticized the aggressively anti-Islamist tone of the network in casual conversations at work, I was accused by colleagues of being "pro-mufti" (religious leader), which I frankly thought was hilarious, considering how liberal I believe myself to be. I had had hopes that I could use my role at the station to promote the idea of a peaceful transition of power that ensured that all Libyan parties, including the Islamists, had fair representation. But I can see now that I was naïve in my thinking. The network's intention was never to respect the democratic process. As executives weighed me down with more and more restrictions and pressure, and tensions rose, I knew that it was time for me to move on. I wanted to be a real reporter, not someone who was actively avoiding sensitive subjects for fear of reprisals. I decided to resign.

I never expected to join Alnabaa, a competing network that was thought to be soft on Islamists. After its executives approached me, it quickly became clear that I was offered a job not for my journalistic skills but for what I represented: they seemingly thought that having a woman on air who did not wear the hijab would give them a better chance of appealing to the broader Libyan public. I wasn't overly concerned, though. I took the job offer almost immediately, seizing the opportunity to gain more experience in TV production and as a journalist. It felt like the right thing to do for my career at the time. I'd just returned from a two-month trip to the U.S. and was filled with excitement and focus. I also felt somewhat removed from the toxic political situation and wanted to steer clear of reporting on it in my new position. Instead, I wanted to create a show that would make a real difference for women in Libya. This was going to be a new beginning for me, I thought.

Surprisingly, Alnabaa agreed to my proposal: I was hired as a show runner, and also took on the role of producer and presenter of *Hawa* (Eve), a weekly show focused on women's issues. My sole request was the freedom to investigate and broadcast whatever subjects I thought were important. Just because the show would center on women, I said, the network shouldn't expect me to focus on makeup and cooking tips—I had a suspicion that this is what they expected of me. The executives agreed, as long as I ran "sensitive" topics by them for approval first.

As I searched for hidden stories about women that I believed were worthy of national attention, I stumbled upon several cases of mothers who had been struggling to keep their families together because of a law that limits the right for Libyan women to pass their nationality to their children. While some progress had been made on amending the law, according to Human

Rights Watch, it stopped short of giving women full rights, contained contradictory provisions, and perpetuated gender discrimination. Regulations to change the law were drafted, but had not yet been brought to the General National Congress for formal authorization. Many members of the GNC felt approving it would be too drastic of a change and that the country had far more urgent matters to focus on anyway.

My team and I worked tirelessly with the GNC's human rights committee to delve deeper into and raise awareness on a topic that had long been buried. I sought out women who had harrowing stories to tell about what the lack of freedoms meant for them and their children. The process was eye opening, not just journalistically, but personally. These women had endured years of hardship, and no one had taken notice—yet they never gave up, even as war raged on around them.

Barring women from giving the Libyan nationality to their children effectively treats them as lesser citizens, and ultimately lesser human beings. In practice, this misogynistic rule penalizes women for choosing to marry non-Libyans, often affecting children in concrete ways as a result. For example, the Libyan government in 2007 ruled that Libyan women who had wed non-Libyan men had to pay about $654 annually for their children's public schooling. In some cases, non-Libyan fathers aren't able to pass along their own nationality to the child if the child is born outside of their home country, spurring a situation in which the baby is effectively born stateless. By contrast, a Libyan man can marry whom he pleases and pass his nationality on to his child.

The women I interviewed all had similar stories: as soon as their children turned eighteen, the family would be broken apart, for they would be considered non-Libyans and were therefore subject to deportation. One woman's two sons were sent to Lebanon when they turned eighteen because their father was Lebanese and diplomatic relations between the two countries were strained in the 1990s.

There was one case that had more impact on me than all the

others combined. For years, one woman had fought for the right to give her children Libyan nationality, as she'd married a foreigner. Although she talked about the subject with me extensively off camera as I got to know her and we prepared for the show—she had bravely agreed to two appearances—I'd noticed she hadn't mentioned her daughter once, even though I knew she had one. It wasn't until the day of filming at the studio that she opened up completely.

During the 1990s, Gaddafi's rule had come under threat by Islamists, and the regime responded to an assassination attempt on the president with repressive measures. Riots were crushed and security was tightened considerably. It was in this environment that the woman gave birth to a baby girl. The baby was born with severe health complications, and as a result was frequently in and out of the hospital. By the time the little girl was three, her health had deteriorated to the point that she required immediate surgery. Hospitals in Libya were overcrowded, so the mother had to make her way to Tunis with her daughter to ensure she could get surgery there instead.

Traveling as a foreigner was a complicated, protracted process. Given that the girl was not Libyan, each time she crossed the border, she and her mother had to go through a lengthy security-clearance procedure. There was also a risk that the family would be barred from returning to Libya. This time around, that lengthy process proved fatal: the girl died in her mother's arms, at the airport.

Following that tragic loss, the woman decided to dedicate her life to raising awareness on issues pertaining to the law to prevent a similar situation from occurring to another family. It was only many years after her daughter's passing that she was finally able to speak about it publicly. As she recounted the tragic events, I could see her choke up, tears in her eyes and sadness in her voice. For a brief moment, the image of a powerful, confident woman who was willing to speak up against injustice faded, and all I could see was a broken parent, filled with sorrow and regret.

This fearless woman, and many more like her whom I was fortunate enough to meet and learn from, helped me come to the realization that I was finally doing something of meaning and value. As Libya was enduring a major conflict, women's rights weren't at the top of the political leadership's list of priorities. By bringing them to the fore, I was making a difference, however small. For weeks, my team and I were given the space to produce powerful episodes simply because the management needed to fill an empty slot on a Saturday evening. The show was initially deemed "soft" and palatable to the network's executives since it didn't tackle political issues pertaining to the war, so we managed to fly under the radar for a long while. We were proud of what we'd created.

Unfortunately, our freedom was short-lived. The more shows I produced, the more confident I became. I wanted to push the envelope, and I was galvanized by the strong women I'd hosted on the show. Slowly, the show gained traction, and its viewership numbers spiked. The popularity shocked the network's executives, who'd expected us to focus on their definition of women's issues, which they considered to be nonpolitical— matters of clothing, makeup, or how to be a good mother or housewife. That flawed definition of women's issues, of course, diminishes the importance of women's rights, the struggle for which is very much political. They also hadn't anticipated that women's issues unrelated to those "trivial" matters would pose any sort of threat to their editorial agenda, or garner so much interest from viewers, as Libyans at the time were focused primarily on matters pertaining to the war. But as people had started taking the show seriously, the management began censoring our work; show by show, story ideas that were deemed "unfit" for the channel were killed.

I continued pushing stories on women's empowerment despite those restrictions, knowing, perhaps, that my employment at the network would reach a breaking point. I pitched a series of episodes on rape, hoping that any discussion surrounding the issue would instigate much-needed dialogue, and help change the outdated way many Libyans looked at and treated victims of sexual assault. The idea was shot down as it didn't fit the network's editorial policies. After that particular decision, my team and I started to feel cornered. We couldn't move forward with our vision, and despite the battles we'd fought and won, it became clear to us that it was time to leave. I resigned, yet again.

Alassema had given me the freedom to tell the stories I wanted to tell, as long as they didn't paint Islamists or Islamism in a positive light. Alnabaa, too, had claimed to give me the freedom to report on the topics that mattered to me, with the caveat that I leave my so-called liberal views at home. Ultimately, both channels were two sides of the same coin, turning Libyans against one another by fueling polarization in a country that had descended into sheer chaos. I didn't want to play a part in that polarization, even though I still wanted to be a journalist.

I joined Reuters in 2014. Reporting for an international media organization allowed me to grow as a journalist and producer without having to worry about bias. As if by design, however, shortly after I started at the newswire, the security situation in Libya deteriorated even further. I had also recently given birth to my first child. Though Tripoli had become a war zone, I tried to trick myself into believing that Libya was a country in which I could be both a mother and a journalist. I would be lying if I said I wasn't scared to cross militiamen yet again, this time without a favorable outcome. When the Libya Dawn party took over the capital in the summer of that year, it was the last straw. I found myself in yet another precarious position in which I was forced to make a difficult choice. This time I had to think of my six-month-old daughter, Sama, not just me, my husband, and my career.

Our only choice as a family, we decided, was to flee Libya. It was time to leave behind all of the risks that had consumed our lives during my short-lived career as a journalist in my home country. Reuters moved me to Tunis to cover both the Tunisian capital and Libya remotely for four months, but the pressures continued to manifest themselves, even from afar. In hindsight, I can see now that becoming a mother was my most significant achievement and my greatest fear: I knew that there would come a time, if I did have children, when I would have to choose between my family and being a conflict reporter. A choice as dramatic as this one—leaving one's life and career behind for the safety of one's children—isn't difficult to comprehend if you've worked in a war zone like Libya. That said, it was one of the most challenging things I've ever had to do.

I'm writing this today from Malta, where I work as a media consultant and have lived with my family for three years. Even though we are safe from the instability that continues to engulf Libya, it's difficult to live in peace when you're worried about friends and family who are in perpetual danger. But we are trying to make the most of what we have. When I reflect on the work that I did back home in Libya, and how much I miss being a journalist, I can't help but contemplate my shortcomings. I was young, and I didn't have a background in the industry. Maybe I would have handled things differently had I known then what I know now—had I seen that the networks' editorial agendas eclipsed objective reporting. But I know that I worked hard and listened harder to all points of view, even inconvenient ones. And for that, I have no regrets.

Breathing Fear

Lina Sinjab

It was the winter of 2011. Like many Syrians, I was closely watching the events that were unraveling across the Arab world. What would come to be known as the Arab Spring had sparked within us a desire for change—not only in other countries across the region, but in Syria, too.

Organizers on Facebook came together to schedule a Day of Rage in my home country, a protest against President Bashar al-Assad that was set to take place in Damascus on February 4, 2011. I didn't think anything would actually happen, but as a journalist, I had to be there and ready nonetheless. My suspicions proved correct: there were more security officers than people in the streets of Damascus that day.

But there was a lot of talk in the capital. Many journalists who were close to the regime started asking locals what they thought would happen if protests were to reach Syria, sending them a clear message that the demonstrators were part of an antistate conspiracy, designed to deepen sectarian divisions and to trigger bloodshed that would ultimately leave Syria divided. That message came from the government, which was indirectly warning people through those journalists that chaos would ensue. No one thought Syrians would dare take to the streets.

I had just come back from Yemen, where I'd been covering an antigovernment uprising in Sana'a. I couldn't believe what I was seeing. Hopeful, brave, and nationalistic Yemenis were out in the squares, determined to fight for change. There was something about that determination that consistently left me speechless: the demonstrators were never afraid. They were speaking their minds fearlessly, while in another square, loyalists of President Ali Abdullah Saleh were staging support for their president. I shuffled between the two sites, speaking to people at both camps. I never, ever thought this would happen back home.

On February 17, however, something inconceivable occurred. Rumors began to spread that children in Dara'a, a city in southwestern Syria, had been locked up in detention centers for having written graffiti on the walls of their hometown calling for change. The news was hard to believe; at the time, it felt like a thing of fiction.

On that day, people spontaneously gathered in Harika Square in the old city of Damascus. After a businessman quarreled with a police officer, who responded by attacking him, protesters started chanting with one voice, *"Al-sha'ab al-souri ma bienzal"* (Syrians won't be humiliated), and filming their surroundings with mobile phones. Hundreds gathered around the businessman, and together their voices became louder and louder. In response, the minister of the interior came to the square, where he told the protesters, *"'Ayb ya shabab, hai mouzahara hai?!"* (Shame on you, men, this is a protest?!) A protest, he says. Shameful, he says! The very thing the minister and his government had feared was happening before him.

But I still wasn't convinced anything would become of the protest. The massacre of Hama in the 1980s and the crackdown that followed remain vivid in the memory of many Syrians, including me, who had been locked in fear since then. (The forces of then-president Hafez al-Assad, Bashar al-Assad's father, had murdered thousands of Syrians in the massacre to quell an antigovernment uprising.)

After the protest in Harika Square, I wrote a piece for the BBC about why there hadn't been an Egypt-style revolution in Syria. Although many Syrians were watching events unravel around the Arab world, they thought that Bashar al-Assad, the young president who had portrayed himself as a reformer, now had a golden opportunity to instigate change at home.

News of the children of Dara'a had become real by then. They had disappeared, and reports suggested they had been tortured: their nails had been removed as punishment for having dared to challenge authority and write graffiti on school walls calling for the toppling of the regime.

A few weeks later, in the middle of March 2011, three significant events unfolded over the course of a week. On March 15 in Hamidieh, a town on the Syrian coast, a small crowd stood under the covered market and chanted *"Allah, souria, hurriye, wa bas"*—a phrase that would become popular during the protests, calling for freedom in the country. The following day, women gathered in front of the interior ministry building, holding up photos of their detained relatives who had disappeared into government prisons for years. The women were beaten up; some were dragged by their hair down the streets. Two days after that, families in Dara'a took to the streets, demanding a change in government and the release of their children. I was stunned. Everything that happened during the week was like a spark. I realized that silence was breaking in Syria. And so was mine.

Growing up in Syria in the seventies meant one thing: breathing fear. Fear was so deeply embedded in our lives that we barely even noticed it. Whenever the topic of the government came up at home, there was silence. I can't recall ever hearing the word *ra'ees*, or "president," in the house.

I attended the same school as Bashar al-Assad and his brothers in Damascus—the school of the "business elite," the educated middle class, and the corrupt power circle of the leadership— although we were there during different years. At school, the son of a military officer could shout at the teacher and kick him or her out of class. In such a scenario, it was more likely that the teacher would disappear than that the boy would face punishment. The wealthy boys and girls at the school were keen to befriend the sons and daughters of military personnel or security officers who were enrolled there. They all came to school in fancy Mercedes driven by chauffeurs.

I looked at the wealthy from a small distance, but never mingled with them, mixing instead with the educated elite of the remaining middle class—we used to walk together to school. One part of the school was comprised of the rich and powerful, while the other part was fearful and helpless. A fellow student's father, a security officer, imprisoned the socialist politician father of another student. Both students attended the same school, but never enjoyed the same power. Such was life in Damascus.

My life was in the shadows, observing the lives of others. There had to be another way to live, I thought, but I didn't know how to do so. I pondered life beyond the strict rules of society imposed upon women, not to mention the untold barriers of fear from the state. That fear unknowingly pushed a hidden desire within me to break free from my silence.

I turned to journalism. I wanted to write about people and tell their stories—perhaps because I was too afraid to tell my own.

But I knew nothing of the rules. I had to learn by doing, while always watching my surroundings carefully so I didn't falter or make a mistake that would put me in danger. First, I started writing about culture, and then society. Soon after that, I started working for international media, reporting on "acceptable" margins of life within Syria, like the economy or minor political developments. In those early years, I never, ever dared to raise questions about what happened behind the walls of prisons in Syria. I was too scared to discuss that reality, let alone write about it. I lived within the red lines drawn by the Syrian security apparatus. The fear that they entrenched in our lives was immeasurable.

Yet there were people who were fearless. Some had just left prison, some had family members who were still behind bars, and others were simply speaking out, calling for an end to such practices. I followed these people and their stories and started timidly reporting on them. With every report, my heart pounded; I knew I was doing the right thing, but wondered when I would be thrown into jail for my work.

I took baby steps into journalism. After I joined the BBC in 2004, I learned to acquire international standards of journalism, but trying to maintain them while also trying to stay safe was never an easy balance to strike. A documentary about music that I worked on was reported to Syrian security as a story on Kurds in the north of the country. Soon after it aired, I was threatened with, and then faced, a three-month suspension on reporting in Syria. I couldn't resume my job until after a connection of mine helped me resolve the situation with the minister. An article I wrote about Riad Seif, a businessman who had been released from prison, was also reported to security, this time as an act of sympathy toward the opposition. (Mr. Seif had been imprisoned in 2001 and again in 2008 for having created a Damascus Spring forum, in which Syrians had gathered for the first time in thirty years to discuss reforms, democratic change, and an end to corruption.) I subsequently faced additional threats, and about three months of being blacklisted from covering Syrian affairs.

And how dare I have questioned the success of the first lady when I interviewed her in 2010 at a conference she sponsored on nongovernmental organizations? At the time, Syria was trying to partner with NGOs, allegedly to work on "rural development, female empowerment, and the promotion of Syrian culture"—and yet many women's rights organizations had been waiting for years to be recognized by the government. I asked representatives from several if they were able to operate comfortably without being under the umbrella of the first lady; that line of questioning was enough to anger the palace. I was summoned, threatened, and suspended from work for another three months.

Most journalists in Damascus are vetted by security and have to show their work to their "sources" and "connections" before they file or air a single word. Everything has to be preapproved. I, on the other hand, had no sources or connections in the country's inner security circle—it was my hard work that had gotten me into the BBC. The fact that they hired me led people to believe that I was in some way "connected." I had a vibrant social life that brought me into powerful circles, yes, but never in a way that meant I could be ordered around by someone or needed to obtain their approval to chase a story. During coffee meetings with the members of the security apparatus who dealt with the press, I always managed to stay on the safe side, never giving anything away, and playing dumb when they said I had to "collaborate." "If I learn of anything that might threaten the safety of the country, I will definitely alert you," I would say. But deep down, I knew they were the ones who posed a threat to our safety.

Still, something inside me kept me going, and I kept pushing boundaries.

In late 2010, I worked on a documentary about corruption and state monopoly in Syria. In the story, I discussed Rami Makhlouf, a tycoon who had monopolized businesses in the country. An economist who had previously brought attention to the issue had spent seven years in jail for speaking out about what he knew. As I gathered evidence for the documentary, I became increasingly anxious, unsure of what would happen when it was broadcast to the public. When it finally aired, it was almost January 2011, and protest fever had already started spreading across the Middle East. I had thought that tapping into issues of corruption would pose a huge risk, but that type of daring reporting paled in comparison to the reporting on the death and killings in the streets of Syria that was to become the norm within weeks.

In March 2011, during the protests in Dara'a and Hamidieh, the vibe in Syria felt different. I had never felt optimistic and happy about my country's future before, but suddenly I was experiencing a feeling of profound connection to the place where I had grown up. The protests spread across the country, and a sense of solidarity among Syrians from all spectrums of society allowed us to feel like we were entering a new era. In that moment, we citizens felt that we belonged to a place where we could say what we thought and play a role in determining our fate.

The first two years of the uprising were filled with hope and energy. Syrians came together, bonded, and assisted one other. Social support systems were established. Women gathered and established networks for people in areas facing regime brutality. Citizen journalists started organizing and sending the news on what was happening across the world via social media and other means.

As Syrians broke their silence and fear, I followed suit, reporting on their bravery and sidelining my own fears from the authorities. I watched them attend protests, come face-to-face with bullets, and face incarceration.

I saw women from Syria's wealthy tier of society drive their Mercedes and BMWs close to the protests, circling security officers and bribing them with cash to free detained men. During one protest, I was holed up in a small area of a grocery shop with fifteen other women and men; the owner had closed the shop's shutters to protect us from the *shabiha* (armed gangs loyal to the regime) and security forces who were firing gas and bullets at the protesters. In the course of my reporting, I sat in the town of Douma with women who were protesting in front of state security, asking for the release of their husbands and sons. Sometimes I found myself walking over fresh blood in the street or in a prison cell where I was being interrogated—people had just been tortured in the exact same spot where I was standing.

But that bravery came with a price, for the protesters and for me. They faced bullets, blood, and arrests. I faced threats and an arrest and was stripped of my accreditation as a journalist.

By early 2013, it was impossible for me to move around. I wasn't allowed into government press conferences or prearranged interviews, and when I was blacklisted, I had to confine my reporting to behind my desk, relying on Skype and WhatsApp to communicate with sources and occasionally going on underground trips to banned areas to see for myself what was unfolding. Since many brave Syrians were determined to continue putting forth their demands, even while facing the increasing brutality of the regime, I felt determined to continue reporting despite the growing challenges.

The anticipation and excitement of change started deteriorating as the death toll rose, cities were destroyed, and hundreds of thousands of people started fleeing their homes. I had to get used to the new normality of life during war.

I spoke to everyone I could on both sides of the conflict: one side was filled with hope and the other was filled with hatred. Those who sided with the regime were opposed to freedom, democracy, and citizenship. I could understand how those tenets were not necessary for the powerful and privileged, but shockingly, some poor Alawite communities supported Assad, too. From the early days of the uprising, rumors had spread in Alawite villages that this was an Islamist movement and that they were the targets. The regime distributed weapons among minorities starting with the Alawites and told them to protect themselves. The authorities played the game of fear and it worked well. Many Syrians were convinced that what had come to pass in those early months was not an uprising but a Salafi radical movement whose goal was to threaten the lives of those Syrians.

I watched dozens of friends leave the city in early 2013. My social circle grew smaller as friends died or were imprisoned and relatives were shot by government forces, and a wave of fear began to wash over everyone again.

In the spring of that year, I, too, was forced to leave the country after enduring several arrests, multiple threats, and a twelve-month travel ban. I had dared to report the reality on the ground—going to places I shouldn't have gone to, speaking with people I shouldn't have spoken with. I had dared to tell the truth.

I thought I would return just a few months later. I hadn't quite realized that the country I had lived in for four decades of my life—my home—would never be the same again.

I bade my farewell to my city, my people, and my life, and soon after endured a long cycle of depression, trauma, and a state of denial, not wanting to believe that I had left. By then, hope had started to fade and calls for change were replaced by the sounds of war: bombings, Scud missiles, and explosions. As I crossed the borders outside Syria, life as I knew it had started to fall apart. I helplessly watched my country disintegrate as the world stood idly by, not wanting to do anything to end the suffering of Syria and its people.

The guilt of leaving was killing me. I hated the fact that I was privileged enough to seek safety, while hundreds of thousands of my own people were not. My personal losses—a home, a job in my country, my house (which had caught the attention of a pro-regime local and was subsequently seized by security forces, who claimed I was not loyal to Syria and therefore not allowed to live there)—were nothing compared to the disasters other people experienced.

I lived in London for three years but felt disconnected from the city. It was hard to bond with anyone or to build a new life there; while people around me chatted about normal, daily occurrences, my mind was occupied with images of death and destruction. I continued covering Syria from a distance, maintaining daily contact with people I knew who were still in the country in order to reflect the reality of what was happening on the ground. I also traveled around to report on refugees from my own country who were living in tents in Lebanon and elsewhere.

Until 2016, I still thought there was a way out of the quagmire that Syria had fallen into. I was also convinced that my life outside of Damascus was just temporary. When a wave of refugees took to the sea to reach Europe, I made the opposite journey, leaving London for Beirut—the closest possible location to home—with the naïve idea that I would be back in Damascus within a year or so. The closer I got to home geographically, however, the further the concept of home started to feel.

Today, five years since I left Damascus, I am still in Beirut. Hope seems completely lost for most Syrians, including me. There's too much killing, destruction, and loss. The diaspora is too big. The damage this war has caused goes far beyond the figures quoted in media about the human, economic, or social costs.

The connection and bonding that Syrians had to their community and their home country is forever lost. There is too much pain and trauma that people are carrying along with them, and only justice can help them heal. Justice for their lost loved ones, for their material losses, for their dignity, and for their diaspora. Only justice for all can bring Syrian society back together.

What we are witnessing today is the rule of the powerful—even if those in power are responsible for the Syrian catastrophe. And that won't bring peace or justice to Syria.

Although I chose to be here, in Beirut, so I could be as close as possible to Damascus, I feel farther from my city than ever before. It is not my city anymore. It is occupied by the winners who have blood on their hands, and by foreigners who are altering its identity. I feel powerless, unable to protect Damascus, and still unable to stop the killing. I sit on my balcony in Beirut and watch the sea, not knowing where I belong anymore. My Syria is gone—at least for now.

Hurma

Zaina Erhaim

Five long, shapeless tops; a pile of loose-fitting, dark-colored jeans; a knee-length coat; and a video camera. Those were the contents of my wardrobe for more than two years, when I lived in the rebel-held area of Aleppo, known as eastern Aleppo city. Few things changed between the seasons, as we had to dress conservatively year-round. However, at some point, I decided to settle my camera into a large safety box we'd bought to protect our passports and precious belongings from being destroyed should the house be bombed.

"Would you really care about your camera and passport if you got stuck under the wreckage yourself?" a friend asked.

"If I were to be buried by the rubble of my own home," I replied, "you'd hear me screaming out the safety box's passcode, demanding that my passport and camera be brought along with me to the hospital." My camera, my passport, and I live or die together.

Conversations about death in my part of the world aren't gloomy or depressing; they're as common as conversations about the weather in the UK. Mind you, I wasn't bothered by the weather while I briefly lived in London for my master's degree. It was the ubiquity of black and gray clothing that I found depressing. I have always disliked dark colors. In my "real life"—my life as a layperson and not a journalist—I have only two to three dark pieces of clothing in my closet, hidden among dozens of green, blue, pink, and red garments. When I reported from Aleppo, the hardest thing for me was putting on a dark headscarf just before leaving the house after I'd carefully chosen my outfit for the day.

Back in early 2011, when the uprising erupted in Syria, I finally started to feel like I belonged in my own country. The antigovernment demonstrations demanding democratic reforms from President Bashar al-Assad represented everything I'd long hoped for: freedom of expression, a free press, elections, and an end to fear. Hundreds of thousands took to the streets to peacefully demonstrate against the regime. Some held olive branches, while others would sing and dance, even at the funerals of those killed during the previous day's demonstrations. Despite the government's crackdown on the movement's leaders, and the looming risk of being shot when protesting in the streets—or tortured to death while in detention—Syrians continued demonstrating until 2012, before the uprising turned into a war. But even after experiencing all of that hope, I found myself fighting the same fight that I had won so many years ago: the fight not to wear a hijab.

If you ask anyone why women in Syria should be covering their hair, they might cite the Qur'an. But why is this rule enforced so much more strictly now than it has been in the past? The answer is simple: many fundamentalist Muslims are now armed, giving them the unlimited power and impunity to suppress women, whom they believe to be the weaker gender.

I come from a conservative community in Syria, in Idlib city, and my family had tried to force me to wear the hijab at fifteen years old. I won that battle: I refused to cover my hair simply because I couldn't see why "all the women in our town do" was enough of a reason for me to do so as well. I will never forget the shame I was forced to feel when I was harassed and called names on the streets. I can't count the number of times I was groped while on my way to school, in broad daylight. Even though I had adamantly refused to put on the headscarf, I couldn't help but feel responsible for being touched inappropriately. But I never gave up.

After the uprising, fifteen years later, I fought the battle again and lost. I had tried to resist. I had thought: I am not a foreign journalist who's in Syria for a short trip to do some reporting before heading back home. This is my home, and I should force these people to accept who I am. I should once again fight the same battle I had fought as a teenager, this time with strange, armed men in a chaotic corner of my country, known as the most dangerous area in the entire world for journalists.

But I and other women activists and journalists had become "minors" in Syria. Any man had the right to check the length of our sweaters, the color of our outfits, who we were moving around with, and who we were talking to. They even had the right to scrutinize the fabric of our pants. Jeans signaled that we were not locals, or that we were activists, since many consider them to be a Western form of clothing.

"Minor" wasn't just a term: I was quite literally treated as one. I needed a man by my side to travel, to be able to move from one neighborhood to another. The chaperone had to be a *mahram*, meaning an allowable escort—a man who has a close blood relationship with me, such as my father or uncle. In my final couple of years in Syria, I had to fake having two brothers (I used their sisters' IDs), four maternal uncles (my mother's surname is not written on my ID, so this was easy), three cousins, and two husbands. It wasn't always funny. When passing through an ISIL checkpoint in Raqqa in December 2013, I was riding along with a thirty-one-year-old doctor—the brother of my friend Sara—and I was carrying her ID. I had to memorize all the information about Sara that I could, since we expected them to interrogate us separately to make sure we were relatives. I sweated profusely until the Tunisian jihadi decided to let us pass.

A year later, at one of the checkpoints in northern Aleppo in

2014, I ran into trouble again. At the time, I was still refusing to wear a headscarf. "Who is she?" the young man asked my male chaperone.

"She's a Syrian journalist from Idlib," my friend answered.

"A journalist? From Idlib? Are you kidding me?" the armed man mocked. "She's obviously a foreign journalist. We don't have any women journalists here."

"Well, I'm from Idlib city—the Dabeet neighborhood, to be exact—and I have a heavy dialect, too. Here's my ID," I interjected, waving the document at him.

"Wow, you speak Arabic well," he said. "Where did you learn it? And this ID could easily be fake."

The idea of an impostor with fake Syrian identification papers who speaks in an authentic Idlibi dialect was, apparently, easier for the armed man to accept than the idea of an unveiled Syrian woman journalist.

After a series of clashes like these with soldiers at checkpoints—many of which caused my male chaperones great distress—I decided to start covering my hair with the Palestinian *keffiyeh*, carefully wrapping it around my head in the way Arab men traditionally do to protect themselves from the desert sun. The change didn't help to lower my profile, however, so in 2015, I started to arrange the *keffiyeh* around my head as if it were a full headscarf, covering my hair completely. By the time I left Syria for southern Turkey for good in 2016, I was wearing a long, dark coat along with a formal, regular hijab.

The only way I could challenge those dim colors while living in Syria was by wearing bright underwear and colored pins on my scarf. They were tiny dots of color, yes, but they made me feel better. I didn't quit using my expensive antiwrinkle cream either. "There's a helicopter hovering above our heads and a barrel bomb could be breaking both of us into pieces at any minute, so why the hell are you worried about aging?" my husband at the time, Mahmoud, would ask. There's a chance we may live through this war and come out of it in one piece, I thought. And if we do, all of the hard work I put into sustaining my skin's elegance will have paid off. I want to live a long life, and to write about what I witnessed so that no one will forget what happened here. And I want to have supple, crease-free skin, too.

During those years, barrel bombs were toying recklessly with my existence.

The regime cut off all roads to the city in 2016, foreshadowing the upcoming siege and blocking the entry of food, medical supplies, and fuel. (At the time, Mahmoud bought a motorbike to reduce his consumption of fuel, which had become rare and expensive. He constantly dreamed about fruits and vegetables because he was sick of eating canned food.)

However, I was fighting on a different front, an internal one. Who was Zaina? Was Zaina the obedient, dependent, modestly dressed woman who cooks delicious feasts in huge pots for her guests? Or was Zaina the powerful, busy, liberated woman who challenged the society around her by becoming its first female journalist? The real answer is that the two women were taking turns without overlapping. The first emerged while she was inside Syria, and the second was liberated one meter away from the HOŞGELDINIZ (welcome to Turkey) sign at the border.

Helmets and bulletproof vests are common in my country: they're used for protection by male reporters stationed at the front lines, or as accessories for people to take photos with. Mine were mostly needed when I went shopping for groceries, or when I filmed from hospitals and schools. Those were the most dangerous places to report from, because they were continually targeted by the Bashar al-Assad regime and its allies, the Russian forces.

I have two particularly precious photos—souvenirs, you could say—of myself in a bulletproof vest. I was with my friend Hamoudi Bitar in the suburbs of Latakia. He was only twenty-one years old at the time, an ambitious architecture student, and he was acting as my fixer, helping me to arrange meetings and travel logistics. We'd just passed some extremist-controlled areas in the Jisr al-Shogour area. Even though we claimed we were cousins, we faced great difficulty when crossing through checkpoints. Hamoudi, in particular, had to bear the brunt of the questioning—why was he traveling on his own with a young woman?

After we'd finished the reporting trip, we drove along the beautiful mountains of Akrad, but I started to feel overwhelmingly depressed. I was where I belonged—my homeland—but I could not accept that I had to be this dependent on someone else. I felt weak. Hamoudi sensed my sadness, and suddenly stopped the car at the edge of the road. "Get out of the car and bring your camera," he said firmly. I thought someone was following us, or that he'd spotted a land mine, until he said, "Take off your headscarf. Enjoy the air in your hair and be yourself," and began to snap some photos of me.

PHOTO BY HAMOUDI BITAR.

Hamoudi was a conservative man from my city, Idlib. All of the women in his family were veiled, and he wouldn't propose to a woman who didn't wear a headscarf. However, in that moment, he supported me, risking his own life to give me a few precious minutes of relief.

In September 2013, a year later, Hamoudi was killed while filming a battle on the outskirts of our city. The journalistic norm of "keeping a distance with your sources" is, to me, an abstract concept, as removed from reality as "living alone on an island." My sources are my schoolmates, relatives, and family members. And those death counts flashing on your screens contain my first lovers, teachers, neighbors, and friends.

During those years in Syria, I felt like I'd been floating, with no past and no stable present. It was easier to deal with that uncertainty when I was in the crossfires of the war. When you face death on a daily basis, you don't plan for tomorrow. Why would you, if it might not come? Wasting your time is not an option. You go about life, knowing you're lucky to be alive. Sometimes when I made plans with friends for the following week, they'd casually add, "If God allows us to stay alive until then." But beyond all of the wreckage are some of my most precious memories. Expecting death gave me the luxury of being an adventurer, even an irresponsible one.

I still considered Aleppo my home. The house I lived in was situated less than 165 yards away from the Syrian regime's barracks, which meant that it was on an active front line. It was a charming house compared with the dwellings of the rest of that part of the city, despite the bullet and shrapnel marks on its walls. Mahmoud and I replaced what was left of the glass windows of the house with compressed plastic to remove the potential danger that flying broken glass could inflict upon us. Death, however, is inevitable in Syria, with or without plastic windows.

It's possible to get used to witnessing daily destruction in your immediate surroundings. I once saw a coffee vendor serving customers while rescue workers belonging to the White Helmets, a civil defense unit, were collecting body parts in front of his shop after an attack. Another time, I had a trivial discussion with a friend shortly after witnessing a bleeding, injured little girl cry out in shock after a missile strike on her school. I cleaned her blood from my car while asking casually, "What do you want to have for lunch today?"

Only now, after stepping away, do I realize how deep the trauma must be for a person to be able to go on with life after witnessing such horrific scenes. When you suddenly stop being in danger, you begin to feel the burden of the trauma you've experienced.

Toughness and resilience aren't unusual for most of the Syrian women I know, especially those who, like me, come from closed-minded communities. We challenge the traditions we were raised with. And we were raised to believe we should be nothing but feminine, likable dependents. We were even made to feel guilty for being harassed on the streets of our hometowns. After deciding to revolt against the patriarchal society I lived in, I had to deal with the consequences of my rebellion. There were many. "You will go to hell." "Surely, you will end up a spinster." "You will ruin the family's reputation and destroy our honor." "You will bring shame to the city of Idlib." These are some of the attitudes that I had to fight.

I have committed all the sins that could potentially be committed in such an awful war zone. I am a Syrian; a woman who lived in the most masculine of spaces; a journalist in a land of warlords; a secularist living among different kinds of extremists and foreign jihadists; and a human rights defender among war criminals, some claiming to be fighting for the other side, and some claiming to be pro-freedom, on my side. All of these combined meant I was far more scared of being assassinated than of being randomly killed by the Syrian army. I would be a *great* target, someone a fighter would be proud to have killed. After my murder, the killer would be guaranteed a place in heaven, where they'd be gifted with pretty girls. They would be a proud patriot because they would have eliminated a voice that threatened the image of Assad's Syria.

One of the few common threads that run through the different parts of Syria (including territories controlled by the Kurds, ISIL, the Assad regime, rebels, Turks, or al-Qaeda) is that if you are deemed a propagandist or a traitor, you must be killed. In my weakest moments, I couldn't even share stories, photos, or bits and pieces of news on my social media accounts. I had to harshly censor myself. My loved ones volunteered to do so on my behalf as well. They would read what I intended to make public, then tell me to either publish or not publish the content. Then I started taking notes of the things that I couldn't make public—at least for now. Over the past four years, I have barely had ten articles published, even though I have written eighty pages of outlines and notes saved in a file on my laptop entitled "Can't Be Published."

Despite having taken all of these precautions, I was still deemed reckless. I was still risking my ability to stay inside Syria for the "useless right of self-expression." While I showed my support for the *Charlie Hebdo* journalists who were murdered by Islamist terrorists in Paris in 2015, for example, other activists in Aleppo were demonstrating against the magazine. They set fire to *Charlie Hebdo*'s emblem because its journalists had once insulted the Prophet Muhammad. Shouldn't we be glad that they were massacred and that their families were suffering, then? I had to be the one and only voice against that sort of extremism, riding against the tide, harming not only myself by expressing my controversial opinions but also my family and friends.

Being a journalist and an activist was never easy. Before the uprising, I had been allowed to work as an activist specializing in gender equality and women's rights, most of the time. But when I pursued an internship opportunity in 2008 that would have allowed me to dig deeper into Syrian civil society, the military security forces interrogated me, giving me clear orders not to get involved in anything related to human rights. In 2015, I couldn't even show my support for a homosexual man who had been thrown by rebels from the rooftop of the Al-Bayan hospital tower in Aleppo for his "crime" of being gay. Doing so could have gotten me killed, as a lesson for those daring to disrespect tradition and religion. In the best-case scenario, I'd have been given a warning and told to disappear to avoid being captured. In the past seven years, I have made major sacrifices and paid heavy costs for what was supposed to be freedom.

And yet still I'm self-censoring. I was first kicked out of regime-held Syria for writing about the violations government forces committed during peaceful demonstrations, and then from Syria itself by the rebels who were rebelling against the regime. In both situations, I had to choose between instant freedom and being able to continue my work in Syria, which at the time included helping citizen journalists, training women, and producing stories about life beyond front lines and war. The option between the two was obvious. "Keep quiet so you can go on": I heard this sort of thing from friends and family every day, before posting on my Facebook page, after deleting the post, before sleeping, and after I woke up (when I always felt particularly depressed, because I'd realize I was turning into a person I couldn't recognize).

There were, nonetheless, advantages to being a woman journalist. If I wasn't a woman, I wouldn't have been invited to the closed segregated women's community of Idlib. And I certainly wouldn't have been able to film the women there moving about freely in their houses and as they worked. I was called *hurma* repeatedly during this time. This Arabic word carries with it multiple insulting connotations: *haram*, or "forbidden"; a form of weakness; someone who is dependent; a minor; a man's tool for pleasure; his property; his possession; her gender role; and, finally, the eternal circle that a woman shouldn't break—fertility and giving birth.

Because I was given access to these women, I stopped being bothered by the word *hurma*. Instead, I was choosing to be *hurma* to be able to capture their stories. I was able to obtain access to a very private gynecological clinic in Aleppo city, which men are not allowed to enter. I went in with my camera, and I was terrified at first. It was a place where women covered themselves up in black from head to toe. And their male relatives could have had me killed for showing their faces on camera (to preserve their "honor," women should be kept hidden from the public eye).

While I was at the clinic, a fifteen-year-old girl wearing a black face veil walked in with her mother. She lifted her scarf to reveal the bright, youthful face of a teenager. Her mother then told the doctor that her daughter had been married for six weeks, but wasn't yet pregnant. She was worried. "What's *wrong* with her?" she demanded. The girl started to blush and looked at the floor. Her mother requested a "pregnancy catalyst," something that would "please" her husband.

Another woman in her midforties visited the clinic with her pregnant daughter-in-law. She whispered to the doctor, "I want to have a baby, too. If I get pregnant, my husband will sleep in my house more, instead of going to his new, younger wife's home."

These stories aren't surprising to me, not only because I come from a community where such anxieties are common but also because I have witnessed firsthand that even empowered women activists who challenge the regime, their families, and tradition voluntarily turn into *hareem* (plural of *hurma*) after getting married.

I was disheartened, though, when a very brave Syrian woman citizen journalist—the only female videographer in northern Syria—got engaged to a married man who was already a father. She didn't mind being a second wife in her early twenties. She wasn't even bothered that he was dividing the nights between the two of his wives, until his first wife found out about her and then divorced him.

From this particular story I learned that being a brave and successful woman journalist doesn't mean that you're necessarily more of a feminist and less accepting of patriarchy. Her example and all the challenges I've faced make me more determined to focus on women in the work that I do. As a consequence of this war, Syrian women are now being stereotyped more than ever: in both local and international media, they're mostly portrayed as victims and dependents who need to be helped. I want to fight those stereotypes.

It's been two years since I left that version of Syria, and I'm still struggling to find my voice and my freedom again. I'm a thirty-two-year-old journalist, but I've reported freely for only two years of my life, between 2010 and 2012, as the uprising escalated into a brutal civil war. The years 2012 and beyond constitute an awful chapter of my personal and professional experience.

I have survived extraordinarily painful conflicts—both external and internal—to be the woman I am today. A man would have been able to do it all quite easily, while I and other women have had to fight for our achievements. And I don't want my daughter to have to do the same.

To be frank, if I were sent back in time to the age of fifteen, when I had that very first argument about putting on the hijab, I wouldn't do anything differently. I would choose to recommit all of the sins that have accompanied my being born into the original sin of womanhood. I would still choose to become a journalist, a secularist, and a human rights defender. I would choose to travel along this same path. Every thought I can change or eye I can open to help people see the difficult lives the women in my homeland live—and the inequality they experience—makes this battle a worthy one.

TRANSITION

Syria Undone

Zeina Karam

January 2011, Syria. The air was thick with cigarette smoke. Men clutching whiskey glasses crowded around the roulette table as the sounds of laughter and coins jingling in slot machines mixed with the soothing voice of the Lebanese singer Fairuz. I was at the newly opened Ocean Club casino in Damascus. Young, smartly dressed Syrians standing around one corner of the bar spoke excitedly about the future.

No one in that room could have imagined that just over a month later, protests would erupt nationwide and the country would plunge into a catastrophic war that would kill hundreds of thousands of people and send millions of others fleeing, many of them drowning in the Mediterranean before reaching safety in Europe. I would spend the next years covering the conflict, chronicling the slow, agonizing death of a country.

My life as I knew it would be transformed.

I think of my life in terms of before and after the Syria war—the latter generally referring to the time when my work overtook almost every other aspect of it. As the war intensified, I became entirely consumed with its coverage, constantly distracted by updates and breaking news. The question of whether I, or we, were doing enough to convey the tragedy in Syria to the rest of the world tormented me.

At night when I can't sleep, my thoughts are often filled with

Syria. Sometimes it's images of babies twitching and gasping for breath. Other times it's a beheading. Sometimes my brain is kept awake simply trying to connect the dots and make sense of whatever dizzying events we had covered that day.

As a Lebanese, covering the war in neighboring Syria was a deeply personal experience—not only because I had lived through my own country's civil war but also because, unlike many of the foreign correspondents covering Syria who had never been to the country before the war, I had been visiting Syria ever since I was a little girl.

My connection to Syria began when I was about ten years old, when my mother drove my sister and me three hours from Beirut to Damascus to visit my aunt, who lived there at the time. One of my earliest memories of Syria is packing the car at my aunt's request with bread, Kleenex, and toilet paper, which were among the basic commodities constantly in shortage in the country. "Bring as much as you can," she told us, knowing that the security guards at the Syrian border would help themselves to some of it—in addition to any cigarette boxes our driver had on hand—as their *baksheesh*, or "tip." It was the 1980s, and Syria, under Hafez al-Assad, was a drab, socialist-style police state, isolated and economically troubled.

I was filled with a mix of fear and anticipation as we left Beirut, driving through the Lebanese mountains into the Syrian capital. Even as a child, I understood enough to know that I was stepping into a place completely different from home, a place where people spoke in hushed tones and where one had to be careful about what was said. Assad's portrait was plastered everywhere—at the immigration hall on the border, on the wall behind the cash register at the grocer's, on buildings, and on car windshields.

I remember walking down the old, covered souk called Hamidieh, taking in the smell of soaps, spices, and perfumes and watching, transfixed, as people walked up and down the maze of narrow alleys and cobblestone streets. I also recall strolling by the Citadel of Damascus, a large medieval palace locally known as Qalaat Dimashq, and buying Damascene sweets from a nearby seller who insisted on knowing whether we were from east or west Beirut, as if that would immediately determine our religion and political affiliation.

Later, as a university student, I visited Syria a few more times. Syria then was an occupying force in Lebanon with some thirty-five thousand troops stationed in the country. There was—particularly among my Lebanese Christian friends—deep-seated hatred for Syria. They told me I was crazy to go there, even crazier for liking it. I told them they were being narrow-minded, and then, inevitably, we'd argue. I had my own conflicting feelings about Syria, but I couldn't understand why they were unable to separate the country's politics from its people—why they couldn't differentiate between the Syrian soldier at a checkpoint in Lebanon and the potential kindness of an ordinary Syrian in Damascus.

On those trips to Syria, I was able to discover more of the country's rich cultural heritage, visiting sites like the ancient Christian town of Maaloula, the Roman ruins of Palmyra, and the Krak des Chevaliers Crusader castle. Those memories would come back to haunt me years later as the country plunged into war and those places became etched in blood.

Within a short time after I started working at the Associated Press in 1996, I expressed an interest in going to Syria and spending time learning about its people and politics. I couldn't wait to step into the country as a reporter and write its stories. It became my beat, taking me to new places like Aleppo, Latakia, and Homs. I felt lucky, and my ties to the country grew stronger as I soaked in its rich history and culture and made new friends.

In June 2000, less than three weeks after Israel pulled out of south Lebanon following an eighteen-year occupation, I was on my way back from the area where UN experts were demarcating the border with Israel when my boss called from the Beirut bureau. "There are reports that Hafez al-Assad has died. Don't come back to the office, drive straight to Damascus. We'll send your clothes later," he said. It was the end of an era. One of the Arab world's most enduring dictators, known for his aloof, iron-fisted ruling style and his transformation of Syria into a regional powerhouse, was dead at sixty-nine.

You could have almost heard a pin drop at the border crossing when I got there two hours later, one of the first journalists to arrive in Syria. Inside one of the rooms at the immigration building, I caught a glimpse of a man covering his face, and realized he was weeping silently. "*Tyattamna* (We have been orphaned)," said the young security guard searching our car when my taxi driver offered his condolences. Although he was hated by many, Assad, having ruled Syria for thirty years, was the only leader many had ever known. A Syria without him seemed unthinkable.

I was apprehensive, thinking about what the next hours would bring. Would there be violence, perhaps a coup? Syria had had a long history of military coups until Assad, then an air force general, seized power in 1970. It was a well-known fact that his son, Bashar, who trained in London as an eye doctor before he was recalled home in 1994, was being groomed for the post, but would that play out in a peaceful transition?

Within hours, however, new posters showing the late president with his son, Bashar, appeared on car windshields in Damascus, along with black ribbons tied to car radio antennas. "Dr. Bashar is now our hope," a woman told me on the street that night, where convoys of Syrians were honking their horns in a show of support and allegiance to the younger Assad. Among the new generation, there was some hope that he would loosen the shackles and inject new energy into the country.

Foreign journalists descended on Damascus to cover Hafez al-Assad's funeral, which was to be the largest in Syria's modern history. Among those journalists was the man who would, years later, become my husband.

He was a press photographer who also worked at the AP, although I hadn't met him yet. Our editors had assigned us a story about the late president's exiled brother, Rifaat al-Assad; there were reports that he might return to Syria to challenge Bashar's claim to leadership, and we were to investigate whether he still had any following in the country. Together, the photographer and I set off for Qardaha, the Assad family hometown about 125 miles northwest of Damascus, where Hafez al-Assad was to be buried.

As a European, my future husband was not familiar with the sensitivities of the subject, so he followed my lead as I set out nervously to interview people in Rifaat's hometown, knowing that mere mention of his name could get us in trouble. We must have approached more than two dozen people, out of whom only two agreed to talk to us; our quest eventually attracted a crowd of government informers who tagged along, listening in to our conversations. As soon as we finished our interviews, we fled the scene as fast as we could and headed back to the hotel. After struggling for hours to find a satellite phone signal, we finally climbed up to the roof to file the story.

My husband and I married ten years later, in 2010. To this day, we remember with fondness the panic over that story that bonded us, including the red-faced, angry hotel manager who came racing up the stairs after hearing about the two journalists on the roof. I guess it set the tone for the conflict that would take over our lives many years later.

Over the next several days, the Syrian parliament cleared the way for Bashar al-Assad to assume the presidency, amending the constitution to lower the minimum age for presidents from forty to thirty-four—Bashar's age at the time. The move was seen by critics as an outrageous break with constitutional laws and one that reinforced the perception that Syria somehow belonged to the Assad family.

A new chapter in Syria's history was beginning.

While he continued with his father's political repression, Assad pursued economic liberalization, transforming the country's climate within the next decade. The more time I spent in Damascus, the more it felt like home, and indeed, some people pointed to the "Lebanonization" of Syria at that time. The Damascus I left before the war was a place buzzing with opportunity. As foreign banks and universities proliferated, young Lebanese executives took up key positions in Syria—an unthinkable prospect only a few years back—and the city was brimming with tourists crowding cafés, pubs, and shopping malls. Beautiful historic houses converted into boutique hotels mushroomed across the old city, catering to wealthy visitors and the expanding rich crowd.

The inauguration of the Ocean Club casino on Christmas Eve in 2010, the first in Damascus since the 1970s, was a major sign of Syria's new openness. Patrons from Syria's privileged elite and middle classes, along with some Arab tourists, flocked to the building near the airport, despite opposition from conservative lawmakers and other critics. It was a far cry from the rigid, closed Damascus of my childhood.

Outside, the world was also changing. A fruit seller in Tunisia called Mohamed Bouazizi had set himself on fire in an act of desperation on December 17, 2010, killing himself and setting off a revolution that caught swiftly across the region in what came to be known as the Arab Spring.

Still, when protests broke out in Dara'a, a city in southern Syria, in March 2011, I was deeply skeptical that they would amount to anything significant. I was in Cairo covering the aftermath of the uprising in Egypt and assisting our regional bureau with coverage of the war in Libya. An Egyptian colleague burst excitedly into the newsroom to announce that the Arab Spring had arrived in Syria.

"Nah, I don't think so," I replied coolly.

In part, my disbelief was rooted in a failed protest only a few weeks earlier. I had gone to Damascus in anticipation of a Day of Rage that activists had been organizing on social media networks against Assad's rule. But the rain-soaked city's streets were deserted, and except for the plainclothes security agents stationed protectively in key areas and on street corners, not a single person had showed up. It was largely due to fear and intimidation, of course, but many people also felt wary of rocking the boat after having seen Libya, and to a lesser extent Egypt, descend into chaos following their own uprisings.

There was also the paradox of Assad himself. As one long-time Syria observer told me early on in the uprising, many Syrians did not necessarily hate Bashar. In fact, many Syrian youth loved him, they were convinced he was an instrument of change, held back by an old guard reluctant to yield ground. A few days later, as the demonstrations in Dara'a escalated, I flew back from Cairo to Beirut and took a taxi to Damascus, still somewhat skeptical that the seemingly snowballing protests were anything like those that had brought down longtime dictators in Egypt, Tunisia, and Libya.

Any skepticism soon vanished, however, after I reached the drought-parched south along with a few other local and foreign journalists. Syrian forces were reportedly using water cannons, batons, and gunfire to beat back protesters in Dara'a who were defiantly marching and shouting slogans against corruption, calling for more political freedom. Checkpoints throughout the city were manned by soldiers in camouflage uniforms and plainclothes security agents with rifles. Antiterrorism police wearing dark blue uniforms were also out on the streets. An ambulance was parked on the side of a road leading to the old city, its windshield smashed. A burst of semiautomatic gunfire echoed in the old center.

When the other journalists and I tried to enter Dara'a's old city, where most of the violence was unfolding, we were turned back and instructed to wait outside the town's ruling Baath Party's head office. A uniformed, heavily mustachioed army major eventually showed up and told us we had to leave right away. "As you can see, everything here is back to normal and it is over," he told us before we were led out of the city, escorted by two security vehicles.

Back in Damascus, pro- and antigovernment crowds were clashing outside the historic Umayyad Mosque, hitting one another with fists and leather belts. That night, I heard that two colleagues from Reuters were missing, and that several journalists had been detained or expelled. I continued working, calling contacts in Dara'a from the privacy of my hotel room in the capital, half expecting security agents to barge in and haul me away any minute. I was very much aware that the breaking news I was putting out was being quoted on Arab TV networks and might get me expelled—or worse. It is at times like this when a journalist has to choose between self-censoring to stay in the government's good graces and continuing to report the facts as they come, risking detainment or expulsion. I never considered the first option.

A few days later I sat down with a group of Syrians to watch Assad's highly anticipated first speech since the unrest had started. There was some hope at that point that somehow the president would strike the right tone or find the right words to temper the protests and stop what by now seemed to be a sure descent into chaos. In an hour-long speech in front of parliament, he quickly dashed any such expectations, blaming two weeks of popular fury on a foreign conspiracy and fabrications in the media. I glanced at a Syrian colleague sitting next to me. "What do you think?" I asked her. She took her time to answer me, her eyes fixed on the screen where members of parliament were standing up, clapping, and cheering Assad's speech.

"I think we have entered a dark tunnel, may God be with Syria," she said, her eyes still fixed on the spectacle on TV.

I had been reporting from Damascus for nine days when the dreaded call came from an information ministry official informing me that I was no longer welcome in the country. I had less than an hour to leave—or else.

I knew there would be no sense in arguing or negotiating. Within twenty minutes, my photographer colleague and I had packed our belongings, paid the hotel, and arranged for the car that would take us back to Beirut. I was filled with a sense of foreboding as we sped down the Beirut Road toward the Lebanese border. We kept turning around nervously to see if we were being followed until we crossed over into Lebanon.

I learned in the following days that I was blacklisted in Syria, which meant that my name was placed at the border crossing as a persona non grata, and that like many other journalists I would be banned from entering the country for the foreseeable future. I was stunned, and could not imagine how I would continue reporting without being able to travel there. But I was not alone. The government restricted media access to the country, refusing to grant visas to most journalists and expelling those already inside. Flashpoint areas like Dara'a and others were largely sealed off, with telephone calls going through only sporadically. Within a few days, even my Lebanese SIM card was blocked from calling Syria. I was astounded by the scope of the clampdown; for many, it harked back to the early eighties, when Bashar's father, Hafez, had crushed an uprising by Islamists in the city of Hama, killing thousands. That time, the government's actions had been almost completely hidden from the world. This time, there were smartphones and social media.

Covering the war from neighboring Lebanon would become the new normal for me. Because of my extensive reporting from inside Syria for many years prior to the war, I already had a list of contacts to tap, although security concerns meant that very few Syrians were willing to talk to me on the phone. Skype, deemed a more secure option, became the go-to social network for communication. One source led to another, and in a relatively short time my colleagues and I had built an enormous list of contacts that we all shared at the Beirut bureau.

Over the years, the list dwindled. One of my saddest moments was scrolling down that list of Skype contacts a few years later and reading the notes we had typed next to the names: "killed"; "imprisoned"; "went to Germany"; "joined al-Qaeda"; etc.

Videos posted on the internet by people inside Syria became key to our coverage and were often our only visual window into events unfolding in the country. That also meant it was ten times more difficult to verify information and make sure that any user-generated content we were putting out was an accurate portrayal of what was happening on the ground. In the early days, we watched, incredulously, as exultant crowds of protesters danced arm in arm, singing *"Yalla irhal, ya* Bashar!"—a simple yet power-ful lyric translating to "Come on, Bashar, leave"—to the beat of a drum. Eventually, as the government escalated its response and the protests became an armed uprising, the videos turned into an endless stream of horror showing protesters being gunned down, massacred victims in pools of blood, villagers digging through destroyed buildings with their bare hands for survivors, and children with grave wounds from heavy bombardment.

As the opposition took over chunks of territory in northern Syria, journalists began entering the country from Turkey, cross-ing the border illegally at enormous risk of arrest, kidnapping, injury, or death. Many have paid the price with their lives. As a Lebanese, I didn't want to jeopardize my chance of being al-lowed back into Damascus someday, and chose not to make the illegal trip from the north despite my overriding desire to be in-side Syria again. Like many others, I continued covering the conflict from the outside. I have no doubt missed out as a jour-nalist on a crucial aspect of the war by not being able to visit opposition-held areas, but in retrospect, as the Syrian army and its allies clawed back most of the rebel-held territory, I think it was the right decision. Many of my colleagues continue to be refused entry to Damascus.

By mid-2012, the war had significantly escalated. The weapons that the Syrian government used in their attempts to crush the uprising progressed from guns to artillery to helicopters and war planes to indiscriminate helicopter-dropped barrel bombs, or "barrels of death," as the Syrians called them. Rebel groups proliferated and got progressively more radicalized as the conflict went on. In the summer of 2012, the fighting spread to the northern city of Aleppo. Syria's largest and arguably most beautiful ancient city split into two halves, a rebel-held eastern part and a government-controlled western part. Death crossings, sniper corridors, and hatred separated the two sides. It was painfully similar to my own country's divide during the Lebanese civil war, and I have often thought back to that vendor in Damascus who wanted to know whether we were from east or west Beirut. History has a strange way of repeating itself.

As the war progressed, so did the way we covered it. Skype gave way to WhatsApp, Telegram, and Facebook Messenger. It seemed every rebel group, every militia, and every activist had their own social media channel. Statements, comments, and videos were posted on Twitter, Facebook, and YouTube. I went to sleep with my phone and reached out for it as soon as I woke up. Almost inevitably, there would be news of some massacre or development that would make my heart drop and jolt me into action. I would often leave work after a twelve-hour shift, only to head back into the office later or get back in front of the computer as soon as I arrived home. I missed out on weddings and birthdays and time spent with family and close friends.

Being a journalist as well, my husband understood the life of a reporter, especially one covering the Middle East. But it wasn't easy for him either. I took my phone with me everywhere. It lit up with notifications at the dinner table, at the movies, and on vacations. He joked that it was stuck to my hand like a magnet. I argued that I couldn't ignore contacts who were risking their lives to talk to me, or that this particular news development was too important. He would look at me, shaking his head like I was crazy. Privately, I struggled with my guilt. Was he right? Was I so immersed and focused on the war that I was starting to think and behave as though nothing else mattered? Would it make a difference? Would anyone remember?

It seemed like every time the conflict appeared to settle into a routine, there would be some huge development that would re-shuffle the deck, pushing Syria back up to the top of the global news cycle. On June 10, 2014, we had just landed in Switzer-land, where we were planning to visit relatives of my husband, when the breaking news flashed on my phone: "The Islamic State group overruns Iraqi city of Mosul, tens of thousands of Iraqi civilians fleeing in terror."

Another nightmare had begun.

Less than three weeks later, the Islamic State group declared the establishment of an Islamic State, or caliphate, in territories it controlled in Iraq and Syria, demanding allegiance from Mus-lims worldwide. Raqqa, in northeastern Syria, became the ca-liphate's de facto capital.

Despite being accustomed to the endless stream of bad news and gruesome videos from Syria, we were not prepared for the brutality of the Islamic State group, which publicized their be-headings, crucifixions, burning, and drowning of their oppo-nents. The dangers for journalists covering the conflict also multiplied. By the end of 2013, dozens of reporters had gone missing or were kidnapped in Syria.

One August night in 2014, I was woken up by an editor in New York, inquiring about a video that had just surfaced on the internet.

"Sorry to call you up so late, but could you take a look at this video I sent you, please?" It was disturbing, he warned.

I was alone at home. I fired up my laptop and clicked on the link, which led me to a video claiming to show the beheading of American journalist James Foley, who had been missing in Syria for more than a year. It was a hot summer night, but I was shiver-ing with cold as I watched the masked Islamic State fighter dressed in black brandishing a knife next to Foley, who was kneeling in the desert in an orange jumpsuit. Struggling to put all personal feelings aside, I typed up the news alert and clicked SEND.

The Islamic State group's barbaric activities became the subject of global fascination and dominated the news, sadly overshadowing the Syria war itself and the suffering of millions of besieged, displaced, and bereaved civilians. Freelance journalists complained that if their story did not have an Islamic State element to it, editors weren't interested.

I remember around that time interviewing an activist who ran an opposition radio station in Idlib for an hour and a half. Afterward, he thanked me for taking an interest, adding: "No one thinks of us as real people anymore. The world thinks everyone in Syria is a walking Daeshi."

I was once again gripped by worry that we were not adequately reflecting the situation in Syria.

We were being pulled in so many directions all the time, from the global catastrophe of the Syrian civil war and the resulting migrant crisis in Europe to the deadly terrorist attacks around the world that were being plotted and claimed by the Islamic State group.

Among the Islamic State's targets were ancient archaeological sites in Iraq and Syria, including the magnificent site of Nimrud in Iraq and the two-thousand-year-old temples in Syria's Palmyra. The group used sledgehammers, bulldozers, and explosives to destroy them, erasing history. The unprecedented scale of heritage destruction was, of course, no more painful than the wanton killing of hundreds of thousands of Iraqis and Syrians. But there was something so cruel about this collective demolition of civilization that left us—particularly journalists from the region reporting on the loss of our heritage—feeling utterly desperate and hopeless.

I was eventually allowed back into Damascus, very briefly in 2012 and then for longer visits in the past few years. For the casual visitor, the city appeared to be more or less the same, relatively untouched by the war. From my perspective, it was completely changed.

Almost none of the people I knew from before the war were still there. Old friends and colleagues had long moved on and settled abroad. People I would have visited before the war were now exiled or imprisoned. There were few young men in Damascus—they were all either fighting with the army or had moved away in search of a life outside Syria. The city was full of internally displaced people from Deir ez-Zor, Aleppo, and other violence-plagued cities. It seemed like everyone was grieving, having lost someone or something to the war. In a way, I was also grieving for the Syria I had known. Traffic snaked in long lines through military checkpoints, blast walls surrounded government buildings, and streets were deserted at night, when the sounds of nearby gunfire and shelling were loudest. Random mortars fired from rebel-held suburbs crashed unannounced into residential neighborhoods.

In April 2016 I traveled to Palmyra, days after Islamic State militants withdrew and thirteen years after my last trip as a tourist. The Roman ruins that had once provided the backdrop for magical summer concerts were sealed off as Russian military teams worked to dismantle land mines left by Islamic State militants. Instead of the European and Asian tourists who filled the place before the war, young Russian soldiers were taking selfies with Palmyra's towering citadel. The nearby town was an uninhabitable wreck. People were coming back to salvage whatever souvenirs and home appliances they could from their destroyed homes. It was a scene that had sadly become all too common across Iraq and Syria. "Our country was a paradise, how did this happen?" a woman asked me after finding her home relatively intact but completely looted.

In May 2017, in the town of Zabadani, near the border with Lebanon, I met a Syrian couple and their ten-year-old daughter who had just arrived for the first time in five years to check on their home. So immense was the destruction in the town that they were having a hard time locating their apartment amid the endless vista of rubble and collapsed buildings. The woman walked over the mounds of rubble and abandoned buildings in disbelief, wiping away tears.

Later, standing inside their charred apartment picking through heaps of trash to find family photos and other mementos, I asked her husband, a forty-six-year-old builder, what he planned to do now. He gazed at the horizon, his eyes watering, and said he would rebuild their home, of course.

"What's a home without neighbors and a town without people, though, is it still home?" he asked. He then smiled sadly and answered his own question: "They will come back, everything needs time and patience."

I felt a lump form in my throat as I tried to hold back my own emotions. Hearing the sadness in this wonderful man's voice as he tried desperately to hang on to hope, I thought of the millions of other ordinary Syrians whose lives had similarly been uprooted in the most brutal of ways, and who were still confused as to how it all happened. There were some who had faith in their president and genuinely believed their country was a victim of a conspiracy; some who, in retrospect, would have never taken part in any antigovernment protests had they known it would lead to this devastation; and some who still believed it was all worth it for a little taste of freedom. Did we do them all justice in our reporting?

On September 21, 2016, a group of AP colleagues and I drove from Beirut to Damascus as guests of the Syrian government. After years of unanswered requests, we finally had an interview with President Bashar al-Assad. I wondered how it would feel to meet in person the man whose rise to power I had chronicled from the very beginning, and who was now at the center of a bloody civil war that had killed close to half a million people and uprooted half of the country's population.

On the day of the interview, a palace car picked us up from

the hotel to drive us to the Muhajireen Palace, a relatively modest white building in Damascus where the president often works and where the interview was to take place. There, at the entrance, was the president, wearing an elegant dark suit and a smile. The battle for Aleppo was raging and there were reports of children dying from malnutrition in the besieged rebel-held suburbs of Damascus only a short drive away from where we were. All that seemed far away here in this beautifully decorated compound. Not surprisingly, Assad projected confidence and composure in the interview. While acknowledging some mistakes, he contested any excesses by his troops, denied his forces were besieging Aleppo, and said Syria will bounce back as a more unified state, pledging to rebuild the ruined country.

Following the interview, we exchanged pleasantries and the president shook my hand with a smile, before posing for the standard, postinterview photos with all of us. There was such a strong disconnect that the war outside almost seemed like it was happening in another nation. I wondered, standing next to the fifty-one-year-old president in this almost surreal setting, when, and how, all this would end for him and the country.

I sometimes think about that night many years ago at the Ocean Club casino and the sense of excitement that prevailed among the crowd of mostly rich, privileged Syrians. I did not think of it at the time, but in retrospect, perhaps there were some clues to the tragedy that would befall Syria.

The glittering casino was celebrated as an indicator of liberalization—a showcase for Syria's gradual shedding of its socialist past. Looking back, I cannot help but think it emphasized Syria's classist divide and the glaring disparity between rich and poor, which was, after all, one of the driving forces of the revolution. It was no surprise, then, that the casino became an early target of the uprising, shuttered in the first weeks of unrest to appease critics after an Islamic backlash. Perhaps Syria's disorderly shift to a more open-market economy amid the rampant corruption and cronyism that defined the political system was too quick, creating opportunities for ambitious businessmen linked to the Syrian political elite, even as it deepened the dangerous societal divisions.

In my job, I frequently get asked about when and how the conflict will end, and whether Syria can ever come back as a unified state. It's terrifying to think about the millions of Syrians who have abandoned their country over the past seven years, many of whom will likely never return. It terrifies me to think of all the people who have died, and all the abandoned cities lying in ruins.

No, I do not think it can go back to what it was, and that is why I feel so fortunate to have known Syria before the war. But I know that one day all this will be over, and people will pick up their lives and rebuild. They will try to move on, just like they did in Lebanon following fifteen years of war.

It will not be the same country or the same people, and there will always be ugly scars, but just like the builder in Zabadani told me about rebuilding his gutted family home: "Everything needs time and patience."

An Orange Bra in Riyadh

Donna Abu-Nasr

When I saw the women selling underwear, I choked up. The depth of my feelings took me by surprise. At the time, I had been a reporter for more than twenty years and thought that two decades of covering conflict in the Middle East had toughened me up. But on that day in January 2012, as I stood outside a lingerie store in a mall in the Saudi port city of Jeddah watching Saudi women finally do what only men had until then been allowed to do, I felt overwhelmed with pride and joy.

Before late 2011, Saudi women weren't allowed to work in stores, so they had to buy their bras and panties from men. This was both embarrassing and impractical for them. A prominent Saudi journalist had brought the issue to my attention back in 2002, when I was still a reporter with the Associated Press, telling me it was something his female relatives had to grapple with. Women were forced to cover up in public, wearing long abayas that hid most of their bodies, while salesmen had the power to undress them with their eyes.

I understood what he meant by this when I walked into a lingerie store in a Riyadh mall in October 2002, a few months after I had started covering Saudi Arabia. I saw a woman totally covered in black with only her eyes showing pick up a lacy orange bra and approach the Syrian salesman. In a whisper, she asked if he had it in 36C.

"Did you say 36C?" the salesman asked, loudly enough for everyone in the store to hear.

"I don't know. I think that's my size," said the woman.

He gave her chest a once-over.

"The past changes," he responded, and advised her to buy a larger size.

I was astonished that such an exchange could take place in public in conservative Saudi Arabia. But when I started to talk to other women about it, they recounted even more shocking stories. One woman told me that a salesman had once held up a pair of panties and, eyeing her hips, stretched the waist with his hands to show they were big enough to fit her. A different salesman had rubbed the underwear to demonstrate how to wash it. Another woman who wanted to buy a strapless bra took her husband along with her in the hopes that his presence would keep the salesman from being too bold. "I felt so embarrassed when he covered the table with bras while everyone in the store looked on. He wasn't satisfied with that. He picked up one of the bras and demonstrated with both hands how it supports the breasts," she told me. "We left without buying any." To minimize interaction with the salesman, one woman said she would cut the sizing label off her underwear and hand it to him with a frown so he could find the correct size for her. Another would buy her panties from a department store, because underwear there was sold in packs instead of individually, which meant she could head straight for the cashier instead of engaging with a salesman and therefore didn't have to bring her husband along for protection. "We've reached a state of submission even when it comes to our bras," said one woman, sighing.

But in June 2011, almost ten years after I'd spoken with these women, King Abdullah partially reversed the ban, allowing women to sell underwear and makeup. His decision seemed like a minirevolution. At that time, before his death in 2015 and the subsequent rise of Crown Prince Mohammed bin Salman, change happened at a snail's pace. King Abdullah, and other leaders before him, were careful not to upset the country's powerful, ultraconservative religious elements, not only because they feared them but also because they needed them. Saudi Arabia follows Wahhabism, a strict strain of Islam that emerged under the guidance of an eighteenth century cleric, Muhammad bin Abdul Wahhab. His descendants hold key religious positions, giving them sway over legal and social policy in the kingdom; in return, they give the royal family legitimacy. This meant that every development, no matter how small, was a major piece of news, and many months or years passed in between.

It's important to look back at those days to understand the enormity of change currently under way in the kingdom. Before Prince Mohammed became crown prince in 2017, it was inconceivable that orders to allow women to drive, singers to perform, and cinemas to open would follow one another at such speed, as they have in the last couple of years. In the past, a shy mention of one of these issues in the media was news. One could assume that Prince Mohammed started doing this for political expediency—burnishing his credentials with foreign powers to ingratiate himself with the West. But it seems that he has also realized that times have changed. Low oil prices and a growing population in Saudi Arabia mean the government cannot go on propping up the economy with subsidies. For there to be economic growth, decades of tradition need to be upended. Women need to become active members of society; Saudis need to spend their money on entertainment at home, not in Dubai or Europe; and Westerners need to find the kingdom attractive enough to invest in.

Over my seventeen years working as a reporter intermittently covering Saudi Arabia, first for the AP and then for *Bloomberg News*, I've been able to witness some of the changes firsthand. But every time I leave the kingdom, I think: If it were that easy for these changes to take place, why didn't they happen decades ago? And who will ultimately be proven right—the prince who's reversing decades-long bans at a pace not seen in the modern history of the kingdom and introducing unprecedented repressive measures, or his more cautious uncles who ruled before him?

Although I'd been to Saudi Arabia twice before—once on a family vacation and once to cover a conference—my trip in January 2002, was different. The kingdom was a mysterious place that rarely granted entry permissions to journalists, let alone female journalists. I didn't have any connections—a family member or an event I had been invited to—to ease me into my assignment, and I didn't know what to expect. Was Saudi Arabia a tightly controlled police state like Libya, where the newspapers were filled with drivel about the late dictator Muammar Gaddafi's supposed supernatural qualities? (A Libyan English-language paper once published a piece that described him as follows: "His teeth are naturally immune to stain, so that when he releases a full-blown smile, the naturally white teeth discharge a radiation pregnant with sweet joy and real happiness for those lucky ones who are fortune [*sic*] to be around him"!) Or would it be like Iraq, where Saddam Hussein's sons had reportedly installed cameras in the rooms of the only hotel where journalists could stay, and my photographer and I were forced to speak in whispers? Maybe it was more like Kuwait, another Gulf state, relaxed despite many restrictions and an alcohol ban. In September 1991, on a first date at a beach in Kuwait City, I spent an evening drinking a fine white wine straight from the bottle as police carried out regular patrols a few meters away. A few days before, I had celebrated my thirty-second birthday with champagne that a colleague had brought into the country from Bahrain, with no problem at all.

But I soon discovered that Saudi Arabia wasn't like any Arab country I had visited. Over the years, the kingdom has surprised me, challenged me, and infuriated me, but it has never bored me. I never imagined I would attend stand-up comedy in an empty pool, go to a "beauty pageant" in which sheep strutting down a red carpet were lauded with poetry, or be shooed away by the religious police—the *muttawa*—for interviewing men or not knowing how to buy a sandwich. I never imagined that behind the seemingly static, literally black-and-white façade of the country, where men wear white robes and women wear black abayas, there existed such an intense energy and pushback against the restraints that stifled society.

The Saudi Arabia I arrived in in late January 2002 couldn't have been more different from today's kingdom, which seems like it's *almost* a twenty-first-century country. I still remember the flight to Riyadh and how apprehensive I was about being a female journalist in a nation as closed off and conservative as Saudi Arabia. True, I am an Arab like the Saudis, but I grew up in Lebanon and had freedoms few Saudi women enjoy, like driving, mingling freely with men, and working in a mixed-gender space. At what point during the flight, I wondered, was I supposed to cover myself with the abaya I had bundled up in my handbag? How was I going to do my job in a country that segregated men and women, even when standing in line at McDonald's? How would I get around in a country spanning eight hundred thousand square miles that was also the only nation in the world that had banned women from driving? What would happen if the information ministry employee who was supposed to meet me at the airport—women at that time could leave the building only with a male guardian—didn't bring with him what we jokingly called the "I'm not a prostitute letter," without which I couldn't check into the hotel? (The letter was a document from a male guardian—in my case, the ministry—stating that I was known to the authorities, meaning I wasn't there to seduce every man in sight. On successive trips, when the ministry letter was late, the hotel circumvented the problem by listing me as a "Mr.")

I was more or less paralyzed during my first couple of days in Saudi Arabia, too focused on what I could or couldn't do and how I looked in the abaya. I kept tripping on the overgarment and had to slow my pace until I got used to it. Riyadh was windy, so I had to learn to bend swiftly and gather the hem together to prevent it from flying into the air—and to make sure I was wearing something decent under it, just in case.

At the hotel, every time I ordered room service, the voice at the other end of the line would promptly say, "Yes, sir," because the person wasn't expecting a woman to call. The hotel rarely hosted women guests traveling on their own for business, and the gym and the pool were off-limits to them. I've seen some women tell the receptionists they were entitled to a discount because they couldn't enjoy these facilities.

On top of learning how to make my way around Riyadh, I had to adapt to the no-gender-mixing rule. For instance, it took me some time to figure out the logistics of how to buy my favorite shawarma sandwich. Restaurants are divided into "singles" sections—for men eating out alone—and "family" sections, which at that time decreed that women without a *mahram* weren't allowed in. Staff at some family sections would bend that rule, but they usually didn't sell sandwiches there—only the singles section did. At first, I would ask a salesman at a nearby patisserie to get the sandwich for me. Then I decided to buy it on my own. I would stand outside the singles section and wave my arms around until a waiter reluctantly came out and took my order. Every time I did this, I would wonder how, in a kingdom so obsessed with shielding women, I found myself in a situation in which I had to expose my arms—as I waved, the loose abaya sleeves would fall back—and in which I was in full view of male diners and passersby for at least ten minutes while my sandwich was being prepared.

Then there was the issue of the male AP photographer who accompanied me on my trips to Saudi Arabia, a dear Bahraini friend named Hasan Jamali. In other countries, working with photographers was a normal part of my duties, but in Saudi Arabia, where unmarried men and women found together in restaurants, cars, or malls were detained, how were we supposed to cover stories together? There was no choice but to risk it. We got away with it, but sometimes, while walking in the mall, the religious police would order Hasan to ask "the woman"— meaning me—to cover up her hair, something that became a private joke between us.

My first story from Saudi Arabia was a scoop. The September 11 attacks had taken place only months earlier, horrifying the world and causing a public relations disaster for the kingdom: fifteen of the nineteen hijackers were Saudi, as was their leader, Osama bin Laden, and the nation was under global scrutiny. In response, Saudi officials had gone on the defensive, arguing that the citizenship of the hijackers was questionable. Since by that point I'd settled in and begun to feel a little more comfortable in the country, I decided to focus my energies on obtaining official confirmation that the hijackers had been Saudi.

I asked our information ministry contact to put in a request for me to interview Prince Nayef, even though I suspected I wouldn't get anywhere. I turned to the AP stringer, seasoned journalist Abdullah Nasser al-Shihri, for advice. He told me to call the prince at home, and gave me his phone number. I was skeptical, but desperate, so I called. It was around 7:30 p.m. The operator informed me that the prince was asleep, so I left him a message, saying I had put in a request for an interview and hadn't yet heard back.

Close to midnight, the information ministry contact returned the call and, in a shaky voice, probably due to his surprise, said I had been granted an interview with Prince Nayef the follow- ing day, at 11:30 p.m. (Saudi royals like to work in the middle of the night, possibly due to the intense heat of the daytime.) Not only was my message actually relayed, the prince had responded to it and granted me an interview. I couldn't believe it: I have seen Arab officials tear up reporters' business cards seconds after assuring them that they would call back.

Prince Nayef was two hours late to the interview at the interior ministry, and his spokespeople said I could have only thirty minutes with him because of the delay. But I ended up spending ninety minutes with him anyway, during which time he confirmed that the fifteen hijackers were indeed Saudi. I left determined to focus on doing my job as a journalist, and to deal with the hiccups as and when they came up.

That incident was an eye-opener. It showed me that behind the rigid façade there was room for maneuvering, and I shouldn't let myself be intimidated by how "different" the country was.

On my first few trips to Saudi Arabia—I visited the kingdom regularly, spending several months a year there before I was appointed AP's first Saudi bureau chief in 2008—I focused on what set the country apart from a social perspective. I often felt like a rebellious teenager because I was virtually breaking the rules every time I stepped out of my hotel room. On some of those trips, my adventures would begin even before takeoff, when a Saudi man assigned to a seat next to mine would balk at the idea of sitting next to a woman. The cabin crew would then scramble to find a female passenger willing to switch seats with him.

One of my first features out of the kingdom was about how Valentine's Day was celebrated in a country where genders were not allowed to mix publicly. Some families were so strict that they did not allow their daughters to meet with male cousins or in-laws once they reached puberty. "Sometimes, while walking down the street or in a mall, I would wonder if the man walking past me was a relative," one Saudi woman told me.

I had no clue if Saudis even knew about Valentine's Day, so in early February 2002, I went into a gift shop across the street from my favorite shawarma place to investigate. There were Valentine's Day gifts in the back of the shop: teddy bears with "Love" on one paw and "Me" on the other; baskets of plastic red fruits and flowers; messages of love expressed in poetry. "Officially, there's no Valentine's Day here, but there are many items you can choose from," said the salesman. Like many residents of the kingdom, he was so used to such contradictions that he said the words with a straight face.

I learned that Saudis buy their Valentine's Day gifts as early as possible, well ahead of the *muttawa*'s raids on shops shortly before February 14, when they would confiscate every red, white, and pink item that they came across in stores. A salesman said he was once detained for a couple of days because he was wearing a white top during one of the raids. "They accused me of celebrating Valentine's Day," he said. Flower shops were also a target at this precarious time of the year. I heard stories of salesmen ordered to trample on red roses. The shops looked bizarre during the few days before Valentine's Day, after the flush of red and pink had been forcibly removed.

Restaurants, meanwhile, received leaflets from the religious police ordering them not to decorate tables with red candles, roses, or tablecloths, dim the lights, or even play music on February 14. At one restaurant, a waiter told me in exasperation that the police had given him a CD with a recording of the sound of running water that he could play for the diners to soothe their nerves, instead of music. But it had the opposite effect. Many were annoyed. "They kept asking us to turn off the water," he said.

I was surprised to find that in such a restricted environment, with no cinemas, mixed-gender cafés, gyms, or bars, young couples still found ways to date. Roughly half of all Saudis at that time were under the age of eighteen, and for them, life was boring. They were under constant scrutiny from the government, which had begun trying to understand, following the September 11 attacks, what drove young men into the arms of militants. On the weekends, the streets were packed with men driving around, hoping to catch glimpses of a woman—any woman—in the back of a chauffeur-driven car. Often, while I was stuck in traffic, young men would slam Post-its or papers with their mobile phone numbers scribbled on them on the window of my car. That was one way to pick up women. Another was to go to the mall and throw the little slips of paper at the feet of women covered head to toe in black. Dating consisted mostly of long phone conversations or meetings abroad for those who could afford it. When Bluetooth became popular, I went to a mall to report on how the technology made it easier for Saudis to connect. I called a man whose number appeared in my vicinity to interview him. He turned out to be eighteen and desperate to hear a woman's voice on the phone.

"I'm old enough to be your mother," I told him.

"I don't care," he said. "Just keep talking."

The longer I was in Saudi Arabia, the more I understood how invasive the presence of the religious police, or *muttawa*—run by the government body known as the Commission for the Promotion of Virtue and Prevention of Vice—is in Saudi life. They were the only men allowed to look women up and down under the pretext of ensuring they were properly dressed, although men were also targeted. One man was chided by a policeman for allowing a Western woman to step onto the escalator before him. Another was berated for having streaks of blond in his hair. "Are you trying to seduce women?" he was asked. A young Saudi woman caught with a newspaper she'd brought in from another country containing an advertisement for the movie *Titanic* was accused of possessing pornography. A Lebanese couple got into trouble after the husband asked his wife if she wanted to have a taste of his ice cream. The *muttawa* couldn't bear the sight of a woman licking the dessert in public. Some women ended up in jail for innocent infractions; when their sentences were over, their families sometimes refused to take them back because they had sullied their honor.

I usually encountered the *muttawa* in the mall. Some ordered me discreetly in English to cover my hair. Sometimes I would argue with them, saying that as a Christian, I didn't have to follow that particular rule. They would respond that Mary, the mother of Jesus, always had her hair covered.

In November 2003, I ventured out to cover the aftermath of a shootout between police and Islamic militants in a very conservative neighborhood of Riyadh. "Cover up your hair properly," my Pakistani driver, Ihsan, told me. I wanted firsthand witness accounts, so I started approaching the men in the area, asking for their names, what they saw, and what they did for a living. I was so consumed with reporting that it took me a while to understand that to conservatives, what I was doing was tantamount to hitting on the men. Some of them avoided me by pressing themselves against the fences of nearby homes, lowering their gazes, and scurrying away. I knew I was in trouble when I heard the screech of a religious police car a few meters away. Angry men got out of the vehicle and were soon joined by even more angry men from the neighborhood. They advanced toward me, unleashing a torrent of what were supposed to be insults: *safira* (a woman whose face is unveiled), *mutabarrija* (made up in a way meant to entice men—I wore only moisturizer), and "You're shamelessly mingling with men." I backed away, trying to process the bizarre, surreal situation. I didn't get all of the witness accounts I had wanted, but I wrote about the shootout anyway, and mentioned the incident in the story.

One of the things I enjoyed about covering Saudi Arabia is how unusual some of the stories were. In October 2008, I saw an announcement in the newspaper about an upcoming beauty pageant for sheep. So I thought to myself, why not? It was an opportunity to witness an undercover aspect of Saudi life. And it was a lot of fun!

The event took place in the desert outside Riyadh at midnight. Its goal was to encourage Saudis to breed sheep for quality. There were two things I didn't expect: first, the stench of dung, which hit me as soon as I arrived at the location; and second, the seriousness with which the entire event was planned. I was the only woman there, but about four thousand men were in attendance. Some of them sat in armchairs near a tiny runway covered with a red carpet discussing what makes sheep attractive. "Height," said one. "No excess fat in unwanted places," said another. "Good stock," said a third.

Then the spectacle started. First there was a show of fireworks, followed by a competition for the best poem in praise of sheep. Then the animals sashayed down the runway as would-be buyers appraised them. The winner was Sana, purchased for $120,630. "I loved the length and width of his cheeks, his long neck, and how the creamy yellow fur falls down his body," said its new owner.

One cool evening in January 2012, I was invited to one of the most unique outings I have ever been to: stand-up comedy in an empty pool at the back of a house in Jeddah. I was on assignment for a *Bloomberg News* story on Saudi youth, and some of the people I had met wanted to show me how they go about defying the country's various bans—in this case, the ban on theaters. About sixty men and women in their early twenties sat on stools, armchairs, and a carpet inside the pool as comedians poked fun at some of the quirks that defined their culture, including how officials black out the arms, legs, and chests of women in magazines. "I bought a Spice Girls CD, and I was surprised to see they were wearing abayas," one joked.

Saudi Arabia was so opaque to me that many rumors, no matter how outrageous, sounded plausible. Once when I was reporting a story on how the kingdom was beginning to acknowledge the prevalence of AIDS cases in the country, someone told me that women, both local and foreign, could not buy condoms. Since most of the women I interviewed had contracted HIV from their husbands, I wanted to check if that was true, so I could add the tidbit to my story. But I also didn't want to get in trouble, so I asked a young diplomat to come along with me.

He brought along a friend, and the two men remained at a distance from me in a big supermarket as I chose a yellow packet of condoms, took it to the Saudi cashier, and paid for it. (I truly felt like a teenager at this point.) No problems at all. I told the diplomat that the transaction was too easy, so he took me to a small pharmacy. As I walked through the door, the diplomat urgently whispered: *"Donna, no!"* The bearded Saudi cashier was clearly very conservative. I ignored the diplomat, who followed me in with some trepidation, chose a purple box of condoms, and went to the cashier, where I dissolved into giggles like a schoolgirl would. The cashier looked up and without a word handed me the plastic bag containing the box. I had never expected to find myself in such a situation, buying condoms in a country like Saudi Arabia.

Before his death in 2015, King Abdullah paved the way for the changes happening now. His decisions to reform were in part due to the calls for modernization in the kingdom following 9/11, and in part due to technological advancements like satellite TV and the internet, which brought the wider world into Saudi homes and made it easier for citizens to circumvent social obstacles. In addition to allowing women to work in lingerie and makeup stores, he allowed them to stay at hotels without a guardian letter, granted them the right to vote and run in elections—though only municipal elections have been held—and sent female athletes to the Olympic Games for the first time in 2012.

I have been to Saudi Arabia several times since Prince Mohammed came into power. One sign of how much things have changed is this headline, published by the daily newspaper *Arab News* shortly after Valentine's Day in 2018: UN-FORBIDDEN LOVE: SAUDIS ENJOY SECOND "RELIGIOUS POLICE-FREE" VALENTINE'S DAY. In decades past, no one would've dared to brag about marking a Western celebration and being totally dismissive of the religious police. Sheikh Ahmed Qasim Al-Ghamdi, a previous *muttawa* chief in the holy city of Mecca, even endorsed the celebration, telling the paper that love was a natural feeling, "a positive aspect of the human being."

When I travel to Saudi Arabia these days, I can see the changes as soon as I land. The dark, drab arrivals hall at the Riyadh airport has been painted white, with television sets playing cartoons. Passport-control officials now sport white robes and smiles, in contrast to dark uniforms and frowns. Young people can be seen everywhere, and their energy is felt at business conferences, start-ups, and ministries. Women are more visible in public and in government and banking jobs.

The transformation made me feel somehow outdated, at least at first. My black abayas, considered bold when I bought them because of their red embroidery and sprinkles of glitter, are passé amid the more relaxed grays and blues that don't fully cover what's underneath them. On an assignment for *Bloomberg News* in December 2016, I went to a variety show in Jeddah where the audience was mixed and Justin Bieber's song "Let Me Love You" blared from giant speakers—this in a country that had banned music and men and women mingling in public. At restaurants, the family sections are still there, but minus the partitions that used to shield each table and made eating out feel like dining in a tomb.

But it hasn't all been good news. There's now a climate of fear in the kingdom that I have previously encountered in repressive regimes but never in Saudi Arabia. Some Saudis I have known for years didn't want to meet when I was on a reporting trip to Jeddah and Riyadh in August 2018, saying it was too risky to be seen with journalists. The shift in their attitude came after the government arrested clerics, critics, and women activists, and detained hundreds of prominent businessmen and some royals at the Ritz Hotel in Riyadh in November 2017. The mass arrests were part of a so-called anticorruption campaign that some analysts have labeled as shakedowns. The developments sent a message to Saudis that the new leadership has little tolerance for free speech and isn't concerned about due process or transparency.

As I'm writing this, Saudi Arabia and its crown prince are mired in an international controversy over the killing of the Saudi journalist and critic Jamal Khashoggi, who moved to the United States in 2017 to avoid arrest and went into self-imposed exile. Khashoggi, whom I met in early 2002, disappeared after walking into the Saudi consulate in Istanbul on October 2, 2018. It took the Saudis seventeen days to finally admit that government agents had murdered Khashoggi following an altercation at the consulate, after first claiming he had left the premises unscathed. That account didn't align with what Turkish officials had been leaking: Khashoggi was tortured and dismembered at the consulate, they said, a claim the Saudis have denied. The episode exposed vulnerabilities for the prince as he faced the toughest questioning of his rule, with U.S. lawmakers blaming him for the murder.

These events have left me wondering whether foreign media can continue reporting more or less freely before they, too, come under some kind of control.

Every time I find myself amazed by the new Saudi Arabia, I recall an incident at a restaurant in Riyadh in December 2016. Music was playing in the background, young women were taking selfies, and there was lots of chatter and laughter, before two totally covered women walked in and demanded that the waiters switch off the music. Although there were only two of them in a restaurant packed with diners, their wishes prevailed, and the music was turned off. Saudis grew up believing that music, gender mixing, women driving, and celebrating Valentine's Day are all *haram* (forbidden by Islam) because they lead to decadence.

These two women had the religious argument on their side and no one dared challenge them. How many in the kingdom still agree with them? No one really knows. But I've asked many Saudis if they're happy with the changes, and everyone has responded with ambivalence, saying, "Yes, but . . ."

Dying Breed

Roula Khalaf

I can't recall the precise moment I decided I wanted to be a foreign correspondent, but I know it had something to do with the Commodore Hotel in Beirut's legendary Hamra district. A scruffy establishment with plentiful booze at the bar and the rare advantage of a working telex line, the Commodore was for years the home base of foreign correspondents covering Lebanon's civil war. Many would make their name during the bloody sixteen years of conflict that erupted in 1975, pitting Muslim militias against Christians, turning factions within each sect against one another, and inviting foreign interventions. In 1982, Israel invaded Lebanon and linked up with Christian militias to drive out the Palestine Liberation Organization. My family temporarily swapped our spacious home a few miles west of the Commodore, on the Mediterranean shore, for a small, dark, serviced apartment a two-minute walk from the hotel, above a celebrated bar called Jack's Hideaway. At times, we visited the hotel lobby, catching a glimpse of the war reporters huddled with machine-gun-wielding militiamen.

The appeal of the hotel had nothing to do with the greater safety we felt in Hamra, which, in any case, was fleeting. I was an anxious teenager who gorged on French novels and was desperate for a cause, while at the Commodore, the women and men were right on the front line. Just thinking of them conjured up images of excitement and intrigue; they embodied a freedom and a purpose that I craved.

It would be more than a decade before I received my first assignment as a foreign correspondent. By a fortunate twist of fate, I was hired to cover another civil war in the Arab world, one that would prove even more brutal than Lebanon's. When I began covering Algeria in 1995, the war in Lebanon had ended, though not before the Commodore had succumbed to its ravages. The hotel was bombed and plundered in 1987 by gunmen who fought outside and within its walls. Soon after, a spate of kidnappings forced the rest of the foreigners, including correspondents, out of Lebanon.

But the Commodore came back to mind on my first trip to Algiers, when I stayed in another war hotel. The Djezair, otherwise known as the St. George, was a charming former Moorish palace where rooms were still referred to by the names of the fabled figures who stayed there, including Winston Churchill. By the time I arrived in Algiers in the fall of 1995, the military had been fighting an Islamist insurgency for more than two years. The rebels had taken up arms after an election that they were poised to win was canceled by the army, a coup that had been applauded by Western allies of Algiers. This was the first Arab spring, nearly two decades before the uprisings of 2011 swept the region. It was also the first time that an Islamist party came within a whisker of power.

That party was the Islamic Salvation Front, or FIS, a ragtag collection of various Islamist tendencies that had come together when Algeria shed decades of authoritarianism and allowed parties to compete in elections. For two years after the military coup, the country was virtually shut off from the world and firmly sealed off from the international media. I was part of the first batch of reporters allowed in by a military-backed regime keen to burnish its image in the face of mounting accusations of human rights abuses.

The ambassador in London who had signed off on my visa took me out to lunch before my trip. We met at an Italian restaurant in Holland Park, around the corner from the embassy. On the menu were delicious pasta dishes and a heavy dose of propaganda. Intellectuals and journalists were hunted down like animals in those days; Algeria was deemed the most dangerous country in the world for reporters by the Committee to Protect Journalists. The regime, too, was killing indiscriminately. The ambassador advised me to keep a low profile by dressing modestly and in dark colors and never straying from the minders that would be assigned to me in order to stay safe. I took his advice seriously, packing the most ragged clothes I could find in my closet. On my first night at the St. George, I was reminded of what a rookie reporter I was when I spotted Nora Boustany, the *Washington Post* correspondent whose work I'd followed for years, in bright-red high-heeled pumps.

I returned to Algeria time and again as the North Africa correspondent for the *Financial Times*. The minders were always present to trail journalists and control their messages. The big question in Algeria at that time was *"Qui tue qui"*—who was killing whom. Officials painted all the rebels with the same brush, and blamed all the violence on what was then called the GIA, the French acronym for the Armed Islamic Group, a radical offshoot of the FIS; opposition politicians were convinced the GIA was infiltrated by the military. Over the years, other reporters and I were bused several times to massacre sites to interview victims, in surreal visits that the government inexplicably treated as touristic road trips. The pattern was always the same: villagers told contradictory stories, leaving us with the impression—although we never had proof—that the massacre site had been thoroughly prepared for our arrival.

Algeria was my introduction to foreign reporting, an adventure that was steeped in tragedy yet unforgettable. Though I haven't visited Algiers for nearly ten years, I can still see its white-washed colonial buildings and the tears of mothers and fathers whose children had disappeared. Algerians have a name for the contempt with which the regime—*"le pouvoir,"* as it is known—has always treated them. They call it the *hogra*. Colleagues who cover Algeria tell me the *hogra* is still entrenched in the Algerian psyche.

Since the war in Algeria, which I covered for more than five years, I have reported on numerous crises and conflicts, from Iraq to Iran, Syria, Lebanon, Israel, and the Palestinian territories. To the memory of the Commodore, I added the dilapidated Rasheed Hotel in Baghdad, the charming American Colony in Jerusalem, and the dreary Sheraton in Damascus. From those bases, I bore witness to momentous geopolitical shifts and told stories of inspiring courage and of wretched failures. I heard of hopefulness, saw the bloodshed, and learned of the despair before I witnessed the cataclysm of the Arab revolutions and their rapid extinguishment through counterrevolutions.

Over the years, however, as I moved on from on-the-ground reporting to running a foreign network for a global news organization that is one of the few that are still committed to serious foreign reporting, I have also watched upheaval of a different sort: the digital revolution that upended the business model of media outlets, putting formidable pressure on revenue streams, spurring new competition from social media platforms, and forcing changes in the ways in which readers interact with newspapers. The vast majority of online advertising spending has shifted from newspapers to Google and Facebook. News organizations that have survived have adopted a subscription model that brings journalists into a more direct relationship with readers. Thanks to reader data, we are now informed about what users are reading, where, how, and for how long.

The industry turbulence has inevitably affected foreign reporting. A foreign bureau is expensive to maintain, especially in a conflict zone. It requires a local staff, drivers, and possibly also a security detail. Yearly costs could run into the hundreds of thousands of dollars.

Because of this, foreign reporting was an early casualty in technological disruption. I often hear foreign correspondents described as a dying breed. Journalists who've had careers like mine wonder whether others will have the same opportunity. "Journalism met the market—and found it uncomfortable," Richard Sambrook wrote for the Reuters Institute for the Study of Journalism at Oxford University. "The truth, that expensive journalism seldom paid its way, was being exposed. International reporting, with its high costs, was often at the forefront of budget cuts necessitated by these changes."

Across the Western world, the number of foreign bureaus run by international news organizations has shrunk. As early as 2011, the *American Journalism Review* reported that eighteen newspapers and two chains had shuttered every one of their overseas bureaus in the last dozen years. Not only did a vast number of local and regional newspapers decrease their coverage of foreign news but television networks also slashed the time devoted to it, narrowing their focus largely to war zones.

One disturbing implication for the crisis in legacy media is the growing use of freelance journalists, often young enthusiasts willing to take greater risks to cover dangerous zones for the promise of a byline. Many freelancers were among the contingent of foreign reporters kidnapped by ISIS in Syria over the past few years.

Ever since William Howard Russell's reports about the Crimean War, the traditional foreign reporting model has been that journalists witness historic events and relay them to the rest of the world. Technology and globalization, however, have knit a more interconnected world. The news business has been disintermediated: a breaking story can be followed, blow by blow, minute by minute, on Twitter, Facebook, and other social media platforms.

No one could have reported on the war in Syria, for example, without closely following the flood of YouTube videos published by rebels, or evaluated the evolution of ISIS without tracking their posts on platforms such as Telegram. Journalists used WhatsApp to contact their sources just as often as they used mobile telephone lines. With access to much of Syria either blocked or too menacing for reporters, an important tool for investigating attacks was provided, particularly in the early years of the civil war, by a Leicester blogger who had never set foot in Syria and had no prior training in journalism. By scrolling YouTube channels from Syria, Eliot Higgins was able to study the weapons used in the conflict, providing reporters and human rights organizations with valuable clues about foreign suppliers. Moreover, as financial constraints have led news organizations to parachute more reporters onto breaking stories rather than base them in countries around the world, information gathered from local sources and citizen journalists has become more valuable.

Social media, local blogs, and citizen journalism have been critical tools in my own reporting, too. During the 2009 elections in Iran, for example, they provided essential information about organized protests that I would not have known about otherwise.

The 2009 elections in Iran promised to be one of the most exciting: Mir Hossein Moussavi, the reformist candidate trying to deny the radical Mahmoud Ahmadinejad a second term, had run an energetic, lively campaign and won the endorsement of reformist and pragmatic factions in the regime. He seemed tantalizingly close to ending the erratic, economically illiterate presidency of Ahmadinejad. I was expecting a runoff in the election, so I waited until the first round before getting on a plane to Tehran. By the time I boarded, however, the results of the first round had been announced: Ahmadinejad had won in an unlikely landslide victory. The "Green Movement" that had burgeoned in support of Moussavi, capturing the imagination of the West, reacted with rage, setting off mass protests—the largest since the 1979 Islamic revolution. My colleagues in Tehran, where the *Financial Times* is one of the rare news organizations to have an office, had been reporting for weeks on the electoral campaign, traveling across the country. Their numerous interviews had left them with a strong suspicion that the election had been stolen.

Although I had a valid journalism visa in my passport, I was told by the authorities in Tehran that I would not be able to report and would have to remain in the office. The preelection euphoria had given way to the gravest crisis in the Islamic republic, as the protests escalated and the authorities unleashed the Revolutionary Guard's Basij militia. In the vicious crackdown that ensued, dozens were killed and thousands arrested. The crisis was also fought online, in a cat-and-mouse game in which activists organized sudden protests through social media and the regime fought back with sporadic blocks to the internet. As important as the online information was, however, my colleagues and I could not do our job without also going out and talking to people, capturing the mood of social angst and fright. As we wrote at the time, Tehran residents were "caught in a twilight zone, gasping for normality amid deepening insecurity and uncertainty."

Two years later, the Arab 2011 uprisings developed spontaneously, for the most part, outside the main opposition parties and without organizational structure.

Foreign reporting has also adapted to shifts in the ways in which societies consume information. Many of us may still watch television news and enjoy long-form reportage in print, but we read spot news on our smartphones all day. The nature of competition has also changed: news competes for millennials' attention with social media browsing, music, and games, all available on a smartphone. Text on its own is no longer sufficient to maintain that attention, so charts, timelines, quizzes, audio, and video are now offered to engage readers.

In the *New York Review of Books*, Lindsey Hilsum, the international editor for Channel 4 News in the UK, writes that younger viewers, who often watch news with subtitles instead of voiceover, aren't very concerned about the correspondent's face or even voice. When it comes to conflict the trend is "towards raw, dramatic video, shot by local activists and journalists . . . often filmed by rescuers with helmet cameras. On the whole the online viewer does not seem to mind that none of this is mediated by an on the spot reporter."

In print journalism, too, readers, particularly younger ones, are attracted to new formats. That has led organizations to combine on-the-ground reporting from foreign correspondents with articles that can be written from desks in London or New York. Let's take the case of a terrorist attack in a European capital. Two story formats are favored by readers on a fast-moving story: a daily post on "what we know so far" and background explanation. Foreign correspondents collaborate with editors in London or New York to write these stories. Before a reporter from the foreign bureau even arrives at the scene, journalists at their desks in London or New York forage through social media to build a fuller picture of the situation, using photos and tweets from witnesses to offer readers early updates on the evolution of the incident.

Does this mean foreign reporters are redundant? Not at all. While their numbers have shrunk, and practical alternatives to reporting in the field are more widely available, there can be no substitute for the knowledge and the firsthand accounts that foreign reporters bring. Indeed, the role is vital in an increasingly complex geopolitical environment where events move rapidly and shift unexpectedly. The direct contact with sources, the ability to see and feel the story on the ground, the off-the-record conversations, the big and small interviews, and the random encounters—all of these remain key to informing the public. In the age of fake news and political manipulation, it is more important than ever for foreign bureaus to be staffed with reporters who develop expertise in a domestic story. The largest media organizations continue to protect their foreign networks, and some of the savviest new media entrants (*BuzzFeed*, for example) have adopted the traditional model and built up new networks in recent years.

Foreign reporting is not about covering conflict, however important it is to reveal the realities of battle. I never thought of myself as a war correspondent, nor did my editors at the *Financial Times*, where I was told time and again that "we don't cover wars." A foreign reporter's task is to convey an understanding of a society, an economy, and a political landscape, providing context for events he or she is reporting on. You can capture a moment through a Facebook post, a YouTube video, or a Twitter thread, but it is the foreign correspondent who tells the story, whether through a tablet, a smartphone, a television screen, or a newspaper.

"To be a journalist is to bear witness, the rest is no more than ornamentation," Roger Cohen, the longtime *New York Times* foreign correspondent and now columnist, wrote in 2009 after covering the mass protests in Iran. "No search engine gives you the smell of a crime, the tremor in the air, the eyes that smolder, or the cadence of a scream. . . . No algorithm captures the hush of dignity, nor evokes the adrenaline rush of courage coalescing, nor traces the fresh raw line of a welt."

Cohen's words remind me of the night in February 2011 when Egyptian strongman Hosni Mubarak appeared on television to announce his resignation. Tahrir Square, the epicenter of the revolution, erupted in collective euphoria. That night, Cairo was a feeling, not a city, a sentiment that could be reflected only by being there. It was late in the evening, and families spontaneously poured out of their homes as if to catch their first breaths. They melted into army crowds and the masses of activists who had been camping out in Tahrir. The aspirations of Egyptians were painted on their smiles, in their cheers and their embraces, and through the mesmerizing sound of a nationalist tune from Umm Kalthum, the late Egyptian diva. The morning after Mubarak fell was quiet, but no less striking. As if to prove to themselves that Egypt had forever changed, and hold on to the thought, the people went back to the square to clean up, carrying their brooms.

There are poignant memories from Iraq before the 2003 invasion that have also stuck with me over years of reporting: the stunted children begging the lone foreigner for a dollar, the obsessive capacity of officials to demand bribes, the unconcealed encouragement for corruption in a state where everyone was told to fend for themselves and taught that the more they cheated foreigners, the better. Few Iraqis ever openly spoke of their hatred for the regime, but many did not need to. I could see the dread and the loathing in the eyes of impoverished Shi'a in Sadr City on the outskirts of Baghdad. I feared they would be driven to revenge the moment the Sunni regime was toppled. The people of Iraq were brutalized by dictatorship and starved by the most draconian international sanctions in history. That society broke, or politicians failed to govern responsibly, shocked those who contributed to bringing down the regime. It came as no surprise to others who, like me, had reported on the country.

Reporting in close, oppressive societies is challenging. And reporters under pressure can be made to feel as though they must adhere to red lines and withhold some of the most sensitive information they uncover. But writing from a distance or relying on exiled opposition sources can also distort a complex reality and perpetuate stereotypes of countries and societies. Take Saudi Arabia, a deeply conservative state that has, until recently, been sparing in its willingness to provide visas for foreign journalists. I've always found the reality of Saudi Arabia more complex than the simple image of an absolute monarchy and breeding ground for extremist ideology. Even without political parties or organizations, I have seen and read more political debate in the kingdom than in neighboring states with more liberal reputations. Over the years, I've witnessed a society in ferment. I've met Saudi liberals who have radicalized and radicals who have softened and become liberals, clerics who spoke to me without once looking in my direction, and religious scholars who have worked on reforming Islam.

My most vivid memory of Saudi Arabia is of a trip I took in the aftermath of September 11 for a special report on the kingdom, planned before the attacks had taken place. It was a revelation. While the world mourned in solidarity with the United States, my dispatches told of a different mood among Saudis. Behind the shock at the attacks lurked a sense of denial about the responsibility of Osama bin Laden, the al-Qaeda chief who hailed from one of the kingdom's most prominent business families. Some young Saudi men admitted to a secret appreciation for bin Laden for having dared to stage the most spectacular terrorist attack in U.S. history, challenging not only the mightiest country on earth but a Saudi regime that was considered too submissive toward Washington. The conversations followed a disturbing pattern: they began with a denunciation of the attacks and sympathy for victims and their families, but drifted toward the end with a throwaway comment that betrayed an admiration for the master terrorist. It was evident at the time that the real target of al-Qaeda was primarily the Saudi regime, and the aim was to force a rupture in relations between Riyadh and Washington.

Would I have understood this without being there? Probably not. The attacks by a group of mostly Saudi hijackers turned the spotlight on radicalization in the kingdom, the religion-infused education system, and the intolerance preached by the puritanical Wahhabi Islam. But while cries of "Why do they hate us?" rang out in the U.S., Saudi Arabia's rulers fretted about having lost their society to the hold of conservative clerics. One crucial facet of the September 11 story was that the Saudi royal family's tricky balancing act—designed to keep the U.S., the clerics, and the people in check—was collapsing.

The upheaval in the media industry is not over, and the future of foreign reporters is difficult to predict. The romanticism long associated with being a foreign correspondent has been fading, as interest in foreign news among Western societies has lessened. Yet we should be under no illusion that media organizations can report the world from the comfort—and distance—of foreign desks, and without investing in foreign correspondents. As Bill Schiller, a former *Toronto Star* foreign editor, says: "If we ever hope to explain what Lyndon Johnson's late presidential adviser Jack Valenti once called a foreign culture's 'ancestral rhythms,' we have to go to where those rhythms play out—and watch as they are rearranged on a daily basis. We've got to get close enough to listen—and understand what we are hearing."

Acknowledgments

My warmest thanks to the nineteen *sahafiyat* in this book and to our formidable foreword writer, Christiane Amanpour, who believed in the project from its outset; all met tight deadlines with grace and wrote honestly and beautifully, inspiring me at every step of the way with their patience and courage. I know that for many of them, taking a step back from their day-to-day work—in some cases while reporting from a war zone—to explore how their careers have affected them personally must have been challenging. I have no doubt that their strength will inspire many young and aspiring journalists around the world, particularly Arab women and women of color.

Of these women, a very special thank-you goes to Nour Malas and Aida Alami, who wrote sample chapters for this collection before I'd even secured an agent. Without them, the project would likely have forever remained in my inbox. Thank you also to Vivian Salama, the former Baghdad bureau chief for the Associated Press and now a *Wall Street Journal* reporter, whose gorgeous essay on leaving Baghdad, which she wrote for my blog, *Florence of Arabia*, convinced me even further that a book like this needed to exist.

In 2008, the late and great David Klatell, my adviser at Columbia Journalism School, encouraged me to write my thesis on private Islamic education in New York City. I had hesitated when I first pitched the subject, worried that covering my own community might in some way tarnish or taint my reporting. Klatell advised me to never shy away from reporting on my people, my country, or my region—whatever or whoever matters deeply to me—so long as I uphold the highest journalistic standards. I have continued to cherish his advice throughout my career as a journalist. My thanks to him for his mentorship, and his deft sense of humor.

My gratitude to the Scripps Howard Foundation, without which I would never have attended Columbia University, nor had the privilege of meeting so many incredible professors and journalists who would later become my friends, peers, and even some of the contributors in this book.

This project was enriched by Jessica Papin's guidance, wisdom, wit, kindness, on-point editorial insights, and endless support and enthusiasm. Thanks also to the entire team of *Our Women on the Ground* supporters at Penguin Books, including Sabrina Bowers, Louise Braverman, Kathryn Court, Nora Alice Demick, Lydia Hirt, Na Kim, Sara Leonard, Randee Marullo, Patrick Nolan, Lindsay Prevette, and Kate Stark. I'm honored and delighted to have worked with the incredible Gretchen Schmid, the editor of my editing with the most discerning eye, who pushed me always to edit and write clearer and better, without sacrificing nuance and passion.

All the rest of my thanks to Lina Ejeilat, Ahmad Ghaddar, Loubna El Amine, Amal Rammah, Sahar Tabaja, David Kenner, Laura Hurst, Natasha Doff, Dave Mayers, Andrea Stanton, André Heller Pérache, Melanie Huff, Maggie Thomas, Jennifer Powell, Juliana Yazbeck, Alice Fordham, Tamara Walid, Kathleen Brooks, Ghada Nouriddin Salhab, Muhammad Darwish, Yara Romariz Maasri, Dalila Mahdawi, Gaia Pianigiani, Erika Solomon, Kassia St. Clair, and Patrick Kingsley for their suggestions, support, encouragement, and editorial advice (and for answering my panicky emails and WhatsApp messages).

A special shout-out to Simon Akam, for always telling me to go for it, and to Sherine Natout, my first and biggest supporter. And finally, to my family, in particular my mother, Mariam—who is incidentally also this book's talented translator—and my sister, Yasmin: the most resilient Arab women in my life.

Notes

Introduction: *Sahafiya*

xiii I come from there: Mahmoud Darwish, "I Come from There," accessed via httpɔɪ//www.poemhunter.com/poem/i-come-from-there/.

xiv her friends advised her: Homa Khaleeli, Aisha Gani and Mona Mahmood, "Ruqia Hassan: The Woman Who Was Killed for Telling the Truth About Isis," *The Guardian*, January 13, 2016, accessed via https://www.theguardian.com/world/2016/jan/13/ruqia-hassan-killed-for-telling-truth-about-isis-facebook.

xv In January 2016, her brother received: Homa Khaleeli, Aisha Gani and Mona Mahmood, "Ruqia Hassan: The Woman Who Was Killed for Telling the Truth About Isis," *The Guardian*, January 13, 2016, accessed via https://www.theguardian.com/world/2016/jan/13/ruqia-hassan-killed-for-telling-truth-about-isis-facebook.

xvi some of the most dangerous: Institute for Economics and Peace, "Global Peace Index" (2018), accessed via http://visionofhumanity.org/indexes/global-peace-index/.

xxiii the region continues to rank: World Economic Forum, "The Global Gender Gap Report" (2018), accessed via http://www3.weforum.org/docs/WEF_GGGR_2017.pdf.

xxiii the most difficult: *Reporters Without Borders*, "RSF Index 2018: Hatred of Journalism Threatens Democracies" (2018), accessed via https://rsf.org/en/rsf-index-2018-hatred-journalism-threatens-democracies.

xxiii the second-deadliest country: Reporters Without Borders, "47 Journalists, Media Workers Killed in First Half of 2018,

RSF Says" (June 2018), accessed via https://rsf.org/en/news/47-journalists-media-workers-killed-first-half-2018-rsf-says.

Love and Loss in a Time of Revolution

20 **"The war in Iraq is indeed"**: Anthony Shadid, "In Iraq, the Day After," *Washington Post*, January 2, 2009, accessed via http://www.washingtonpost.com/wp-dyn/content/article/2009/01/01/AR2009010102079.html?noredirect=on.

On a Belated Encounter with Gender

50 **"I have been pressured"**: Carol Hanisch, "The Personal Is Political," 1970, accessed via http://www.carolhanisch.org/CHwritings/PIP.html.

55 **"cool young women"**: In Aishwarya Subramanyam, "I Get So Annoyed When 'Cool' Young Women Say They Are Not Feminists: Arundhati Roy," *Huffington Post*, July 2016, accessed via https://www.huffingtonpost.in/aishwarya-subramanyam/arundhati-roy_b_10770790.html.

55 **"Power," she writes, "can be invisible"**: Avery Gordon, *Ghostly Matters: Haunting and the Sociological Imagination* (Minneapolis: University of Minnesota Press, 1997).

56 **"Death is the sanction"**: Walter Benjamin, "The Storyteller: Reflections on the Works of Nikolai Leskov," in *Illuminations* (London: Pimlico, 1999).

Spin

69 **The fact that I am writing**: Gustavo Pérez Firmat, "Dedication," in *Bilingual Blues* (Tempe: Bilingual Review Press, 1995). Used with permission.

Three Girls from Morocco

125 **Dear Muslims, Immigrants, Women**: Facebook post, accessed via https://www.facebook.com/shaunking/posts/dear

-muslims-immigrants-women-disabled-lgbtq-folk-and-all
-people-of-colori-love-/1193182187387364/.

Words, Not Weapons

138 **damned are the thugs:** *Al Sahafa*, September 26, 2013.
146 **"Islamic regimes are concerned":** Shamael Elnoor, *Al Tayyar*, February 2, 2017.
146 **"This vain woman thinks":** Al-Tayyib Mustafa, February 12, 2017, accessed via http://assayha.net/play.php?catsmktba =16748.

Between the Explosions

169 **Our memory is far from an ideal:** Svetlana Alexievich, *The Unwomanly Face of War*, trans. Richard Pevear and Larissa Volokhonsky (New York: Random House, 2017).
183 **"We look at the past from today":** Svetlana Alexievich, *The Unwomanly Face of War*.

An Orange Bra in Riyadh

241 **"His teeth are naturally immune":** Quote appeared in a special, English-language issue of *Al-Zahf Al-Akhdar*, a Libyan newspaper, in September 1999.
250 **Un-forbidden love:** *Arab News*, February 15, 2018, accessed via http://www.arabnews.com/node/1246766/saudi-arabia.

Dying Breed

256 **most dangerous country in the world:** Committee to Protect Journalists, "Algeria Government Restrictions on the Foreign Media" (1999), accessed via https://cpj.org/1999/09 /algeria-government-restrictions-on-the-foreign-med.php.
258 **"Journalism met the market":** Richard Sambrook, "Are Foreign Correspondents Redundant?," Reuters Institute for the Study of Journalism at Oxford University, 2010, accessed via https://reuter

sinstitute.politics.ox.ac.uk/sites/default/files/2017-12/Are%20
Foreign%20Correspondents%20Re dundant%20The%20chang
ing%20face%20of%20interna tional%20news.pdf.

258 **eighteen newspapers and two chains:** Jodi Enda, "Retreating
from the World," *American Journalism Review,* December/January
2011, accessed via http://ajrarchive.org/article.asp?id=4985.

260 **"caught in a twilight zone":** Roula Khalaf and Najmeh Bo-
zorgmehr, "Tehran Enters Twilight Zone," *Financial Times,*
2009, accessed via https://www.ft.com/content/4ef2c51e-6013
-11de-a09b-00144feabdc0.

261 **"towards raw, dramatic video":** Lindsey Hilsum, "The Smartphone War," *New York Review of Books,* April 2018, accessed via
https://www.nybooks.com/articles/2018/04/19/syria-smart
phone-war/.

262 **"To be a journalist is to bear":** Roger Cohen, "A Journalist's
Actual Responsibility," *New York Times,* July 6, 2009, accessed
via https://www.nytimes.com/2009/07/06/opinion/06iht-ed
cohen.html.

265 **"If we ever hope to explain":** Bill Schiller, "Even in Digital
Age, 'Being There' Still Matters in Foreign Reporting," September 2010, accessed via http://niemanreports.org/articles
/even-in-digital-age-being-there-still-matters-in-foreign
-reporting/.

About the Contributors

Donna Abu-Nasr is *Bloomberg*'s Saudi Arabia bureau chief, responsible also for Bahrain and Yemen. Abu-Nasr has covered Saudi Arabia intermittently since January 2002, first as a reporter for the Associated Press before opening the agency's first bureau in the kingdom in 2008. She started her journalism career with the AP in Beirut in 1987. Since then she has reported on politics from most countries in the Middle East, including Syria and Yemen. Abu-Nasr also spent three years in Washington, D. C., starting in 1996. She joined *Bloomberg News* in Bahrain in 2011.

Aida Alami is a Marrakesh-based freelance journalist who's frequently on the road, reporting from North Africa, France, and, recently, the Caribbean. She regularly contributes to the *New York Times*, and her work has also been published by the *NYR Daily*, *Middle East Eye*, Al Jazeera English, and *Foreign Policy*. She earned her bachelor's degree in media studies at Hunter College and her master's degree in journalism at Columbia University. She mainly reports on human rights, politics, immigration, and racism. Alami currently is directing a documentary feature on antiracism activists and police violence in France.

Hannah Allam is a national security reporter at NPR, focusing on extremism of all kinds. Before that, she spent two years covering U.S. Muslim life as a national reporter at *BuzzFeed News*. Previously, Allam spent a decade at McClatchy, serving as Baghdad bureau chief during the Iraq War and Cairo bureau chief during the Arab Spring uprisings. She has also reported extensively on national security and race and demographics. Her reporting on Muslims adapting to the Donald Trump era won national religion reporting prizes in 2018. Allam was part of the McClatchy teams that won a Polk Award for Syria reporting and an Overseas Press Club Award for exposing death squads in Iraq. She is on the board of the International Women's Media Foundation and was a 2009 Nieman Fellow at Harvard. She lives in Washington, D.C.

Jane Arraf is an award-winning international correspondent with National Public Radio, based in Cairo and covering Iraq and other countries for the U.S. broadcaster since 2016. She previously held posts at CNN, Al Jazeera English, the *Christian Science Monitor*, and Reuters, as well as assignments for NBC News and *PBS NewsHour*. While her work has taken her all over the region and indeed beyond, she has reported extensively on Iraq for more than two decades. She was CNN's first permanent Baghdad bureau chief starting in 1998 and senior Iraq correspondent from 2003 to 2006. Her coverage has included the Iraq War in 2003, the battles for Fallujah, Najaf, and Samarra, the rise of ISIS, and the country's humanitarian situation. Arraf is a former Edward R. Murrow Press Fellow and a Peabody Award winner. She studied journalism at Carleton University in Ottawa.

Lina Attalah is the editor and cofounder of *Mada Masr*, a Cairo-based news website. She has worked as a journalist and editor for more than a decade, reporting mostly in Egypt but also in Syria, Gaza, Iran, and Sudan. Prior to *Mada Masr*, Attalah was the editor of *Egypt Independent*, another Cairo-based news website. She holds a degree in journalism from the American University in Cairo.

Nada Bakri is a Lebanese journalist who covered the Middle East for more than a decade for newspapers including the *Washington Post*, the *New York Times*, and the *Daily Star*, an English-language daily published in Beirut. Bakri was based in Beirut and Baghdad throughout her career, covering major events, including the 2006 July War between Israel and Hezbollah and the Arab Spring. Bakri graduated from the Lebanese American University with a bachelor's degree in journalism and received a master's degree from Columbia Journalism School. She currently lives in Cambridge, Massachusetts, with her son.

Shamael Elnoor is a Sudanese columnist and editorial board member at *Al-Tayyar*, an independent daily newspaper, where she has worked since 2010. She holds degrees in psychology and philosophy from the University of Khartoum, as well as diplomas in media and diplomatic studies. Elnoor has been a journalist for more than a decade, having worked at a number of local Sudanese media outlets, including Al Shorooq TV and *Al-Jarida*, a newspaper. She regularly writes about subjects including corruption, civil liberties, political Islam, war, and conflict.

Zaina Erhaim is a Syrian journalist and senior media specialist with the Institute for War and Peace Reporting. She received the first Women Rebels Against War: Anita Augspurg Award as well as the Peter Mackler Award for Courageous and Ethical Journalism, and was named journalist of the year by Reporters Without Borders in 2015. Her reporting has also earned her recognition from the Index on Censorship, Thomson Reuters, and *Arabian Business* magazine, which has listed her as one of the Arab world's most powerful women. Erhaim has directed two series of short films focusing on the experiences of women during war. She currently resides in London, where she is a Ph.D. candidate for media and gender studies at City University.

Asmaa al-Ghoul is a Palestinian author and journalist who writes for *Al-Monitor*, a U.S.-based website specializing in Middle Eastern affairs. Al-Ghoul, who previously wrote for the Ramallah-based *Al-Ayyam* newspaper, was born in Rafah, Gaza. At eighteen, she won the Palestinian Youth Literature Award, and in 2012, she was awarded the Courage in Journalism Award by the International Women's Media Foundation. Al-Ghoul has also worked for the Samir Kassir Foundation, which promotes media freedom in the Arab world. She is the coauthor of *A Rebel in Gaza: Behind the Lines of the Arab Spring, One Woman's Story*, which was translated from French into English in 2018. Al-Ghoul currently lives in France with her son and daughter.

Hind Hassan is a correspondent for *Vice News Tonight*, covering news in Europe, Asia, and the Middle East for the TV program.

Since joining *Vice News*, she has reported on a wide range of global issues, from the humanitarian crisis in Iraq and the battle against ISIS to the rise of populism in Eastern Europe. Hassan was part of the *Vice News Tonight* teams that won a Gracie Award for best news program in 2018. Prior to joining *Vice News*, she was a reporter at Sky News and a producer at Al Jazeera English during the Arab Spring. She is based in London.

Eman Helal is an Egyptian freelance photographer. Her work has been featured in various local and international media outlets, including the Associated Press, the *New York Times*, CNN, *Polka* magazine, and *Stern* magazine. Helal was a Human Rights Fellow at the Magnum Foundation, an international photographic cooperative, in 2013 and 2016. In 2014, she won first prize at Egypt's Press Photo Awards. The following year, she participated in the twenty-second edition of the Joop Swart Masterclass. And in 2016, she received the Portenier Human Rights Bursary for her work on sexual harassment and human rights issues. Helal is currently based in Cairo, after spending a year studying at the Danish School of Media and Journalism.

Zeina Karam is an Associated Press journalist who has reported on conflict and transformation in the Middle East for two decades. She is currently the AP's news director for Lebanon, Syria, and Iraq, in charge of the agency's video, text, and photo coverage. Karam was among the first foreign reporters to enter Syria after the Arab Spring protests erupted in 2011 and has covered the conflict on the ground and from her native Beirut. She played a leading role in the writing of a 2015 AP series of stories, "Inside the Caliphate," which explored life under the Islamic State group. She also coauthored, alongside the Associated Press, the book *Life and Death in ISIS: How the Islamic State Builds Its Caliphate*.

Roula Khalaf is an award-winning journalist and the deputy editor of the *Financial Times*. Prior to this role, she served as the *FT*'s foreign editor and assistant editor. Her promotion to foreign editor came after she served for more than a decade as the *FT*'s Middle East editor, overseeing the launch of the Middle East edition and leading coverage of the financial crisis in the Gulf and, later, the Arab Spring. Khalaf joined the *FT* in 1995 as North Africa correspondent, and before that she was a staff writer for *Forbes* magazine in New York, where she focused on corporate reporting accounting. Khalaf holds a master's degree in international affairs from Columbia University. Her series on Qatar won the Foreign Press Association's Feature Story of the Year in 2013. She was named Foreign Commentator of the Year at the Editorial Intelligence Comment Awards in 2016.

Nour Malas is a Syrian American journalist who has worked for the *Wall Street Journal* for the past ten years. As a Middle East correspondent, she covered stories on business, culture, and societies in transition in the Arab world. Her reporting has included the Arab Spring uprisings and the rise of a new global terrorist group; the people and communities caught in resurgent terrorism and war; and refugee crises that tested borders and security in Europe and beyond. She joined the newspaper's U.S. reporting team in late 2017. Malas is a graduate of the American University of Beirut.

Hwaida Saad is a Beirut-based reporter and news assistant at the *New York Times*, where she has worked since 2007. She earned a degree in public relations from Lebanese University in 1993 and a master's degree in education from Saint Joseph University, Lebanon, in 2008. She went on to hold various teaching, PR, and administrative roles. Following the assassination of former Lebanese prime minister Rafiq al-Hariri in 2005, Saad had a short stint at the *Boston Globe*, spurring her career in journalism. At the *New York Times*, she has covered Lebanon and Syria extensively, writing about ISIS, the regional humanitarian crisis, and beyond.

Amira Al-Sharif is a Yemeni freelance photographer whose work focuses primarily on women, their lives, and their occupations. Her photography has been exhibited in countries including the United States, the United Kingdom, the Netherlands, Sweden, and Spain. Al-Sharif has worked for publications and organizations including the *Yemen Observer*, *Yemen Times*, Oxfam International, and UNICEF. She holds a diploma in documentary photography and photojournalism from the International Center of Photography in New York and a degree in English from Sana'a University. Al-Sharif has won awards for her work at the Yemen Ministry of Tourism.

Heba Shibani is a Libyan journalist and news producer. She has held positions at a number of Libyan and international media outlets, including Reuters, Libya TV, Alassema TV, and Alnabaa News TV. She has also worked as an international correspondent for Libya's Channel in the EU. The civil war in Tripoli forced Shibani to flee Libya along with her family, in part due to her coverage of the conflict. Shibani currently resides in Malta, where she works as a media producer.

Lina Sinjab is a Beirut-based Syrian journalist and writer who currently works as a correspondent for BBC News. Prior to relocating, Sinjab was the BBC's Syria-based correspondent since 2007. She has previously worked as Middle East regional editor at BBC World Service as well as a World Affairs reporter based in London. Her work has appeared in a number of global media outlets, including *Newsweek* and the *New York Times*. Sinjab holds degrees in English literature from Damascus University and read law at the Beirut Arab University before earning a master's degree in international politics from the School of Oriental and African Studies in London. She has covered the Syrian uprising and its aftermath extensively, including the refugee and humanitarian situation and the rise of ISIS. In May 2013, Sinjab won the International Media Cutting Edge Award for her coverage of Syria.

Natacha Yazbeck is a Dubai-based Gulf and Yemen correspondent for Agence France-Presse. She has covered Lebanon, Syria, and Saudi Arabia for the French news agency. Yazbeck holds master's degrees in sociology and communications from the American University of Beirut and the University of Pennsylvania, respectively. She is currently a doctoral candidate at the Annenberg School for Communication at the University of Pennsylvania.